BREAKING BLUE

Real Life Stories of Cops Falsely Accused

BREAKING BLUE

Real Life Stories of Cops Falsely Accused

SEAN "STICKS" LARKIN

With Michael Lewis

LAW & CRIME BOOKS

DEDICATION:

To anyone who has ever been falsely accused, the pages of this book are dedicated to you and to the truth.

CONTENTS

INTRODUCTION

Let's get one thing straight off the bat. The truth is, not all cops are good. This should hardly come as a shock.

Why do I say that?

Law enforcement officers are human beings. In other words, we're just like you. We have families: spouses and children, fathers and mothers, brothers and sisters. We have friends we care very deeply about, communities we love, and dreams we're pursuing. We go through good times and bad times. We celebrate wins but we also make mistakes.

Being a police officer is like being an apple. The population of police officers is like a barrel of apples. And in any population, you're bound to get a few bad apples mixed with the good.

When it comes to cops, I can tell you without hesitation, the good apples want the bad apples tossed from the barrel. If there's one thing good cops can't really stand, it's a bad cop. Trust me on this.

Unfortunately, recent events have conspired to make some people suspicious, or even afraid of cops. Not bad cops; I mean all cops.

Right now, the good cops are paying the price for isolated instances of atrocious conduct. We're all getting tarred with the same brush. And that's not right.

It's not just unfair. It's ignorant.

That's part of why I wrote this book.

But you might be asking, "Who is this guy?"

My name is Sean Larkin. A lot of people call me "Sticks."

I know, it's a curious nickname. Here's how I got it:

Ever since I was a kid, it's been my dream to become a cop. Back in the mid-90s, I was a twenty-one-year-old college student studying criminal justice. I'm from the Bay Area but went to college in Tulsa, Oklahoma. So I figured the best way to gain some real, practical experience was to intern with the Tulsa Police Department.

That's how I started doing *ride-alongs*.

They're just like you see in the movies and TV shows. Basically, you embed yourself with cops while they're working their everyday shifts. A ride-along gives you a chance to see what the work of being a police officer is really like. So every Friday and Saturday night, I'd ride with two officers from Tulsa PD, Thomas "Luke" Sherman and his partner, Mike Eckert, aka "Eck."

One night, we got in a car chase with some gangsters. Eck drove like a bat out of hell. The siren was wailing. Our lights were flashing. The suspects' car screeched to a stop, a door snapped open, and somebody bolted out.

I don't know what got into me. We were all hyped-up, our adrenaline flowing. Picture me. I was this skinny college kid wearing a ballistic vest, no gun or handcuffs, no baton. I just had a flashlight. Still, I jumped from our car and gave chase.

I dove for the suspect's legs, brought him down, then got on top of him. Told him not to move. I was proud of myself for that.

When Eck caught up, he turned to me, glaring. He called me a "fuck stick." He was right to be angry.

I wasn't a cop. I was only a kid doing a ride-along.

From that night on, I was Fuck Stick.

Later, when I went through the Tulsa police academy, Eck was one of my instructors. He knew that a person's reputation is everything when you work in law enforcement. So he shortened "Fuck Stick" to "Stick." Which, once I got out on the streets, became "Sticks."

The new name stuck like glue.

To be clear, nobody in my private life calls me Sticks. I'm just Sean or Dad to my family and kids. But for anything work-related, it seems like everyone knows me as Sticks. Hell, even the mayor of Tulsa calls me Sticks. It's a little unnerving.

In 2016, I was offered a job with the team of *Live PD* and *Live PD Presents: PD Cam* on the A&E network.

The producers asked me, "What do you want to be called? Should we call you Sean? Detective Larkin? Sticks? What?"

"Sticks," I said. "Just call me Sticks."

It couldn't be anything but.

I joined the Police Department in my home city of Tulsa, Oklahoma, twenty-four years ago. Most of my career has been spent working in specialty units tasked with investigating or solving a specific crime issue. For instance, a specialty unit might handle narcotics investigations. Or violent crime. Or domestic abuse. Its members might serve warrants, rescue hostages, or work to disrupt criminal street gangs.

Don't let the details confuse you. In the end, specialty units all have the same purpose: the purpose of the police. We're there to protect and to serve. We're there to make our communities better, safer places where everyone can work and live.

I was asked to join *Live PD* and *Live PD Presents: PD Cam* because both programs showed cops across the country doing their jobs ... *Live PD* in *real time* and *Live PD Presents: PD Cam* directly from an officer's point of view via their body or dashcam.

I had the book's printers italicize *real time* because it's important.

When you show the real work of police officers—the truth, the whole truth, and nothing but the truth—it's a fact that you're going to see some action. By this, I mean car chases, takedowns, hot words spoken, even occasional guns being fired. That's all part of being a cop in America.

But you're also going to see the nuances of the job. How being a police officer is like walking a tightrope, minute by minute and year after year. Our men and women in blue are in a constant state of tension. Consider the questions they deal with each day:

- Will the next suspect I deal with turn violent?

- Will they spit at me? Insult me? Stab me? Shoot me? Kill me?

- Will they do those things to my partner? Or even worse, to an innocent person?

- Will I get to go home to my spouse and my kids when my shift is finished today? Or will they get that call, the one that every relative of every police officer has nightmares about?

These are all dire questions. But there's another that's just as important. It's the question that made me write this book:

Will I be treated fairly?

Meaning if roles get reversed and I, a police officer, have to defend my methods, my professionalism, my integrity, and my reputation ... will I be presumed innocent until proven guilty?

Or will people leap to assumptions?

Like I said, I know this is tough to talk about now. 2020 was a tough year to be a cop. The media broke story after story alleging police brutality or behavior unbecoming of the badge.

I won't list the incidents here, we're all aware of them. In many cases, I found it astonishing that police officers were being accused of murder and criminal activity before the facts of what took place were even released to the public. Celebrities, athletes, politicians, and social justice advocates were demanding that officers be charged, calling for changes to how policing in America should be conducted ... before they knew what had happened!

Am I saying the police were in the right in every one of these instances? Absolutely not. But it's amazing to me that, these days, the police are often considered guilty of wrongdoing before all the facts of an incident have been gathered and reviewed. "Innocent until proven guilty" is a bedrock principle of American law and American life. It stems directly from guarantees made regarding due process in the Fifth and Fourteenth Amendments of the United States Constitution.

When someone is falsely accused of a crime, civilians will cry, "I'm innocent until proven guilty!" They are right to do so. But this begs the question: aren't police officers also innocent until proven guilty?

I wrote this book to give you a glimpse of what life as a police officer is really like. And maybe to change your mind a bit about justice.

Specifically, I want you to consider if justice is served when cops—good cops— get wrongly accused. I want you to understand the price we pay for wild accusations and whether or not that price is fair.

As you're about to read in these pages, police officers, like civilians, can become the target of injustice. And that has to stop.

It has to stop now.

Why am I so passionate about this subject? In part because it happened to me. I was once falsely accused. I recount how that happened in Part One of this book.

This incident made such a huge impact on me, I went out and got my first tattoo. That way I would remember what happened the rest of my lifelong days.

I got the tattoo on my left bicep. It covers that whole part of my arm. It's a picture of Lady Justice.

Yes, you've seen her before. She stands in every courthouse across our nation. She's blindfolded. Wearing a robe. She's got the sword in her one hand, the scales in the other.

My tattoo artist was José "Inkfather" Sanchez, one of the best in Tulsa and possibly nationwide. But I had José do my version of Lady Justice with a twist.

Normally, Lady Justice is shown with her arm up, holding a balanced scale. Balanced scales symbolize weighing the evidence. How truth and fact should prevail over things like opinion and supposition. But on *my* Lady Justice, the scales are tilted to one side. She's not balanced at all.

I asked José to include another pivotal difference.

Normally, Lady Justice wears a blindfold. The meaning of this should also be clear. True justice is impartial. She doesn't factor in things like race or a person's appearance. She treats everyone the same. But on *my* Lady Justice, the blindfold hangs down. She has one eye covered, the other is peeking. In other words, she's not blind at all. This reflects my view of the courts.

Don't get me wrong. In my view, America has the best system of justice of any nation on the planet. I've already mentioned that, here in America, every person is innocent until proven guilty. Thanks to the Sixth Amendment of the United States Constitution, every person accused of a crime is guaranteed a lawyer to help him or her with their case. The Sixth Amendment also grants us the right to face our accusers. Plus, there are countless appeals that a person can file if convicted of a crime. And this is all scratching the surface.

And yet, despite all that, I can't honestly say the American system of justice is perfect. No system is. The truth is, our justice isn't impartial—or anyway not all the time. The *idea* of justice is one thing, but that's all it is: it's just an idea.

Remember the sword Lady Justice always holds? That sword is meant to symbolize punishment. She holds her scales up since the weighing of evidence should come first. But she holds her sword down because, in a perfect world, punishment follows what the weighing of evidence dictates.

The fall of the sword is a sentence delivered. It should be swift and precise. But in my experience, the sword of Lady Justice is far too often used to cut corners. She often gets very important things wrong.

Maybe the worst part of all, she makes mistakes. And sometimes these mistakes affect the very same people who try to uphold her.

Yes, I mean the police.

And yes, like I said, I know about this since it happened to me.

That's Part One of this book.

Part Two presents eight stories where hard-working cops from around the country stood falsely accused.

I want you to know what happened to them. How they paid for their calling.

How justice sometimes turns a blind eye toward the people who serve her best. Maybe then, we'll start to see cops a bit differently. Maybe then, we'll put aside prejudice, blanket assumptions, and blatant misinformation ... and start to see our heroes in blue for the people they mostly are: the unsung heroes of our communities, our society, and our nation.

The overwhelming majority of U.S. law enforcement officers are public servants through and through. They're our first responders, warriors for peace on the front lines of our society. And when it comes to describing them, all the old sayings hold true:

- They're the first ones in and the last ones out.

- The people who run up the stairs when everyone else is running down.

- These are the men and women who put their lives on the line every day for our communities.

For you.

It's true what they say. If you prick us, we bleed. But think about this. It's the pivotal difference:

- More often than not, when a cop bleeds, we're not just shedding blood. We're bleeding for you.

So, read on. I want you to hear these stories and factor them into your thinking.

In telling my own story, I've set down each conversation as accurately as I can recall it. When possible, I use the real names of colleagues and criminals in an effort to be transparent. If I change someone's name, I note that I'm using a pseudonym. This was done for reasons that have to do with privacy, ethics, or legality.

The stories of other officers are the product of careful research. The same rules above hold true for these tales. In the cases noted, I interviewed the officers involved personally and use transcripts from their conversations to help tell their side of the tale.

I certainly hope that you'll keep these stories in mind the next time you hear someone telling you that all cops—all police—are in desperate need of reform.

Justice must work for everyone if indeed we call it justice. And certainly, it should work for those who labor so hard to defend it.

SEAN "STICKS" LARKIN
Tulsa, OK
November 2020

PART ONE:
MY STORY OF BEING FALSELY ACCUSED

CHAPTER ONE:
CANDY FOR THE GOLDEN CHILD

In 2009, I was supervising the OGU, or Organized Gang Unit, for Tulsa PD. As the name very likely implies, this unit was tasked with checking out credible threats posed by organized groups of criminals—gangs—and working with other authorities at the state and federal levels to maintain safety in our community.

Now please don't go thinking that Tulsa must be infested with gangs to have its very own full-time Gang Unit. Turns out almost every decent-sized American city has a unit that monitors gangs. Law enforcement personnel often refer to them as GSUs or Gang Suppression Units.

Put differently, good police work is less about guns and riot gear, more about gathering information and using it wisely. If you know something's going to happen, who's thinking of doing it, where and when, you can stop almost any act of crime or violence before it even gets started. That's the best-case scenario. That's what we shoot for. And, to be honest, it's damn hard.

Because that quote from Friedrich Nietzsche holds true. If you stare into the abyss for too long, you often find the abyss staring back. Cops who are constantly checking on gangs see a lot of bad things on a regular basis. They're talking with criminals, day after day. This can twist them around. Not always, of course, but it happens. It's a bona fide risk, and one we take very seriously.

I mention all this to set the stage.

One day in 2009, my captain called me in for a meeting. "Sticks," he said. "Sit down."

My captain at the time was a gentleman by the name of Nick Hondros. Nick was a legend on the department. He'd worked in the narcotics world for pretty much his entire career, and anyone that came through the Special Investigations Division loved and admired him.

He was on the backside of his career by then, but he still worked longer and harder than just about anyone in the department. He also took more notes than the rest of the department combined.

I mean that. If Nick was on the phone or you were talking to him, he was writing down what was being discussed. But what's funny is that Nick *never* forgot *anything*. As in, *ever*. Still, he wrote everything down. To this day, I have never seen anything like it.

Captain Hondros told me an investigation had launched to look for corruption in our department.

"So who's running the investigation?" I said.

I assumed it was going to be run by a federal agency and, if anything came of it, the U.S. Attorney's Office in Tulsa would prosecute it.

"Eastern District of Arkansas," he said. "It's a joint operation: Little Rock U.S. Attorneys working with Tulsa FBI."

I nodded. That made perfect sense to me. With a population of just over 400,000, Tulsa's a pretty small town. Our U.S. Attorneys and the officers from our specialty units all knew each other from working together. From what the rumors were, the very cops that were being investigated were some of the ones who testified in court on a daily basis. That meant a potential conflict of interest. Ethics demanded that our U.S. Attorneys recuse themselves from any investigation into these officers.

Captain Hondros wanted me to keep my guys on track. Keep them motivated. Keep doing the job of reducing violent crime in Tulsa. We felt confident that the officers working within our division were a bunch of hard chargers that busted their asses day in and day out chasing bad guys. Hondros told me to let him know if I heard anything from that day forward, good or bad. He knew we had good officers. But if someone was in fact doing something illegal, he wanted them caught.

Nick Hondros also knew how I felt. We both felt strongly that bad cops have no place in police departments.

The job was the thing. We were there to keep people safe, so that's what we focused on. Me and my team.

AN INCREASINGLY SHAKY SITUATION

Unfortunately, things started heading south almost at once. Like I said, we were officers in a specialty unit that dealt with organized gangs. This meant we had day-to-day, intimate contact with our underworld informants.

These were people who had their ears to the ground. As a matter of course, they told us everything they heard. And what they heard wasn't good.

"Yo, Sticks!" said one of my contacts. "Yo, man, the feds are out here. They're askin 'bout you, man. You an, like, your whole unit."

I also heard:

"Sticks! Man, the feds are all over the place! What'd you guys do, man? These dudes are serious."

Then there was:

"Sticks. What's up with the FBI?"

Meanwhile, the other guys in my unit—and colleagues from other units— were hearing the same things from their informants. And this was just what we heard on the streets.

Within our own department, rumors were flying around like crazy. It seemed like every minute, some new and increasingly wild allegation got thrown. So the burden of proof had already caved in. The main doctrine of justice was already shot.

We weren't innocent until proven guilty, we'd already been found guilty in the court of public opinion. At times, it honestly felt like someone would stop by our office and throw us in jail.

Some of the officers in our unit began showing the strain.

"Relax," I told them. "Stick to your job. Remember what we do here. Get back to work. Keep doing the best that you can."

I'm proud to say everyone in my unit kept showing up for work. They didn't miss a beat. They went out on the streets, put themselves in grave danger, and basically busted their butts, same as they'd always done, and still do today.

Violent crime in Tulsa was up. We wanted to bring that quotient down.

"Just let the feds do what they do," I said. "It's really got nothing to do with our job."

We meandered along for a couple of weeks. Then somebody tipped off the media. Suddenly, we had reporters calling the department and reaching out to officers they knew in the department. To call the situation aggravating would be an understatement.

Our job became a real circus, that's what I'm basically trying to say. Actual detective work isn't like what you might see on TV. It's silent. Painstaking. Careful. Most of the time, you're collecting data. Moving slowly, incredibly slowly, you hang each bit of evidence like an ornament on the Christmas tree of your mind. You're waiting for something to click into place, that final piece of the puzzle that tells you, This Is What's Going to Happen. Or maybe: This Bit of Evidence Here Allows You to Get a Warrant and Make the Arrest.

But all that effort and painstaking care was suddenly tossed out the window once the carnival rolled into town.

The media kept up its hunt almost daily. Meanwhile, the feedback we got from the streets grew increasingly shocking in nature.

One time I heard: "Yeah, Sticks ... so, like ... the FBI? ... See, they're askin around, sayin, 'Hey, man. Like, tell us who the dirty cops are, okay? Do that an ... '"

"Yeah?" I said. "And what?"

"Well, they's sayin if we tell them who the dirty cops are, like ... that people might be gettin their cases dismissed."

I couldn't believe my ears. This happened not once, but multiple times. We heard it from our informants. Suspects with cases pending against them were saying it. We heard that convicts already in prison were saying it. Even the kids hanging out on the streets.

Everyone reported the same thing. Federal agents were saying they could help them out with their cases. Also that people were talking about suing the City of Tulsa for potentially massive payouts if only they started offering names.

That's when I knew the justice candy had started to drop.

What do I mean by that?

Imagine it's Halloween. The kids from the neighborhood come to your door in their costumes, wide-eyed, holding their goodie bags open. Has this ever happened to you?

You know what those kids often say to get candy? Anything. Anything at all.

They know how the game is played. So do criminals.

Think about that for a moment.

Imagine you're a career criminal. You've got a record as long as your arm and you've got a case pending against you in state or federal court.

Now imagine that some federal officer comes along and flashes a badge in your face. This officer announces that he or she can potentially get your case dismissed or help get your sentence reduced. All your troubles will magically disappear ... if only you go on record saying something, *anything* about dirty cops.

The key word here is *anything*. Some of the deals the feds were cutting required no proof. To get their cases dismissed, these informants just had to lie. They just had to make the investigators believe that they'd been falsely arrested. In many cases, this isn't hard to do. It gets even easier if the person telling you the story is really and truly motivated.

But there's a problem with that. You can probably see it. Most of these people the feds were approaching were criminals. And criminals don't often have any problem telling a lie. Especially when their freedom's at stake. Especially when the pot has been sweetened with potential monetary gain.

Listen. I know that criminals lie at the drop of a hat because I've spent half my life around them. Call it an occupational hazard. These are people who've figured out intricate ways to get whatever they want—illegally, most of the time. Most of them are grown adults who, either by means sophisticated or crude, have never worked a legitimate job in their lives. They'd rather burglarize your house, sell drugs, or rip off your bank account. That, to them, is an honest day's work.

In all my years of associating with criminals, I've also learned a thing or two about their psychology. If you give them an inch, they'll take the whole mile then snicker and laugh, then they'll take a bit more. If you ask them to lie, for instance, they'll do so cheerfully. Then they'll embellish, often to crank up their cred on the streets, with their peers, their families, their enemies, allies ... anyone they want to impress.

Bottom line: you can never rely on what criminals tell you. Especially when they're telling you something to get themselves out of trouble.

To get to the truth, you have to vet all your sources and back up your backups. You dot all your I's and you cross all your T's. Get redundant about your redundancies.

And yet, based on what we were hearing, the feds weren't doing that. We got wind their procedures where slipshod: less about truth and more about making a collar.

We all felt nervous about this. Understandably so, I thought.

Anyone who has been a cop in a proactive unit knows that bogus complaints come in from time to time. It's part of the job and honestly not the end of the world.

"Hey, just relax," I told the squad. "The truth will come out. In the end, it always does."

If only I'd known how wrong I was, I'd never have uttered those words.

INTRODUCING THE GOLDEN CHILD

My colleague, Jeff, had a female confidential informant. Most of us called her "the Golden Child." Why? Because the information she passed to her handlers always checked out. As in, *always*.

For instance, if the Golden Child told you that Suspect A had a pound of marijuana wrapped in a packet he kept in the trunk of his car, you could pretty much bet it would be there if you pulled the guy over and looked in his trunk.

If the Golden Child told you that Suspect B kept an arsenal of handguns under her kitchen sink, you felt confident asking the judge for a warrant.

If the Golden Child had spoken, there was no better word than that.

It's hard to describe how rare this is, or how valuable. An informant who provides consistent, reliable, actionable intelligence about criminal activities can boost the efficacy of any law enforcement effort. In the process, he or she also makes the officer they're working with look amazing in the eyes of their peers.

The Golden Child's real name was Rochelle. Rochelle and I knew each other well. She'd actually been my informant six or seven years prior.

Back in 2004, I was an investigator for a unit called UDNSC. This stood for Uniform Division North Street Crimes. Basically, we were a street patrol squad. We investigated drug dealers, prostitution, and gang activity—all of it street level stuff, and all of it had to take place within our division's geographical boundaries.

Rochelle and I started working together when UDNSC started investigating her boyfriend. I'll call this guy Dub Foster.

Dub was a member of the Bloods. They're one of the most infamous criminal street gangs in the United States. You'll find sets of Bloods in cities from coast to coast.

Founded in Los Angeles back in the 1970s, the Bloods were dirtier, more violent, and more ruthless than any LA gang at that time, which is saying a lot. For instance, when dealing with rival gangs, the Bloods had a "take no prisoners" attitude. Corpses would litter the streets of LA when the Bloods would go on a spree.

And they were territorial as sharks. A gang of Bloods could swallow up whole neighborhoods, holding the streets like feudal warlords. No one who lived in these neighborhoods ever talked back. They never tried brooking dissent. They knew what would happen to them if they did.

Dub and Rochelle shared a house together. Since Dub was a Blood, this house was the frequent target of rival gangs. The serious stuff included drive-by shootings that happened at practically any hour.

One such attack claimed the life of Dub's brother. I'll call this brother Ricardo. Ricardo was sleeping one night on the couch when a car roared past firing shots from an SKS Soviet-style semi-automatic carbine into the house. Ricardo never woke up. The bullets tore right through the wall of the room he was in and killed him, just like that.

What's crazy is that Ricardo was from a criminal street gang called the Hoover Crips. And the Hoover Crips were the Bloods' rivals in Tulsa. So the guys that shot up Dub's house were also Hoover Crips. Meaning, they'd accidentally killed one of their own. That's how gangster life plays out sometimes on the streets. It's pretty ugly.

At UDNSC, we'd heard a lot about Dub and Rochelle's house. We knew about the gang attacks, the homicide of Ricardo, and so much more. But we'd also heard that Dub was dealing drugs from that house. We wanted to shut that down.

That's how I started working with Rochelle. When you boil everything down, she was a young woman who grew up most likely in the wrong place at the wrong time. So many teens and young adults we come across in the gang world would most likely be normal citizens if they were raised by different parents or in a different part of the city. They just wouldn't have the exposure to draw them into the gangs and the world of the streets.

But, like I said, all this happened in 2004. Back then, Tulsa PD was facing a budget crisis. We weren't alone in that. Nearly every other PD in the country was feeling the crunch, as well.

Suddenly, our department experienced a rapid and alarming decline in the number of patrol officers it could field. The solution? Disband units like ours. Put its officers back in uniform. Put those uniforms back on the streets.

This made perfect sense at the time. The truth is, you can't run a police department without patrol officers. They're the backbone of any local law enforcement agency. They drive the marked units you see cruising the streets. They handle the calls for service. In any community, they're the most visible law enforcement presence, the constant reminder that someone is out there, ensuring that people are safe and sound.

I didn't like reassignment one bit. We had a great squad, plus violent crime and drug houses were still plentiful in the area. But we had no choice. We had to stop. This meant that Rochelle and I were no longer working together. I had to chalk the whole thing as a loss.

But then, out of nowhere, it seemed, she showed up in my world again five years later.

THE FEDS ATTEMPT TO FLIP DEMARRIO

By that point, like I said, I was the supervisor for OGU. My colleague, Jeff, had taken over as Rochelle's handler, and been doing that a few years. Jeff, who was being investigated by the feds. Jeff, who was under my supervision. Jeff, who was my friend.

But Rochelle hadn't skipped a beat in the five years or so since we'd last worked together. The information she passed us through Jeff helped OGU make a series of busts for drugs and illegal possession of firearms. The Golden Child was showing her stuff and the City of Tulsa was benefiting greatly from her largesse.

But by that point, she wasn't with Dub anymore. Her new boyfriend was a guy named Demarrio, and this became important.

Demarrio had a lengthy criminal record. Most of his charges were drug related. In fact, by 2009, he'd earned himself a life sentence in a state prison.

You have to understand: his offenses weren't really that huge. But the state of Oklahoma passed a three-strikes law back in 1989. This law mandated life without parole for any conviction of drug-trafficking, provided the offender had two previous felonies for drugs. Which Demarrio did.

To be clear, Demarrio and I never met. To this day, I still couldn't tell you who he was if he walked in the room, shook my hand, took a seat, and asked me to have a beer. But it turned out our fates were entwined.

One day, I got a call from Jeff, who told me Rochelle had reached out to him. Evidently, the FBI had gone to visit Demarrio in prison.

Allegedly, these federal agents asked Demarrio to give them dirt on Jeff. Any information at all, they said. Just pass it along and they could potentially help Demarrio get his sentence reduced. They'd even hinted to Demarrio, Rochelle told Jeff, that they might even work something out where Demarrio eventually went free.

Think about this for a moment. The feds had offered to help free a man who'd gone to prison for *life*. In exchange ... for what? Telling anything, including lies, about a police officer the feds wanted to nail.

To his credit, Demarrio was confused by all this. He told Rochelle that it didn't make sense to him.

In the first place, he didn't know Jeff. They'd never met; they knew nothing about each other. He didn't even know Rochelle had been working with Jeff until the feds told him. This, in my opinion, was reckless behavior on the part of the agents. It's a top priority of any informant's handler to keep their identity quiet. People on the streets threaten, shoot, and even kill people they suspect of being snitches. So why were the feds coming to Demarrio and telling him Rochelle was an informant?

(Yes, I'm aware that I'm mentioning Rochelle here, while writing this book. And yes, I'm saying she was an informant. The difference is that she went on to testify in court. Her name was in the media throughout everything I'm about to describe.)

In the second place, Demarrio was getting plenty of conflicting advice. His fellow inmates were urging him to say anything to appease the feds.

Just do it, they told him. Do whatever it takes to secure your release.

A few of them even mentioned the feds had made similar offers to them. And all of them planned to cooperate. Meaning they'd lie about Jeff, but who cared about that? They cared about getting their sentences reduced. They cared, first and foremost, for serving themselves.

When I heard all this, I went to Captain Hondros's office and knocked on his door. "I think we've got a problem," I said.

He told me to please have a seat and asked me to brief him, which I did. His pen kept moving the whole dang time. As I mentioned earlier, this guy was a bear for taking notes.

At the end of my spiel, Captain Hondros got right down to business. "What do you think Rochelle would say to recording a phone call?" he asked.

"What do you have in mind?"

"Well, you mentioned that Demarrio has a contraband cell phone. Somebody smuggled it to him in prison?"

"That's right." This happens all the time with inmates.

"So." My captain stared at the wall. "Let's say we record a conversation between Rochelle and Demarrio. You think she would go for that?"

"My gut reaction is she would, Captain."

We shared the idea with Jeff and he, too, thought that Rochelle would do it.

Again, to be clear: my department had good reason to believe that an incarcerated person was possibly going to lie to the FBI about fellow officers in the Tulsa PD. The motive? To get his life sentence reduced.

Rochelle agreed to the plan, so we had an equipment officer pull us a telephone recording device. This device was given to Jeff who, along with his partner, brought it to Rochelle. They instructed Rochelle on how to use it and waited to hear what happened next.

Within a week's time, Rochelle called Jeff. She told him she'd recorded a conversation with Demarrio. Jeff contacted me as his supervisor. I, in turn, called the captain to let him know Rochelle had recorded a call with Demarrio.

The captain told me to arrange to meet Rochelle in person and pick up the tape at that time.

I still had her number in my phone so I called it. "Rochelle," I said. "It's Sticks. How're things?"

She wasn't surprised to hear from me. Jeff had already called to say I'd be reaching out.

"Where you want to do this?" she said.

I recommended a combination gas station/quickie mart we both knew. But she had a condition.

"I'm going to be out rolling around with someone," she said. "I can't let her know we're meeting up."

As I mentioned a few pages earlier, protecting an informant is something that Tulsa PD takes very seriously. Again, if criminal elements discover someone's working with the police, they might assault or even kill them. This is especially true when dealing with criminal street gangs like the Bloods.

"I've got a way we can do it so we won't even look each other in the eye," I said. "You ready? I want you to do it like this ... "

A HANDOFF AT THE QUICKIE MART

Later that evening, I met a corporal from narcotics in the parking lot of our division. I'll call him Mike. That's his first name. I can't share his last name. He still works undercover.

We were each wearing plain clothes. We took Mike's undercover vehicle to the gas station and went inside.

At the appointed time, Rochelle came in.

Okay, so maybe we *did* look each other in the eye. But the exchange only lasted a second or less.

I hadn't seen her in several years but she basically looked the same. Being a cop and working the same area is kind of funny at times. You literally watch the transformation that people make from teens to young adults and so on. I had known Rochelle long enough to see that change myself.

Precisely as arranged, Rochelle walked over to a counter near the soda fountain. She was pouring herself a big Coke when I noticed her lay a microcassette on the counter right by the coffee lids. She was clever. She placed it in a spot where no one could see it if they weren't looking for it.

As she walked away, I moved into position and took the cassette Rochelle had left there, slipping it quickly into my pocket.

The transfer was a complete success. There was no way anyone could have known what we were up to. By the time Mike and I circled around toward the front of the store, Rochelle was already gone.

A few weeks after I grabbed the tape, Rochelle called me personally. Not Jeff. She called *me*. Right away, I knew something was up.

I could hear it in her voice. She was scared.

Rochelle told me that the FBI had come to speak with her. They wanted her to testify in front of the grand jury.

I thought, Here we go.

Fun fact: a grand jury convenes after a federal investigation is initiated by a U.S. Attorney's office, or after a federal complaint is filed by the arresting agency. A typical grand jury is composed of sixteen to twenty-three panel members. This process is kept very secret to protect both the jurors and the case. The grand jury is not administered by a judge or magistrate. Long story short: it's a pretty big deal.

Rochelle and I spoke at length about her testifying. This might strike some readers as odd. But the truth is, law enforcement officers often develop decent working relationships with their informants.

It's been my experience that many informants have never enjoyed positive, stable role models in their lives. It can be very gratifying to see how they react when an officer treats them with care and respect. In many cases, this is all they need to see themselves in a different light: less like a gangster or street thug, more like a decent, upstanding member of the community with a potentially bright future ahead of them.

Over the years, I've been contacted by many informants I've worked with. They ask me for advice on everything from matters of finance to relationship troubles. Memorably, one of them asked me to help him vet which college basketball picks he was putting in his NCAA tournament bracket. Another invited me to his graduation from HVAC school. Another time, a gang member informant asked if I wanted to go to a WWE Wrestling match when it came to town.

FYI, I did go to the HVAC graduation. But not the wrestling match.

Rochelle was no different. Yes, she was an informant and associated with the criminal street gangs we were trying to prosecute. But she also trusted us to help guide her through the normal world of being a productive adult.

Hell, Rochelle was taking classes at a local school. She once called me up to ask for help over the phone with her homework. I remember it was some class that had to do with finance. She needed help understanding the difference between debits and dividends.

But now she was scared, and she asked me about exercising her Fifth Amendment rights. I told her I didn't know if that was possible in the grand jury. But if she did have to testify, she needed to tell them the truth.

That's how testifying works. Under oath, you swear to tell the truth, the whole truth, and nothing but the truth. Anything less would be perjury.

My statement regarding the truth turned out to be somewhat prophetic. Because not very long after that, several officers from Tulsa PD, including myself, got subpoenaed to testify before ... you guessed it. The same federal grand jury the feds wanted Rochelle to appear before.

I remember rolling my eyes and thinking the same thing.

Here we go.

FINDING MYSELF IN THE CROSSHAIRS

Thankfully, back while I was still enrolled in the police academy, I joined the Tulsa Fraternal Order of Police, Lodge 93. I say "thankfully" because one of the benefits of membership is your option to sign up for Legal Defense.

Basically, Legal Defense is a group of attorneys that represents members in good standing however they need it. This can be particularly helpful during criminal or departmental investigations—inquiries where the reputations, rights, and careers of officers hang in the balance.

Officers pay for Legal Defense separately, with their own money. In that way, it's kind of like insurance. You pay for it, hoping you'll never need it. But if you need it, you're glad you have it. In my opinion, every officer in the country should sign up for Legal Defense.

Now going before a grand jury is a big deal, especially if you're a police officer. Which is why, along with several other officers who'd also received grand jury subpoenas, I called up Legal Defense.

Every officer in the Tulsa PD knew the attorney I dealt with. In this book, I'll call him Syd Webb. That's not his real name, but I like how it sounds for an attorney.

Syd Webb represented cops in everything from sexual misconduct allegations to shooting cases and administrative actions. As it happened, I'd actually used Syd before. Earlier in my career, I'd been a member of our department's Special Operations Team, or SOT, more commonly known as SWAT, or Special Weapons and Tactics.

We'd been called out to a residence after a male subject shot a female citizen multiple times. When the first officer arrived on scene, the suspect shot at him. Luckily, he missed. After hours of trying to contact the suspect and receiving no response, we tactically opened the front door of the residence. When we did so, we were met with gun shots. Several of us returned fire. The suspect was shot and later taken into custody.

Following any officer-involved shooting, there is a criminal investigation and then an administrative investigation. The criminal investigation looks at whether the officer was justified in his or her use of force. Questions abound but the primary point of interest is this: Were any laws broken? The administrative investigation looks at whether or not any departmental policies were violated. It also tries to determine if there are any training issues that need to be addressed.

Syd guided me ably through both the criminal and administrative investigation. He even had me laughing at times, which I appreciated.

And so, a few days prior to the grand jury, a bunch of officers who'd gotten subpoenas met with Syd to talk about the grand jury.

"So my basic strategy is this," Syd said. "I'll ask the prosecutors to grant you immunity prior to questioning."

One of the guys said, "What exactly does that mean?"

Syd explained that immunity means any testimony you give as a witness can't be used against you. However, if the prosecutors acquire evidence substantiating that you've committed a crime independent of your testimony, that means the witness may then be prosecuted.

We all understood what he meant after that. Syd was telling us that, if we'd done something wrong, immunity before the grand jury was no Get Out of Jail Free card. This was, and is, as it should be.

I vividly remember the day I testified. I was called to take the stand on the same day a few of my fellow officers did. We didn't witness each other's testimony, however. That might have been prejudicial. For this reason, only one witness at a time was allowed into the room to be questioned.

Here I should also pause to point out that I never signed an immunity letter. When it came time to testify, I had nothing to hide and felt that I didn't need the immunity protection. Rightly or wrongly, I went into the grand jury not one bit worried about what was ahead.

The prosecutors talked to me about my relationship with Rochelle. How would I describe that relationship? They asked me what was the purpose of my working with her as an informant for the Tulsa PD? When was the last time I'd seen her? And so on.

I testified that the last time I'd seen Rochelle was the day I went to the gas station/quickie mart accompanied by a plainclothes corporal from narcotics to pick up her cassette tape. The same tape on which she'd recorded a conversation between herself and her boyfriend, Demarrio.

The prosecution then launched question after question about my relationship with Jeff. What did I know about his activities as an officer in my unit? How did I come to understand that Demarrio had been approached by federal agents? Or that Demarrio was allegedly told his sentence might be commuted if he provided information on Jeff?

In the course of this back and forth, it became clear to me that Rochelle hadn't told the federal prosecutors about recording her conversation with Demarrio. Didn't matter. They knew now thanks to my testimony. It was also very obvious to me that the federal prosecutors were not happy about it one bit.

The prosecutors then asked why my unit had wanted Rochelle to record her conversation with Demarrio. So I told them what I knew. That we'd been appraised that Demarrio was going to lie. That his lie would allege that an officer who worked for me, Jeff, was corrupt. Furthermore, I stated that, as far as we knew, Demarrio was going to lie for no better reason than to get his sentence reduced. And that we, as a police department, whose reputation means everything to the community we protect and serve, felt Demarrio's account of these events should be documented.

Here's one of the things you learn early in your career as a police officer: When you testify in court, keep your responses short. You don't want to elaborate and give the defense—or in this case, the feds—anything that they can twist and turn on you.

We went step by step through questions on how the recorded conversation between Rochelle and Demarrio came to pass. I told the prosecutors everything I knew about the entire process, as well as everyone that was involved in it.

The day after I testified, the grand jury heard from Mike, the narcotics corporal who accompanied me to the quickie mart. When I heard this, I knew that the feds were being thorough. They wanted all sides of the story. Any angle was worthy of coverage. They'd even subpoenaed a copy of the micro-cassette, which we dutifully turned over for their consideration.

Now, the way I'm telling this story, it might sound like everything happened really fast. But let me be clear. It did not. Legal proceedings rarely do.

Months rolled by. We heard that the slate of witnesses before the grand jury got longer and longer as more people from inside and outside the law enforcement community were called to testify.

But during all this, my unit was busy with our caseload. Things got to the point where we hadn't the faintest clue what was going on with the grand jury. We only knew it was still convened. Subpoenas were still being filed. The FBI was still interviewing people. On and on like that it went.

Meantime, as I mentioned, the media was having a field day. "Innocent until proven guilty" might hold true in our courts. But the media often operates under a different set of assumptions. Our local newspaper in Tulsa ran headlines which, in my opinion, were directly biased against the Tulsa PD.

One of the things I particularly found offensive was the amount of information that was being fed to the media about the case. Keep in mind that prosecutors and the police both serve the judicial system. And the judicial system, in turn, is supposed to serve justice. It was therefore infuriating to read coverage that seemed to imply that officers had been prejudged as suspicious, if not outright guilty. Prejudged by the very same people who are supposed to keep every citizen in Tulsa safe!

Now look. The reality is that cops and prosecutors sometimes find themselves at odds with each other. It's not uncommon. In this case, however, there seemed to be great animosity. To say we weren't fond of each other would be an understatement.

THE PLOT THICKENS

Eventually, the grand jury spoke and the FBI arrested a handful of police officers, including Jeff and another police officer who worked in my unit. I'll call him Barrow.

The stakes could not have been higher. These were two professional law enforcement officers who worked under my direct supervision. They were hard working cops. They were responsible for putting a lot of very violent people in prison throughout their career. They were also my friends.

Immediately, I felt an obligation to see that they were properly represented as they looked to their defense. They were both fathers. Jeff had a wife at home. I was worried for them, for their families. I was worried for their careers.

The following day the courts held a detention hearing. This is a pretrial hearing where a judge determines what type of bail, if any, should be extended to the defendants.

During this hearing, an FBI agent testified that he believed Jeff and Barrow should be held without bail until their trial. But in order for that to happen, the court had to rule that the defendants were dangerous and/or that they posed a flight risk.

I wasn't able to witness this agent's testimony myself. Our chain of command at Tulsa PD made it clear: no officers from our division were allowed to attend the detention hearing. However, a couple of close personal friends who aren't in law enforcement went. When it was over, they called me on the phone, in disbelief.

They told me about all the allegations the feds made against Jeff and Barrow. Then they told me that my name was also mentioned by an FBI agent.

"What?" I said. "What do you mean?"

I heard my friend say this: "He said ... well, he testified. This agent told the judge that, at one point, you and Jeff had ... you know, allegedly .... well, you kidnapped a man and held him at gunpoint."

I'm pretty sure I stared straight ahead with my jaw hanging open. "He said *what*?"

"Sticks, this agent ... it came out in court. You're part of the case. They said you were a ... " He paused and tried to recall the term. "A ... not indicted ... you weren't indicted. But you were still a 'conspirator.' Is that the right word?"

My heart sank. "Unindicted coconspirator?" I said.

"Uh huh. I think that was it."

I couldn't believe my ears. In the first place ... I'd kidnapped somebody? Held someone at gunpoint? This wasn't the truth, it was fiction ripped out of a TV cop drama. It was a story I might have found mildly entertaining had my reputation not been at stake.

And not just mine, as things turned out.

This bogus story was one of the factors that helped sway the judge, who decided that Jeff and Barrow would be held without bail until after their trial. They couldn't go home. Couldn't work. Couldn't earn an income. Couldn't be with their families. Instead, they would have to sit in jail like the criminals they had been trying to take off the streets of Tulsa.

But now I knew my own situation had become very grave. Being labeled an unindicted coconspirator is no laughing matter. I'd heard the term before, of course, but I wasn't precisely sure what it meant. Or, more importantly, what implications it bore.

Now that I understood my position, I contacted a veteran corporal in my department, Dale Francetic. Dale was a guy I admired. Over the course of many years, we'd worked cases together, off and on.

In 2007, we actually worked together in the same squad. This corporal was legendary in the department. A transplant to Tulsa from Michigan, he still maintained a bit of his northern accent. He was a huge man with long dark hair and a gnarly long beard. He honestly looked like he belonged behind the bar at some shady establishment serving up three-dollar wells and two-dollar beers.

Dale was also one the brightest and hardest working guys I'd ever been around.

"Who's the best criminal defense attorney in Tulsa?" I said.

Dale didn't hesitate. "That would be Allen Smallwood," he said.

I knew the name but had never faced him in court. There was a damn good reason for that. The bad guys I was arresting, mostly street gangsters, couldn't afford Mr. Smallwood.

I called his office to make an appointment.

A short time later, I made the trip to his law office. It was located just south of downtown Tulsa, maybe eight blocks from the federal courthouse. It was an older home that had been converted into a business, the same as all the other homes on the block.

When I met with Mr. Smallwood, I immediately saw why my friend said he was one of the best in the business. An older gentleman, not particularly tall, he was soft spoken and confident. Over the years, he'd been in federal court numerous times. I remember being impressed with that.

Let me tell you, there is a *huge* difference between being an attorney with time in a federal courtroom and time in a state district courtroom. If it turned out I needed an attorney, I had a gut instinct that Allen was the guy for me.

Allen told me he was already well aware of the case I was involved in. Partly because of the nearly daily media coverage. But also because of the regular scuttlebutt traded by attorneys and other courthouse staff.

Did I mention earlier that rumors were flying around like crazy?

Smallwood told me that other officers involved in the case had already contacted him. But he told me, "Frankly, if your friend hadn't vouched for you, I wouldn't have taken your call. Now why don't you tell me your side of the story."

So I did.

When I was finished, Smallwood sat back in his chair and studied the ceiling. Finally, he said, "Here's how we'll leave this, assuming you agree. If you get arrested, I will represent you. Based on what I heard, you've done nothing wrong. Nothing at all."

At that point, I asked Smallwood what his fees would be should I need to hire him. It's tough to describe how discouraging I found his answer.

I'm a cop. We don't make much money. This guy was one of the best defense attorneys in the city, so he charged like a guy who's the best.

I remember I left his office feeling simultaneously elated and discouraged. Elated because Allen Smallwood said it sounded to him like I'd done nothing wrong. Discouraged that, should somebody else think differently, I could be arrested. That would be bad enough. But I'd also be impoverished for daring to defend myself with somebody who was skilled.

It was an awful fix to be in. The kind of thing I wouldn't wish on my worst enemy.

In the end, I called up my parents and asked them for help. That's a humbling experience, and something no adult ever wants to do. But I felt I had no choice. I didn't have the money to hire Mr. Smallwood myself. But I was being victimized by the system. And that was simply untenable.

My parents lived up to every good thing I've ever thought about them, which is saying a lot. They agreed to help put up the money should my circumstances come to that.

This put me a little at ease. But only a little. The situation was basically this: If I fell from the frying pan, into the fire, my mother and father would catch me. Even so, I was going to get burned.

The whole situation was too dang hot for me to come off unscathed.

CHAPTER TWO:
A LYING SUSPECT

Now as I mentioned, the wheels of justice turn slowly on a normal basis. But the case involving Jeff and Barrow was declared a "complex case." This meant that federal prosecutors had been given more time to prepare for a trial.

The trial for Jeff and Barrow wasn't set to begin for more than a year. In the meantime, I had work to do. By which I mean, I had my job supervising the OGU, and we had plenty of cases pending.

I'll be honest. It was hard for me to concentrate on work when I had this sword hanging over my head. My job, my career, and my reputation were at stake. Plus, my friends and coworkers were sitting in the Tulsa County Jail. If there was any good side to that, it was the fact that they'd been isolated from the other prisoners for their own protection.

Complicating matters, attorneys for the defense made it clear they wanted to meet with me several times. Their intent was to prep me as a witness for the defense. Which essentially meant I was constantly working.

The hard grind ruined my personal life. It destroyed my time spent with family and friends. There was no more blowing off steam. No more basketball games. Less time to work out and stay healthy. Now it was work, work, work from the moment the sun came up until long hours after the sun went down.

Looking back, I'm not sure how I did it. And yeah, I came to resent it. But during all this, I reminded myself that Jeff and Barrow were sitting in jail. Not seeing their kids. Not working and so on. I never let work slack off. My job at OGU was important. My officers, our informants, my department—everyone living in Tulsa—they were all counting on us. They count on the police. How could we let them down?

As part of the discovery process, I met Jeff and Barrow's defense team at their law office. It was actually located just a few blocks east of Allen Smallwood's office. There, we were allowed to read through the full investigation—to see everything the prosecutors had against Jeff and Barrow and, tangentially, myself, plus anyone else who'd had allegations made against them. This included all testimonies that witnesses gave to the FBI.

The defense team didn't show me the entire case, just the parts pertaining to any involvement I was alleged to have with the officers. That's when I first understood the real gravity of my situation. I was involved in not one but three separate allegations

The first allegation was witness tampering. The feds were making a case that, by having Rochelle record Demarrio, Jeff and I had been trying to interfere with an FBI investigation.

To this day, I have no idea why I was singled out in this charge. Meaning: several other police officers were involved in that case. For instance, there was Mike, the narcotics corporal who went with me to retrieve the cassette. And my captain, who first suggested that we record Rochelle's phone conversation with Demarrio. There was also the administrative sergeant who went to the equipment officer to get the recording device.

Did the feds go after any of them? Were any of them called unindicted co-conspirators? Were their names being dragged through the media? Were defense attorneys accusing them of being a dirty cop when they testified?

No. They only went after me. This was especially infuriating since I'd been the one to tell the feds about the recording in the first place!

Now let me be clear: I'm not crying over spilled milk. I'm not saying that any of my colleagues should have been labelled an unindicted coconspirator. I'm saying that none of us should have been. As I mentioned, I wouldn't wish what I eventually went through on my worst enemy.

I just found the whole ordeal strange, that's all. To this day, I still can't make sense of it all. It just doesn't figure to me that I was the only law enforcement professional who took part in a completely legitimate operation to somehow get fingered as an unindicted coconspirator.

THE SECOND ALLEGATION

The FBI's second allegation was the kidnapping charge, which was totally bogus. Frankly, the feds should have known better.

Why? There were numerous reasons as things turned out. But the biggest and most glaring was that the alleged kidnapping victim was a subject by the name of ... let's call him Will Patton.

Will, Jeff, and I had a long history together. See, Jeff had been my partner back in 2002. And during our time working together, we arrested Will on charges related to drugs and lying about his identity.

Drugs and lying? Those are two big no-nos as far as the courts are concerned. But it turned out, this incident wasn't Will's first time lying to avoid answering for his own criminal activity.

His first strike happened years prior. Back then, he'd been arrested on the same charge: false personation. On that occasion, his felony charge got reduced to a misdemeanor obstruction. He was still convicted. But only his felony convictions could be used against him for sentencing in any future cases he managed to accumulate.

So Will already had one foot in the door, so to speak. In early 2010, our Narcotics Unit opened an investigation on him. In the course of this investigation, Will once again got arrested. This time he was found to be in possession of controlled substances. And this time around, he was also busted for being a felon in possession of a firearm.

Any way you read this, it was a bad situation for Will. But he was lucky. He got arrested right as the feds were starting to probe into Tulsa PD.

Now remember, the papers were screaming that officers were probably dirty cops. Meanwhile, the feds were all over the streets telling criminals they could get out of trouble—and sometimes even jail. How? All they had to do was dish up dirt on cops.

From what we heard through our contacts, this little deal was the only thing card-carrying criminals were talking about.

Will may have been a convicted felon, but he wasn't stupid. He saw how this situation might work directly to his advantage. Lo and behold, it was Will who told investigators how Jeff and I allegedly kidnapped him. He said this occurred in north Tulsa.

Reading his account of the alleged kidnapping was like reading a Robert B. Parker novel, or possibly one by Mickey Spillane. For instance, in his deposition, Will stated that, one night, he'd been walking down the street in north Tulsa, minding his own business (of course), when, suddenly, this car roared up beside him and screeched to a halt. I was behind the wheel, Will said, and Jeff jumped out of the passenger seat.

Will's account stipulated that Jeff and I were both wearing black police jerseys. Many department's wear these. They're similar to football jerseys but with police logos on them.

Turning a page, I kept reading.

To hear Will tell it, Jeff forced him into our car. After which, Will said, we drove him north to a gun range which, based off his description of the location, was situated just outside the Tulsa city limits.

Once at the gun range, Jeff evidently ordered Will out of the car. Will testified that he had no choice. Jeff, he said, had drawn his service weapon, cocked the hammer, and aimed the barrel directly at Will's head.

The story went on to say that Jeff ordered Will to give up any information he had pertaining to local drug dealers. Will testified that he offered a few names—information anyone would have had, he said. I thought this was another clever detail. It was basically a way for Will to justify why Jeff and I—according to him —took him safely back to the city without casting himself in the role of a snitch.

You see what I'm getting at? A made-up story can be a double-edged sword. Sure, it might get the feds to commute your sentence. But what happens if you win that particular favor by testifying that you ratted out your friends? You might not wind up in jail but you've just increased the chances that you'll wind up dead in an alley somewhere.

When I finished reading the transcript, I looked up. The defense attorneys were waiting.

"What do you think of it?" one of them asked.

"This is total bullshit," I said.

"Tell us," they said.

And so, while the attorneys and their investigator took notes, I ticked off what I knew to be the holes in Will's story.

"Let's start with Jeff and me," I said. "Not only did Jeff and I not work together during the time Will is saying this happened, we didn't even work in the same division."

"Can you give us details on that?" asked one of the attorneys.

So I did. "Jeff and I quit working together in the fall the year prior. The next summer, I was promoted to sergeant and left the Gilcrease Division. Jeff stayed back in Gilcrease while I transferred to Mingo Valley."

While researching this book, I found out that Will was incarcerated and was released from prison after I had already been promoted and transferred to another part of the city away from where he alleged we'd kidnapped him.

Anyway, the defense team nodded at my explanation. They knew that Gilcrease is responsible for police services in the northern part of Tulsa. Mingo Valley handles the city's eastern portion.

I said, "I worked in Mingo until going into the Special Investigation Division."

The defense team's investigator put it together real fast. "Meaning that, when Will alleged you and Jeff kidnapped him, you in fact hadn't worked together for ... what is it? Two years or so?"

"Give or take." I nodded.

"Did you guys, like, hang out together off duty? Anything like that?"

I shook my head. "Who has time for that? We each have kids. We had our own things going on. We didn't start hanging out again until we were reassigned to work together again in 2008."

We all knew that everything I'd just said could easily be verified through a quick check of our work records. It would have been next to impossible for Jeff and me to have found time to meet each other across town. And would we really go to such trouble for the dubious purpose of throwing Will into the back seat of a car so we could drive him out to a gun range and threaten to blow his brains out in exchange for him giving us information about drugs?

"To gain what?" I said. "Hell, drug houses were everywhere back then. Why would we need someone that wasn't a trusted informant telling us where dope houses were?"

One of the defense attorneys seemed dubious. "But you and Jeff were working together when Will talked to the feds."

"That's true," I said. "I'm his supervisor in Gangs. We reconnected when I took over OGU from Van, my predecessor. Jeff was already part of the unit. I was happy about that."

"Why?"

"One: Jeff's a good cop. He busted his butt since he came on the department to reduce drugs and violent crime in a part of our city that was plagued with it. Two: We'd worked together before. I know how he operates and he knows how I work. We don't bump heads. We get the job done. Again, that's gold for a supervisor."

Then I pointed out another flaw in Will's testimony.

"Uhm ... also? He's full of shit about the black jerseys he said we were wearing when Jeff and I supposedly picked him up."

An attorney raised his eyebrows, urging me to continue.

"A lot of departments around the country do black jerseys," I explained. "But the jerseys we'd been issued back in Street Crimes ... they were bright green. So were our windbreakers. That was something we copied from the Los Angeles County Sheriff's Office. Never in my life have I been in possession of a black jersey like Will is describing."

Heads bent, the lawyers scratched notes while I continued.

"There's also the matter of the gun range," I said. "Frankly, this one burns me the most. The feds should have checked this right off the bat."

One attorney piped up. "The range Will said you guys took him to is off 56th Street North."

The gun range Will was describing was officially outside the city limits, a private facility. The Tulsa County Sheriff's Office had used it once upon a time. But as far as I knew, it was strictly for private use and gun hobbyists.

I told the defense team I'd never been out to that gun range in my life. But I knew where it was because it was out near our police academy.

The defense team's investigators later interviewed the gun club's owner. In doing so, they discovered the club had a private drive whose gates were locked every night just prior to sundown. Access was tightly controlled, the club's owner said. The number of people with keys did not include anyone from Tulsa PD or anyone associated with Jeff or myself.

The owner also stated he'd never seen nor heard of Jeff or me. When told Will's story, he thought it was ludicrous. Simply impossible.

"Now let's talk about guns," I said. "Will claimed that Jeff drew his service pistol, aimed at him, and cocked the hammer. Am I correct?"

Heads nodded around the table.

I tore right into this story. It was another example of total bullshit.

Will must have been watching too many movies. You know what I'm talking about. The suspect pulls out his gun and has to either rack the slide to chamber a round or he uses his thumb to cock the hammer.

Moments like these are added to scripts for intensity's sake. They're there to heighten the drama. Problem is, life doesn't work that way. People who carry firearms for a living don't do this stuff. It simply doesn't happen.

There was also, I pointed out, the tiny matter that, at the time Will alleged Jeff and I had abducted him, the official sidearm Tulsa PD issued to everyone in the department was the Glock 22c semi-automatic. But the Glock 22c doesn't have a hammer. It uses an internal firing pin.

Before we carried Glocks, all officers at Tulsa PD carried the Smith & Wesson 4046. I knew that weapon well. It was heavy as a boat anchor and a pain in the ass to clean. Hell, it's the weapon I went through the academy with and used during my first few years on the department. It was a good gun. But there was no hammer on that one either.

I should point out that even Tulsa PD's undercover officers carry hammerless firearms.

There was also this: Will testified that he'd never told a single person about his alleged kidnapping. Not his family. Not his girlfriend. Not his buddies. Nobody at all.

So we should ask ourselves, What makes more sense? That Jeff and I did what Will alleged we did? Kidnapped him, threatened him, all that? Or that he lied to the feds because he was hoping to save his own ass? And the feds wanted a corruption case so badly, they were willing to overlook Will's obvious lies. Either that or they did a horrific job following up on what Will told them.

In sum, the factors I'd described to the defense team were glaring evidentiary errors, holes so big that even the greenest detective should have been able to drive a truck through them. But the feds hadn't bothered. Instead, they'd taken the word of a career criminal. Why? Because it was convenient for them. I can only assume that, in their minds, they thought they were angling straight for a bust that would make them all look good.

Remember what I said back in Chapter One? The sword of Lady Justice can be used to cut corners. In my opinion, that's exactly what was happening here. I could see no other possible explanation.

And I don't mind saying ... at that very moment? I did not like the feds for that.

No, sir.

Not one damn bit.

CHAPTER THREE:
THE TALE OF MCFADDEN

The third and final allegation leveled against me as an unindicted coconspirator came from a disgraced federal agent named Brandon McFadden. McFadden worked for ATF, the Bureau of Alcohol Tobacco and Firearms. I call him "disgraced" because he'd been busted for stealing and selling confiscated drugs.

Go back to the very first lines of this book. Didn't I tell you? Not all cops are good. Brandon McFadden clearly was not. He'd abused his position and broken the law, and for that, he was sentenced to twenty-one months in federal prison. He was looking at a very long sentence in federal prison.

But being a federal agent, he knew how to work the system in his favor.

In our judicial system, the United States Code, or USC, establishes minimum and maximum sentences for federal offenses. These are the sentencing guidelines you may have heard about in the news or seen in movies or TV shows. When a judge passes sentence, they can't assign a defendant anything less than the USC minimum, nor more than the USC maximum guidelines.

Except ...

Judges are allowed to make what are called "variances" and "departures." A variance occurs when a judge passes sentence outside the normal sentencing guidelines based on specific factors set forth in the USC. A departure is a little bit different. Departures are granted when a judge weighs certain factors against the policies of an independent agency of the judicial branch called the U.S. Sentencing Commission.

In general, variances are easier to obtain for a defendant. They tend to be looser and can be argued more successfully.

An "upward" variance or departure allows a judge to pass sentence above the maximum federal guidelines—provided that certain boxes are checked. A "downward" variance or departure allows a judge to pass less than the minimal federal sentence. Again, when circumstances allow.

Let me give you an example.

In the federal case of *U.S. v. Alsante*, a convicted child rapist, James Alsante, was prosecuted for failing to register as a sex offender. By law, Alsante had to register himself with the sex offender database. But he didn't. So the prosecutor on that case pressed the judge for an upward variance and an upward departure, meaning a sentence above the maximum statutes of the U.S. Code.

The prosecutor argued that Alsante should be used to set an example for other convicted child rapists. She asked the judge to consider that Alsante was a repeat offender. And to drive home precisely the danger he posed to society, she read aloud from detailed accounts of Alsante's past crimes. That must not have been easy.

Furthermore, she argued that Alsante's failure to register as a sex offender showed his intent to prey on more children. He'd been ordered to register by law, but failed to do so. Why?

Registering is not a hard process. You don't have to walk over broken glass in your bare feet for six miles to do it. You just have to sign up and present certain court papers. The process is so straightforward, one could only intuit, the prosecutor said, that Alsante's refusal to participate meant he disdained the offender registry. Or that he saw registering as an active deterrent to him raping more children.

Either case, of course, was unacceptable, she argued. The court agreed. In the end, the judge granted the variance but denied the requested departure. Alsante's sentence was raised due to the mitigating factors the prosecutor presented.

You can probably see what all this meant to Brandon McFadden. Like I said, he was a federal agent. He understood how the system works.

He knew he'd been busted. He knew he was going to jail. But he also knew how he might get his sentence reduced.

If he behaved in a way that allowed his attorneys to argue for a downward variance, a downward departure, or both, he might get to see his family again.

For instance, I heard later on that McFadden had admitted his guilt in the matter of stealing and selling drugs. Admission of guilt is a key box to check off if you want to secure leniency.

Also, as far as I know, his theft and sale of the drugs was his first offense. That's another good box to check off.

Finally, he was willing, he said, to provide any information he had on other illegal activities.

As fate would have it, this is where I came in. Even though McFadden was lying.

MCFADDEN, THE ICEBREAKER

The whole thing was utterly strange since McFadden and I didn't have much of a history. I had only been around him a handful of times, and most of those had been in passing, while in the division. Honestly, I can't think of a single incident or case prior to the incident I'm about to relate where McFadden and I had been together.

This is how we met.

A few years before this whole fiasco, McFadden transferred into the Tulsa area to work with the Tulsa PD. That's not uncommon. Federal agents often work very closely with local cops. Sometimes they get embedded in joint task forces created to combat violence or drug trafficking in key geographical regions. These task forces often boast officers from various state and local agencies plus at least one federal agency.

McFadden and I first met back in 2007 when I transferred into the Special Investigations Division. I was in Narcotics back then and I supervised the evening shift.

Narcotics was a great unit to work in. Our investigators worked undercover, which meant we wore blue jeans and t-shirts to work. We drove regular vehicles on assignment. Facial hair and hair worn long was not just allowed, but encouraged. I even grew a beard during that time. But I basically looked like a cop with a beard so I shaved it off and let all the investigators do all of the undercover work.

At any rate, the point was to blend in with the people we were tracking, the criminals we hoped to bust. As a rule, most people who buy and sell larger amounts of drugs aren't wearing suits. They don't wear cufflinks. Don't wear starched, collared shirts, if you know what I mean. Or at any rate, not in Tulsa.

As ragged as we probably looked, we were deeply, intensely focused on minimizing large scale drug traffic in our city. This was during a time when a particularly powerful new form of methamphetamine was coming up from Mexico. It had the street term of "ice" because that's what it looked like: clear, jagged fragments of crystal.

But however strong it was, the price for this form of meth was far lower than the same amount of cocaine. Which meant that ice was all over our streets and we wanted to shut that down. At the very least, we strove to reduce its presence as much as we possibly could.

McFadden and I got to know each other professionally. I knew who he was. I'd seen him around the division. I was aware that he'd helped a few other officers make a few sizable busts that took drugs out of circulation.

One evening, while I was still working in Narcotics, I got a call from Jeff. Yes, of Jeff and Barrow fame.

"Hey, Sticks. You available right now?"

"For what?" I asked.

"Well, I just worked the day shift, I'm off at the moment. But you know that guy from ATF? McFadden?"

"I know him."

"He's doing a follow right now."

A *follow* is what it probably sounds like. Using surveillance techniques, a member of law enforcement follows a suspect to see what he or she is up to. For reasons I hope are obvious, this is typically done in an undercover vehicle.

"Who's doing it with him?" I asked.

Jeff said, "No one. He's on it by himself."

"Why?" I said.

That didn't make sense to me. Tailing gang members or suspected drug traffickers can be dangerous work. We typically don't do this sort of thing solo because, if things go south, there's no one to turn to.

"He said he just got a tip from a CI," Jeff said. CI is short for confidential informant. "Said he wanted to hop on it fast before it got cold. But now he's asking for backup. I'm heading that way but I'm coming from home. I figured you've got an unmarked car and might be free to help."

Looking back, I don't think I even had McFadden's number. I had to get it from Jeff. Once, I had it, I gave McFadden a call and related what Jeff had told me, just to make sure we were on the same page. Then I asked him how I could help.

McFadden confirmed that a CI had given him information on a guy that was selling large amounts of meth. McFadden wanted to follow the guy to see where he was staying. We coordinated quickly and I hung up.

After catching up with McFadden, he and I located the suspect's vehicle and followed it to an apartment complex in east Tulsa. There, we witnessed the suspect enter a second-floor apartment. For a while after that, we watched as, in a short period of time, several people stopped by to pay a visit.

What stuck out to me was that none of the visitors stayed for more than a couple of minutes. They went in and, very quickly, they came back out.

Now, obviously, having visitors isn't a crime. However, given the right circumstances, behavior like this often indicates that sales of drugs are taking place. That was certainly McFadden's opinion on what we were witnessing. Mine, too.

After combining the short-term traffic we'd seen with the information McFadden received, the idea was brought up to do a consensual investigatory encounter known in the police world as a knock and talk.

A knock and talk is exactly what it sounds like. Law enforcement personnel approach a domicile where suspected criminal activity is underway. They knock on the door and ask to speak with anyone living at that location. It's an overt way of letting potential criminal offenders know they're under scrutiny.

During a typical knock and talk, the lead officer identifies who they are and why they've come to that location. At this point, anything can happen.

Sometimes, the head of the household comes to the door and explains very calmly and rationally why there's been so much foot traffic. At other times, however, the officer may witness illegal activity taking place. It could be drugs being sold or consumed. It could be firearms displayed suspiciously, like in abundance. Property known to be stolen might be visible to the officers. You get the idea.

If any prior intelligence makes it seem logical, or if something the officers witness during the interview leads them to think illegal activity is taking place, they can ask the suspect if they'll consent to have them search the residence. The suspect, of course, has the right to say no. Meaning, they have the right to prohibit law enforcement from gaining access to the residence. However, very often, the officer or officers will come back after getting a search warrant, if applicable. This is considered the proper procedure.

It's important to note that, legally speaking, an officer can't force his or her way into a residence, nor can they intimidate a person in any way toward consenting to a search. Such conditions constitute illegal search and seizure. For this reason, knock and talks are often done by detectives and undercover officers. As plainclothes cops, they aren't as intimidating as, say, an officer dressed in full uniform.

That last point is considered critical from a legal standpoint. Because, should a suspect admit officers to his or her residence, they can't later claim in court that the reason they did so was because the police officer's appearance intimidated them.

"You up for it?" McFadden was asking me. He meant the knock and talk.

I told him I was good with it and we headed to the exterior stairs of the apartment.

The apartment was typical of east Tulsa. Meaning, it wasn't Shangri-La, it was one of those lower-rent, in-and-out communities so prevalent in our country these days. I'd actually lived just a few blocks from that apartment complex when I was in college.

McFadden and I took our badges out. I wore mine on a chain around my neck so civilians would know we were law enforcement personnel once they opened up the door.

McFadden knocked once, twice, three times. There was a moment where nothing happened. Then we heard someone moving inside.

You know that moment when you can feel the presence of another human being scoping you through the peephole? That happened.

A few moments later, the deadbolt clicked and the door swung open.

We made contact with a Hispanic male, probably in his early to mid-20s. I remember he was honestly one of the biggest Hispanic guys I'd ever come across. Like, I'm six feet four and this dude was taller than me. He also outweighed me by fifty pounds or so. I mean, yeah, the guy was soft looking. Not obese or fat. He could definitely stand to lose some weight. But he was freaking huge!

McFadden went into his spiel. He introduced himself as from ATF, then motioned to me and said quite clearly that I was with Tulsa PD.

The apartment was tiny but well-kept. The floor plan was pretty straightforward and I appreciated that because McFadden motioned that I should take a spot in the living room. It was a good call. From there, I was able to keep an eye on just about everything except the bedrooms, which split off from the living room, one on each side.

During his talk, McFadden asked the man if he lived there. The man stated that he did. We'll call him Sperry.

More talk ensued. McFadden asked Sperry if he'd give us permission to search the apartment. Sperry wasn't pleased with this. In fact, he looked more nervous than ever. His English wasn't fluent but he understood us. And he agreed.

McFadden looked at me. "Stay here, keep an eye on him. I'll check the bedroom." He'd already determined which of the two bedrooms belonged to Sperry.

With that, McFadden and I split up. I was searching the living room area while making small talk with Sperry. A few minutes later, McFadden came out of one of the bedrooms holding what looked like a large quantity of ice in one of those extra-large Ziploc plastic freezer bags.

McFadden brought this find to Sperry, set it down in front of him, and asked what it was, where he got it. The usual questions. Sperry snapped tight. He refused to answer. In fact, if I remember correctly, he acted like he'd never seen the dope before despite the fact that, seconds earlier, it had just come out of his bedroom.

At that point, we knew what to do.

"We're placing you under arrest," McFadden announced.

I remember tensing up just a bit.

This might be a common reaction for cops. After all, we were in this guy's apartment and had just found trafficking amounts of methamphetamine. At the time, I think it was the most drugs, I'd ever seen in person. I thought Sperry might try to fight us. Remember, he was huge. Either that, or he would try to make a run for it.

But no. Sperry kept cool. He stood there, tense but still, and kept darting his eyes all around while we cuffed him, made sure he was comfortable, and talked about what to do next.

At one point, I jogged my chin at the fat bag of ice. "How much do we got there, you think?"

McFadden raised his eyebrows. "Couple pounds, easy," he said.

I remember whistling low. At that point, ice was selling for maybe eleven grand a pound.

I took a few moments to call in the arrest to my captain as well as some of the other guys in my squad. It was a fat seizure for those days and we wanted everyone to know what we'd found.

By this time, Jeff and another officer had arrived at the apartment to assist us. Evidence was collected and information was gathered, just as would happen with any other knock and talk that yields good results.

Jeff, McFadden, and I had started to question Sperry more extensively. Very calmly, very peacefully we proposed that he might want to help us out. His arrest would still take place, of course. We assured him of that. But whatever information he could provide us would be greatly appreciated.

As I mentioned, Sperry's English wasn't perfect. Still, we were able to communicate with one another just fine.

Sperry took a moment to think about what he'd asked him. Then he said, "What do you want to know?"

"Whatever you've got." McFadden smiled and jogged his chin at the ice. "Let's start with where you got that."

A BUST GETS BUSTED

The procedure we followed was hardly unusual. It's common for Narcotic and Gang Unit officers to parlay with suspects they arrest. These negotiations always have the same goal. On our end—the cops' end—that goal is information. Tactical intelligence.

Names. Places. Dates. Times. Amounts of money. Amounts of drugs. The intent of people who push said drugs. Their associates in business. Their lovers. Their family members. What kind of dog they have. When they walk the dog.

Basically? Anything and everything helps. Armed with such information, good cops—the good apples—fight to keep the streets clean.

When passing along such intelligence, the suspect has a different goal, of course. That goal is to mitigate punishment.

From the moment we've arrested them, they know their lives have changed. At the very least, they're going to jail for a while. Even if they're released for some reason, the resulting procedures and scrutiny will complicate their dealings for years, if not the rest of their lives. At worst, they'll stand trial, get convicted, and go to prison.

In other words, they need help in whatever form it arrives. We like to extend a bit of that help so it works to our mutual satisfaction.

Personally, I like to think of the suspects we arrest as dominoes. Flip one over, he leads to the next. If that domino falls, he can get you another. If allowed to run its course, the line climbs higher and higher. It can go all the way to the top.

That's how the big busts are made. You don't start at the top. You start at the bottom. One bust that leads to another.

We asked Sperry a bunch of questions like, "How much methamphetamine have you recently sold? How much did you pay for it? How much are you selling it for? Who supplied you the product?" And so on.

Though a bit tight-lipped, Sperry seemed agreeable to answering these questions. Then we asked if he'd be willing to drive around with us and point out his supplier, plus any locations he knew to be connected to the dope game. Sperry agreed, so that's what we did.

Jeff, Sperry, and I all got into one of the undercover vehicles we were assigned and drove around Tulsa to talk about the illegal dope business. During this trip, Sperry pointed out a few locations where he said drugs were being kept or sold. Most of these locations, we already knew about. But a few came as new information, and we were glad to have his input.

The biggest obstacle came when we asked Sperry where he'd gotten his ice. He said his supplier was a white guy living in a mobile home park. Here our bullshit detectors went off big time.

Sure, it was possible he was telling the truth. But based on my training and experience, he was probably telling a lie.

At the time, most white methamphetamine users in Tulsa were making their own product. They would gather the ingredients needed from local stores and make what's known as a one pot.

A one pot is basically a meth lab that criminals can manufacture inside a plastic two-liter soda pop bottle. This method is fast. If you know what you're doing, it only takes ninety minutes or so to cook up a batch of meth. And the ingredients required are all easily, legally obtainable. A lot of them are household items you probably already own, like canisters of propane fuel, lithium batteries, Sudafed, and so on.

But many of these ingredients are toxic. Under the right—or wrong—conditions, they can also be highly volatile. So as quick and easy as one pots seem, they can also quickly and easily go very wrong. Highly flammable, they've been known to burn down the residences where meth addicts cook them. There's also the danger of toxic residues plaguing the residence where the meth was cooked, or the immediate community.

All this invalidated Sperry's claim. The meth he said he'd bought from a white guy in a trailer park couldn't have come from a one pot. He had too much of it, for one thing. For another, and much more critically, Sperry's meth was too pure to have been cooked in a soda bottle.

The ice that was then flooding Tulsa had come up from Mexico. We were sure about that. It was still relatively new to the area but it had a totally different look—a different texture, different color—than the local stuff we saw coming out of one pots.

Also, based on training and experience, I knew that Hispanics typically get their product from Mexico. Doesn't matter if it's meth, cocaine, weed, or heroin. They stick to suppliers they know, meaning Mexicans or Mexican-Americans.

So it didn't ring true that Sperry would be doing business for pounds of ice with some Caucasian dude—in a trailer park, no less. Given everything we knew about the local market in Tulsa, this just didn't fit.

McFadden and I were driving around with Sperry when my cell phone rang. I recognized the number as one of my fellow officers who worked the day shift at Narcotics. He was a hard-charging narco officer by the name of Woody.

Woody primarily focused all his work on large-scale Hispanic drug traffickers. I'm talking about the guys bringing loads and loads of dope into Tulsa. He was damn good at it, too.

"What's good Woody?" I said.

He sounded upset. "Sticks, I just heard about a large seizure of ice in east Tulsa." He gave me the address. "You were in on that?"

I shot a glance at Sperry. "Sure was. What's up?"

Woody cursed. "Sticks, I been on that apartment for weeks. Got search warrants signed. In my hand as we speak."

I think I rolled my eyes. Not good, I thought. That's not good at all.

But Woody was still talking. " ... Got an informant, told me the guy there, holds a lot of dope."

I nodded. "We found what's probably gonna be two pounds or so."

Woody groaned. "I was planning to serve the warrants first thing in the morning."

"Sorry, brother. This was McFadden's deal and I had no idea. I helped him on a follow and we ended up at this apartment."

Whenever possible, it's considered professional courtesy that an investigator not interfere with another officer's leg work, let alone horning in on a bust. Especially one that took so long to arrange. And one that yields such incredible results.

There are bragging rights at stake, that's true. But it's also an officer safety issue. You don't want officers from different units or different agencies working the same house. If the investigators are undercover, wearing plain clothes, other law enforcement personnel could mistake them as bad guys, especially if they see a firearm. This has happened with tragic results in other parts of the country.

For this reason, our division had a deconfliction board at the time. If any officer was working a case at an address, or had a search warrant for an address, they posted it on the deconfliction board. Unfortunately, in this situation, we helped an ATF agent with a follow that just so happened to lead to a location that one of our best narcotics investigators was already holding paper for.

"Wait a minute," I said. "You mentioned 'warrants.' As in plural?"

"Yeah." Woody sighed. "One for the place you just hit—"

"Right. Sperry. Who's the other one for?"

"It's either his supplier or his partner."

I glanced at Sperry, who, like I said, I suspected of lying to us on precisely that point. "Who do you think's the supplier?"

Woody gave me a name. Let's call him Chad. I jotted his name down and flipped my book closed.

"I'm still gonna run the warrant on Chad tomorrow," Woody said.

"For sure."

Woody sighed. "You owe me one, Sticks."

"No question. Again. Sorry, brother."

I thumbed off the call, and felt bad. Well, not overly bad. Woody was a buddy I'd known for a couple of years. He had great informants and he'd hit plenty of search warrants with large seizures during his time in Narcotics. I knew he was pretty upset he hadn't made this recovery himself. But I also knew his ego would survive.

Bottom line, he wanted those drugs off the street. And regardless of who had just done it, steps had been taken in that direction.

Of course, I couldn't mention this information to Sperry. If he found out we knew who his supplier was, that would be the first call he'd make once he was booked into jail.

Instead, we just played it cool and told him we'd look into the places he pointed out. We also promised we'd chat with the prosecutor assigned to his case about how much he'd helped us that night.

A short time later, Sperry would be booked into jail. McFadden and I finally left to go home.

SUSPICIONS INCREASE

Early the next morning, as planned, Woody and his team executed the search warrant on Chad.

I can't speak much to the details of that. When it all went down, I was home and finally catching some sleep. But the next time I got to division, I saw that Woody had called. He had new information.

"Turns out Chad is a talkative man."

"Oh yeah?" I said. "What'd he tell you?"

Chad had told Woody that he and Sperry were in business together. Sperry would typically keep the drugs at his place. This made sense considering the quantity McFadden and I discovered in the east Tulsa apartment.

But Woody went on. "Chad also said there was cash at Sperry's place."

"Okay," I said. "Maybe we missed it somehow. We didn't tear the place apart. I'll check on it and get back to you. Thanks."

When Jeff came on shift, I told him the story. When the apartment had been searched, I know for a fact we didn't go into full search warrant mode. Typically, on a search warrant, you search every nook and cranny looking for hiding spots. Dope dealers become professional hiders. They come up with all kinds of ideas on where to hide money and their dope.

What's funny is they typically hide their stuff not from the police so much, but from their own associates. Fellow bad guys. There are so many robberies, home invasions, and burglaries that take place in any city. Many are nothing more than a criminal getting their dope and money taken by a fellow criminal.

Still, after hearing what Woody had to say, I grabbed a younger officer in my squad and asked him to accompany me down to the Tulsa County Jail to interview Sperry a bit further.

Together, we roused Sperry. He'd been trying to sleep in his cell, which is actually pretty tough to do. Jails aren't constructed for getting a good night's sleep, especially for guys as large as him.

A deputy got him out of his cell and sat him down in a nearby interview room. I told him that officers had served a search warrant on his buddy Chad and we wanted to talk about it.

"Chad said there was cash at your place and you guys were in business together," I said.

Sperry shook his head. "Naw, man. He's lying. The officer is lying."

"Why would he do that?" I asked.

"I dunno." Sperry shook his head. "You're asking the wrong damn guy. Ask him."

"We will. But just so we're clear. We know you were selling the ice for days."

Sperry just stared at me.

So I tried again. I asked him a few more times about the money that was said to be in the apartment. Also about his relationship with Chad. Sperry denied it all. He clearly didn't want to talk about his friend and repeatedly denied having any money there.

Since we were getting nowhere, I signaled for one of the deputies working the jail to escort Sperry back to his cell.

"You think about this for a bit," I said. "And remember, we're still here to help. The more information you give us—truthful information—the more we'll testify that you were very helpful when it's time for court."

The other investigator and I got up and left the room. After saying good-bye to some colleagues, we left the jail and found ourselves back at the division where several of us discussed the discrepancies between Chad and Sperry over the money and dope.

Was there really money in Sperry's apartment and we just hadn't found it? If so, had Sperry used one of his phone calls to have someone go to his place and get the cash out of its hiding spot?

Or was the reality of the situation that Sperry held the dope while Chad kept the money? This is actually a very common arrangement among dealers. A stash house will hold the dope and the supplier will keep the money or hide it at another location.

If that was the case, did Sperry call Chad from jail to tell him he'd gotten caught with the dope? And hearing this, had Chad then moved the money from his own house to some other place? Or had something else happened to the money?

There were too many scenarios and they all seemed possible. Perhaps even likely.

We weren't sure what to do next.

CHAPTER FOUR:
JUSTICE WORKING AGAINST ITSELF

Keep in mind, this incident with McFadden happened more than a decade ago. As you may imagine, I've thought about it a lot since then.

I'm sure you know how the human mind works. It picks over every injustice, the way our fingertips pick at old scabs.

When you get dealt an injury as deep as this one turned out to be, it leaves a mark. That mark can be permanent.

I've had plenty of opportunities to assess each of the three allegations levelled against me as an unindicted coconspirator. Frankly, they all hurt me in their own way. But this McFadden one really gets my mind spinning.

FACT: I barely knew McFadden at the time we conducted our knock and talk in east Tulsa. I didn't even have the guy's phone number. That's why Jeff called me that day at the office and asked me to help with the follow.

FACT: That knock and talk was the first time McFadden and I had ever worked together. Again, we had no prior relationship other than me seeing him in our division a few times as best as I can remember. Therefore, it strains credulity to think we were associated in some criminal enterprise.

FACT: McFadden wasn't even with Tulsa PD. Technically, he was on loan from a federal agency to a unit that wasn't even mine at the time. Again, this speaks to the notion that we had no relationship. It therefore doesn't make sense that we'd conspire to pull off a crime.

ANOTHER FACT: McFadden was alone when he found that fat bag of ice. I don't think I honestly even once went into that bedroom the entire time we were there. Therefore, if he'd boosted some drugs, which it turns out he did, he did so all on his own.

Looking back, it was McFadden's idea that I stay in the living room with Sperry. McFadden's idea that I search the other bedroom (I think I found a small bag of marijuana in there). In other words, by my best recollection, McFadden had purposely engineered the bust so he could search Sperry's room by himself. I just didn't see it at the time.

These were the biggest questions that kept flowing through my mind. But then there was this one:

Who in their right mind would believe that I, as a law enforcement professional promoted to the position of supervisor, an experienced police officer with a great personnel file and a clean record with internal affairs, would ever participate in, or knowingly allow, misconduct to take place?

If we can't assume competence and integrity in our trained, career law enforcement personnel, why should we even have them?

HONOR AMONG THIEVES

Now, look. I know that some of you reading this book might come from the private sector. So maybe you read that argument I made above and you're thinking, "Are you kidding? In the world I live in, people in positions of authority abuse their power all the time."

I get that. And yes, those examples abound.

Just think of Ken Lay, who founded Enron. Remember him? In 2006, Lay was convicted on nineteen federal charges, including four counts of securities fraud, two counts of wire fraud, and three counts of making false statements to a bank. But before all that, he was Man of the Hour, a knight in shining armor whom everyone deemed beyond reproach.

In the end, this Man of the Hour, this Golden Boy cost his shareholders $74 billion. That's not counting the billions of dollars his employees lost in their pension funds. Or the damage he caused to the American financial system by forcing people to question its integrity.

You could also point to Jack Abramoff. In 2006, Abramoff pled guilty to conspiracy, fraud, and tax evasion. He was one of the top lobbyists in our nation's capital. But that all came crashing down when prosecutors showed he'd cheated casinos run by Native Americans out of $85 million in fees. And that was just the tip of the iceberg.

Abramoff had also bribed a Republican member of the U.S. House of Representatives from Ohio. Memorably, he'd also initiated a fake wire transfer to the tune of $60 million that resulted in the murder of a private citizen.

While we're on this subject, what about Bernie Madoff? In late 2009, this Wall Street titan, a man beyond reproach, pled guilty to eleven counts of securities fraud, money laundering, and theft from an employee benefit plan. In other words, Madoff wasn't the wizard of Wall Street most people took him to be. He was, in fact, crooked as hell.

His sentence for running one of the worst Ponzi schemes in American history was 150 years plus $170 billion in restitution. As no small aside, Mr. Madoff's son, Mark, committed suicide over his family's disgrace.

So, yeah. In the private sector, perhaps, people lie and cheat and steal all the time. And I don't mean to sound like a prude so I'll say this again. Bad apples show up in every barrel. Even in law enforcement.

McFadden was one of them.

Eventually, McFadden alleged to the feds that I'd watched him steal drugs and he'd offered me money. Does this make sense?

Let's break it down.

What I'm really asking is, does it make sense that I'd throw out everything I had—my reputation, my pension, my job, my career, my morals, and my self-esteem—to participate in a federal crime with a guy I barely knew for a payoff that probably would have amounted to a couple thousand bucks?

Come on.

Here's another thing to consider. I'd been on the job roughly ten or eleven years by the time McFadden and I pulled that knock and talk in east Tulsa. During those years, I'd learned a lot. I knew the realities of the street and the realities of law enforcement.

All of which is to say that, had McFadden approached me with any hint of criminal solicitation, I'd have assumed he was part of a sting. Specifically, that he was a federal agent embedded in Tulsa PD for the express purpose of catching local law enforcement engaged in illegal activities.

Traps of this sort are common enough. The law enforcement grapevine tends to buzz with them now and then. But, knowing this dynamic is often at play, does it make any sense I'd participate in a blatant crime that involved a federal officer? No. That defies logic. It thumbs its nose at common sense.

But the prosecutors ignored all this when it came to assessing my name in connection to this case. They were more intent on ram-rodding through any charges that could make me or other officers look bad. In the process, they made my unit and my department look bad. All so they could tick off a win for their office. All so they could hoist up their card, shout "Bingo!" and win a prize.

That's what burns me the most. I think their investigation began with good intentions. But then it steamrolled into something different once every bad guy saw it as their get out of jail free card. The feds wanted victory, and it felt to me that they were cool with victory regardless of the cost. But that sort of ethic turns toxic, and fast. It doesn't work in business, nor in politics or family life. And it sure as hell doesn't work when dealing with people who serve the law.

What I'm trying to say is the feds' whole rationale for naming me as an unindicted coconspirator was rotten to begin with.

Take the charge involving Rochelle. The feds had alleged I was involved in witness tampering.

Really? How?

Our chain of command had asked if our informant would make a recording; the informant agreed to this. When the informant asked that we preserve her safety while exchanging a piece of evidence, we fulfilled that request. And remember: Tulsa PD hadn't been shy about sharing evidence. When the feds requested a copy of Rochelle's tape, we gave it to them. None of this rises to the charge of witness tampering. It amounts to good police work.

And what about the second allegation, the one involving Brandon McFadden?

Remember that old saying, "Good lies are grounded in truth"? That, in a nutshell, is what McFadden tried to pull off.

Consider the truth he used to underpin his lies:

Was there an actual incident involving myself, Jeff, and McFadden? A documented incident where we conducted a knock and talk in east Tulsa?

Yes.

Had drugs been present at that incident?

Yes.

Had the drugs been methamphetamine?

Yes.

Had an arrest been made at that incident?

Yes. We arrested Sperry.

But the rest of what McFadden alleged was a passel of lies bound up with the twine of untruth. In many ways, he was doing what Will had done. Will was a career criminal and McFadden was a federal agent. But both had been arrested on charges they were going to jail for. Both were trying to save themselves from spending a good deal of time—and in McFadden's case, maybe the rest of his life—behind bars.

By the way, it was my understanding that McFadden changed his story multiple times. Meaning, whatever he needed to say or do to save his own ass, he would say it or do it. And the prosecutors, to get what they wanted, accepted McFadden's lies while knowing full well (I believe) that he was lying.

And what of Sperry? He later testified in court that he did have cash in his apartment at the time the knock and talk occurred. But by the time he took the stand, he'd also been interviewed by the feds. And who knows what they offered him to potentially get his sentence reduced?

Bottom line: Was there cash in Sperry's apartment?

I don't know. I know I didn't see any large sums.

How much of this drug that poisons our streets across America was there when we arrived, before McFadden allegedly took some?

I don't know that either.

What I *do* know is that McFadden brought roughly two pounds of ice out of Sperry's bedroom in what appeared to be, as I mentioned, one of those larger Ziploc bags. And that's what we later turned into the property room.

But the third and final allegation burned my butt most of all. This was the kidnapping charge that involved Will Patton.

Will's account had absolutely nothing at all to back it up. Literally nothing. Not one shred of evidence. Not one single witness.

Frankly, Will's story had all the veracity of an alien abduction, minus the probe that got shoved up his ass. Plus, his ridiculous claims were made by a convicted felon facing enough federal charges to send him away for a significant amount of time. But the feds seemed totally cool with that. Amazing.

You know why I say that? Because the double standard at work was head-spinning. Had any officer across the country walked into a prosecutor's office and tried to file charges based on Will's account, they would have been laughed right out of the building. I mean that.

In fact, I guarantee that any cop or prosecutor reading this book is nodding in agreement. Anyone with a half a brain could have debunked Will's myths on their own, and within a matter of minutes. But the prosecutors didn't.

That was outrageous. And yet? Will's tale worked. Meaning, the prosecutors let Will go. That's right. You read that correctly. They dismissed all charges against him as thanks for the lies he'd told under oath. Will Patton had successfully hustled the system. He walked away free as a bird. And I wouldn't be one bit surprised if this victory over justice later emboldened him to pull off even more crimes.

The ultimate point I'm trying to make is that both the investigators and prosecutors seemed to turn a blind eye to pieces of evidence that didn't fit their indictments. In politics, that's called cherry picking the facts. It doesn't work in that sphere and it sure as hell doesn't work in the law.

Except when it does.

Except when innocent people—innocent cops, in this case—get falsely accused.

And that, as they say, is the hell of it.

As I mentioned, this whole episode pissed me off so badly, I went out and got my tattoo. That's how burned I was at the way good cops were being treated. But again, it's not just cops. I'd feel the same way about any innocent person who was falsely convicted.

In late 2010, I had my altered version of Lady Justice permanently etched on my body. Then I went back to work, same as any other day.

The trial for Jeff and Barrow was set to begin in 2011. When it finally did, they'd sat behind bars without bail for fifteen months.

You read that right. Fifteen months.

And me? In a very real way, I'd been kept in my own kind of jail.

It was a prison of disillusionment that our system could be so inept.

AN INFORMANT GETS BUSTED

In May 2011, immediately prior to Jeff and Barrow's trial, I was on the job, on a routine day, when my cell phone rang. I checked the screen.

It was a Tulsa County deputy that I knew, but we hadn't spoken for months. He was a good guy and a hard worker who loved chasing dope and gangsters.

"Sticks," he said. "Listen. Reason I'm calling, I'm out on Queen Street right now. Got a search warrant on an old informant of yours."

"Who's that?"

"Lindsey Hicks?"

This is not the informant's real name. In this case, I've changed it to protect his safety.

"Uh huh," I said. "What about him?"

The deputy I was talking to was right. Lindsey and I had a history. Though still in his early-20s, Lindsey was already a convicted felon. His criminal history and convictions were mostly in drugs, but he was also a high-ranking member of one of Tulsa's Crip-based street gangs.

Lindsey was young enough that I'd watched him grow up on the streets. I'd seen him weather the storms of coming up poor and running with really bad crowds in Tulsa. This kid was a criminal, sure. He knew it and I knew it. But the way I saw it, that was mostly a matter of circumstance. His older brother and everyone he hung out with were gangsters. The power of peer pressure or family pressure is huge. In Lindsey's case, I felt it had to be accounted for.

He and I had a relationship I'd describe as friendly, even brotherly at times and in its own way. This sort of thing is actually very common despite what the media tends to show.

Like I mentioned regarding Rochelle, law enforcement officers and their informants tend to grow close. The relationship isn't personal. There are lines that cannot be crossed. Still, there's affection. There's a lot of caring involved. Above all, there's a real concern that this person who's trying to help you out, often by risking their life and their limbs, should come to no harm for going that extra mile for law enforcement.

"So I'm serving this warrant."

The deputy's words snapped me back to our conversation. "Where are you doing it?" I asked. "At his trap spot?"

A *trap spot* or "trap" is street jargon for the location a drug dealer sells dope from. Typically, it's not his own house.

The deputy grunted an affirmative. "You know where Lindsey might hide his drugs or firearms? We're searching the place and we can't find a thing. But we know he's got stuff hidden. Everyone says so."

I told this guy the truth. "I'm sorry, I don't know anything about it."

I stopped short of saying that, if I'd known where Lindsey had dope and guns stashed, I'd have run a search warrant on him myself.

I could hear the deputy shrugging on the other end of the line. "Okay. Well. Had to try. Call you back if we find anything."

"Yeah, thanks," I said, and hung up.

Later that day, the deputy called me again. "Outside," he said.

"Where?" I said.

"Backyard. It was up in the downspout that runs down the side of the house. We also found some guns under the empty house right next door."

I heard then that Lindsey was being booked into the Tulsa County Jail. I remember I told the deputy to tell Lindsey he was a dumbass. The deputy said he would do so. We got off the phone.

In case this is all new to you, this is the life of working informants. They get in trouble and they get arrested. For sure, the choir boys aren't the ones helping you solve violent crimes in your city. You need informants who have dirt on other people. And typically, the way they get this dirt is by associating with guys and girls who are dirty. Folks who are actively involved in committing crimes at various levels. That just comes with the territory and everybody knows it.

DISHONOR AMONG FEDS

Now like I mentioned earlier, it's very common for law enforcement officers to work part-time security gigs. We make extra cash that way. This doesn't just happen in Tulsa, by the way, it's sort of a nationwide phenomenon.

Various businesses and events will pay officers to provide security in uniform. Police departments condone this because, in a very real way, the public is supplementing the department's budget. Having more uniformed cops on the streets means they're mixing with citizens. No matter how you slice it, this is always good for the community.

On the day this all went down, I was pulling this sort of part-time gig with one of my best buddies, Vic Regalado. Vic actually went on to be the Sheriff of Tulsa

County where he still works today. He and I were partnered up working an annual music and art festival called Mayfest. We both used the money we made from the festival to take our families on vacations during the summer.

Vic and I were sitting in my patrol car watching DVD's when my cell phone rang and I checked the screen. It was Lindsey. I lifted the phone to my ear.

"Hey, Lindsey. What's up?"

I'd barely gotten these words out when he said, "They on yo' bumper, bro."

I think I stared out my windshield and blinked. "Say what?"

"The feds, man. They want your ass."

"What do you mean?"

Lindsey said, "Them Sheriffs took me away from my house ... took me down to some place that I, like, never seen before, yo!"

"Not Tulsa County Jail?"

"Naw, man. That was after. I'm talkin before!"

To hear Lindsey tell it, his journey to get booked at Tulsa County Jail got interrupted by a little side trip. This was unusual.

"I get to this buildin? They take me inside to a room. There were feds there wanted to talk to me," he said.

"No kidding." My voice rang flat and cold. I could tell where this was going.

"Yeah, dude. Two guys from the FBI. One of them looked like a Luigi motherfucker. They're like, 'Yo, Lindsey. We just wanna talk to you.' I'm like, 'Yeah? What about?' Then they're talkin bout you! Askin questions. They're sayin yer dirty an shit."

"Are you kidding me?" I was pissed. "I'm not dirty, I'm sick of this shit!"

"Thas what I told 'em! I was like, 'Sticks? Dude, Sticks ain't dirty!' Man, but these feds were like, 'Naw, naw, he's dirty.' And then they're like, 'Lookit. This bust they arrested you on? We can help your case out.' An I'm like, 'How?' An they were like, 'Tell us bout Sticks.'"

Lindsey went on to outline how this particular pair of federal agents grilled him on everything we'd ever done together as handler and informant. True to my good opinion of Lindsey, he told them the truth.

"Dude!" Lindsey said. "They was, like, 'He ever give you drugs to sell for him?' I'm like, 'Naw, man.' So they're like, 'How bout stealin' money or dope from you?' An I was like, 'Naw, man. Naw, he didn't.' So they asked me if the deals I did with you was legit. I told them they was. I said you didn't get down like that."

"Are you shitting me?" I asked.

"Yo, Sticks, man. I figgered it out. I know why mother fuckers say shit to the feds all the time. It's cause they basically put that shit in your mouth! They give you the ideas on what to say."

Just think about this for a minute.

My informant was telling me that federal agents were so interested in busting cops, they were basically force-feeding him ideas on something he could make up and say. Lies that would not only end the career of a hard-working law enforcement officer, but would also put a known criminal gang member back on the streets in exchange. Does that make sense to you?

It would be an understatement to say I felt betrayed. It would also be an understatement to say I was angry. Frankly? I was furious.

I was also, right at that moment, a little bit scared.

"Lindsey," I said, very carefully. "What did you tell these guys."

He knew right away what I was asking. I heard the change in his voice. "Yo, Sticks," he said, a bit quietly. "Like I said, man. You always been straight with me. And like ... I always appreciated that, you know what I'm sayin? So I'm keep'n it a hundred, okay?"

On the streets, when you *keep it a hundred*, it means that you're keeping it real. Not lying. You're telling the truth. And you live or you die by that truth. Whatever happens after ... well, at least you know you've earned it. Right or wrong, good or bad, you reap what you sow. Even on the streets, kids know there's a kind of salvation in that.

I thumbed off the call.

In the end, Lindsey went away for the guns and the drugs that officers found on that search warrant. He did his time in a state prison and he came out more mature. A little bit wiser, a bit more likely to think through his options before he makes a mistake.

I wouldn't say he's an angel now. But he paid his debt to society for his crimes that day. And I hope he's started to change for the better. That's what the system's supposed to encourage.

We bumped into each other a few years after he got out. And we still talk now and then. To this day, I'm grateful for what he did. I'm grateful he told the truth. That he wasn't a coward. That he had a sense of honor and pride.

I like to think exercising those traits on my behalf, or anyone's really, was one of the things that might have led him to a new understanding of life.

CHAPTER FIVE:
AN UNDESERVED STAIN

The Latin term *annus horribilis* means "a year of incredible suffering." My annus horribilis actually lasted fifteen months. Technically, that's a bit longer than a year. But then, technically, what can you do?

As I mentioned, the trial for Jeff and Barrow took place fifteen months after those two officers were denied bail. That's another way of saying they stayed in jail for fifteen months while awaiting their chance to defend themselves. This, to me, was a great injustice. As was the fact that I, who was innocent, had to deal with the burden of being branded an unindicted coconspirator.

In the final assessment of life, the greatest currency any person can spend is their time. We're all on this earth for the blink of an eye. To take away more than a year of somebody's life, and for what I considered the most spurious of justifications ... well, that just makes me angry. And it leaves me shaking my head.

Doubly so when the people who stole that time—the federal agents and U.S. Attorneys—were supposed to be fighting on the same side that Jeff and Barrow and I were on. The side of justice.

But maybe the worst part of all boils down to these two words: "not guilty."

After nearly twenty-four hours of deliberations, Barrow was acquitted of all eight charges filed against him. I'll say that again: all eight charges. In the final assessment, a specious case brought by the feds disenfranchised a man of his basic human rights while depriving the city of Tulsa, Oklahoma, of a twenty-six-year veteran police officer. Doubtless, the whole affair cost local, state, and federal taxpayers millions of dollars.

I guess Lady Justice was sleeping or something.

And Jeff? He had fifty-three charges levied against him. He was acquitted of all but eight. The eight counts included six counts of perjury and two counts of civil rights violations. All counts stemmed from two cases.

In the end, he received forty-two months in a federal prison with three years' probation. With credit for time served—and thanks to Jeff behaving as expected; meaning, in an exemplary fashion—he was a free man in about two years' time.

Keep in mind that Jeff and Barrow were held in isolation for fifteen months because they were deemed dangerous. This despite the fact they were never convicted for the crimes that supposedly made them dangerous.

But this is also very important: neither Barrow nor Jeff were found guilty for the three counts where I was listed as an "unindicted coconspirator."

In other words, we were right all along.

In other words, as far as those counts were concerned, all three of us were victims of justice.

According to Title 9-11.130 of the Department of Justice's Manual, its recommended that federal prosecutors do not name unindicted coconspirators unless doing so is absolutely required.

I quote:

"In the absence of some significant justification, federal prosecutors generally should not identify unindicted coconspirators in conspiracy indictments. The practice of naming individuals as unindicted coconspirators in an indictment charging a criminal conspiracy has been severely criticized in United States v. Briggs, 514 F.2d 794 (5th Cir. 1975)."

The statute goes on to read:

"Ordinarily, there is no need to name a person as an unindicted coconspirator in an indictment in order to fulfill any legitimate prosecutorial interest or duty. For purposes of indictment itself, it is sufficient, for example, to allege that the defendant conspired with 'another person or persons known.' In any indictment where an allegation that the defendant conspired with 'another person or persons known' is insufficient, some other generic reference should be used, such as 'Employee 1' or 'Company 2'."

The statute goes on to illuminate that even "non-generic descriptors," such as a person's "actual initials ... should not be used."

Why?

Clearly to protect the identities of people like me. People whose reputation, as things turned out, should never have been dragged through the mud in the first place.

Innocent until proven guilty, my ass.

The statute continues:

"If identification of the person is required, it can be supplied, upon request, in a bill of particulars. See JM 9-27.760. With respect to the trial, the person's identity and status as a coconspirator can be established, for evidentiary purposes, through the introduction of proof sufficient to invoke the coconspirator hearsay exception without subjecting the person to the burden of a formal accusation by a grand jury.

"The prohibition against naming unindicted coconspirators should not extend to persons who have otherwise been charged with the same conspiracy, by way of unsealed criminal complaint or information. In the absence of some significant justification, federal prosecutors generally should not identify unindicted coconspirators in conspiracy indictments. See JM 9-16.500; 9-27.760."

All of which can be summed up neatly like this: There was absolutely no reason for the FBI and U.S. Attorneys to name me as an unindicted coconspirator in the three allegations I mentioned. But they did. And to this day, I have no real comprehension of why.

All I know is the damage was done. To my life. To my reputation. Even, somewhat, to my faith in our system of justice.

For years afterwards, if somebody Googled my name, the first search results they got back had to do with the corruption trial. No context was offered. My commendations, my promotions, my sterling record on and off the force ... none of that was the focus. Only guilt by association on charges that finally turned out not to be true.

It's now been more than ten years since that investigation took place. Even now, I occasionally hear suspects, or those who aren't really fans of the police, accusing me of being a dirty cop. And of course, they'll specifically mention the prior allegations.

Imagine this for a moment. Imagine that somebody told a big whopping lie about you—a lie that maligned your character, demeaned the directional ability of your moral compass, and created a false narrative about your ability to do your job.

Now imagine this lie gets disproven. Imagine the relief that follows that. You think you've finally awakened from the nightmare.

But no. It turns out you haven't. Because the only thing some people remember is the bad stuff. That's the reality.

I bet you know exactly what I'm talking about. It's sort of like that joke about the Scotsman in the bar. Ever hear it? It goes like this:

"A man walks into a bar. He sees a bedraggled old coot leaning over his drink. This guy is a ruin. He's totally soused. He looks like he's been on the bottle for years.

Apropos of nothing, the old codger lifts up his head. In a thick Scottish accent, he calls aloud to everyone and no one in particular:

'There's no such thing as truth in a name!

'Once upon a time, I built me a great big factory. The products made in me factories got sold all over the world! Ah, but did they call me MacGregor the Factory Builder? *Nooooooo!*

'So next I built me a shipyard. The ships we made weathered great storms and sailed over each a' the Seven Damn Seas! But did they call me MacGregor the Ship Builder? *Nooooooo!*

'So then I built me a bank where we made money hand over fist. The loans we made helped people buy houses. We helped families save for retirement. Ah, but did they call me MacGregor the Banker? *Nooooooo!*'

The old man slammed his fist on the table so hard that his glass of whisky tipped over. Furious, drooling, he screamed at the bar.

'You know what they call me *now*? A' course, you do, damn it! *Everyone* knows!

'All it takes is a lie. *One lie*!

'Some bastard nobody heard of told the world I went out to a meadow one night and *got intimate with a sheep*!'"

That's it. That's the end of the joke.

Did you laugh?

I did the first time I heard it. But that was long before 2010.

After 2010, believe me ... I wasn't laughing anymore.

Recently, I got a phone call from a prosecutor with the Tulsa County District Attorney's Office.

"Officer Larkin?"

"Speaking," I said.

"This is ADA Smith."

I just made this name up. I honestly can't remember the name of the assistant district attorney who called me that day. The phone call, however, was real, and it's burned indelibly into my mind.

"What can I do for you, Mr. Smith?"

"Got a case here, pending a prelim."

A *prelim* is short for *preliminary hearing*. This is an event that takes place in a courtroom, and it's basically just what it sounds like. State prosecutors present evidence hoping the judge will agree they have sufficient cause to justify a trial.

Unlike a grand jury, however, defense attorneys are also present at a prelim. They get to challenge witnesses and contest the state's evidence hoping to convince the judge that a trial would be a waste of everyone's time.

This ADA continued. "This is regarding the case where your unit served a search warrant on Shaunday Mullins."

The ADA asked if I remembered that case. Boy, did I ever.

In October 2018, my unit was passed reliable and corroborated intelligence. A convicted felon, the aforementioned Shaunday Mullins, was said to illegally possess firearms and narcotics with intent to distribute. Those are two big no-nos for anyone. But they're especially bad for a convicted felon.

Our department had a history with Mr. Mullins. The last time police went out to arrest him, he'd barricaded himself in his residence and verbally threatened them.

There was also this: An informant had told us that Mullins kept saying he wasn't going back to prison. As in ever. Law enforcement officers take such threats very seriously. When coupled with Mullins's previous behavior, it led us to believe that, if we ever went out to arrest Mr. Mullins again, he'd try to shoot us all dead in the streets.

After weighing our options carefully, our department decided the only safe course of action was to have our Special Operations Team execute the warrant.

I've already mentioned SOT. Again, most people know a Special Operations Team by the more generic term SWAT, which stands for "Special Weapons and Tactics." Basically, SOT is a law enforcement unit that's highly trained in the use of tactical deployment and various weapons.

As you may imagine, we only send this unit into situations we deem highly dangerous. Our old friend Shaunday Mullins fit the bill. And it turns out, we were right.

On the day the search warrant was executed, our team pulled up to Mr. Mullins's residence in an armored personnel carrier. Mullins eventually emerged with a weapon and shot at the officers. The SOT returned fire and, during the gunplay that followed, Mr. Mullins was shot and killed.

Inside the residence, officers located firearms and trafficking amounts of methamphetamine. Mullins's live-in girlfriend was present and subsequently charged for these felony crimes.

Once I'd relayed to the ADA that I was familiar with the case, he said the following.

"I don't see your name on any of the reports."

There was good reason for that. "I wasn't there," I said.

"Well, I just got a call from her attorney and she's saying her client said you stole money and jewelry from her purse. The attorney says she is going to the media with it tomorrow."

In disbelief I asked, "Are you joking?"

"Her client says that when she was arrested you took her purse from her and that her money and jewelry weren't turned in or in her purse when she got out of jail."

I remember raising my voice. "I wasn't on the warrant! I wasn't even in town when the warrant was served!"

This, for me, was a no-brainer since I knew exactly where I was when the warrant was served and Mullins met his fate. Not only was I not in Tulsa that day, I wasn't even in the same time zone. I was in Manhattan, New York City, at A&E Television Network headquarters.

"What I remember," I told ADA Smith. "I was taping an episode of *Live PD Presents: PD Cam*. I was on set and my cell phone rang. It was one of my squad mates, Tyler Cox. He was calling to let me know what went down."

Like I said, I remember it perfectly. When your squad is part of an operation where shots are fired, it's one of those deals when you look back over your career, you will always remember.

Smith sighed. He could see where this was going. "So you had nothing to do with the warrant. Nothing at all."

"Not true," I said. "Prior to running the warrant, Cox came to me to discuss Mullins's history. We both agreed it was a high-risk warrant. For that reason, we decided to use SOT, and I'm glad we did."

"Can you prove that you were in New York when this happened?" Smith asked.

"I'll supply whatever you need to show I was there," I said. "Witness accounts, receipts. Hotel confirmation. Pay stubs. Airline tickets. Just give me a couple of days."

"Okay, then. Thanks."

We hung up.

THE PROFESSIONAL BECOMES PERSONAL

I mentioned this story because I want you to ask yourself a question.

Why do you think Mullins's girlfriend and her defense attorney tried to pull off the move they did? Was it because they knew my record is spotless and I've never once had a single credible complaint lodged against me? Or was it due to the fact that, despite having a spotless record with no sustained complaints, my name still shows up on Internet searches related to a corruption trial?

I bet you know the answer to that.

Some people sense potential weakness in a person and do anything they can to exploit it. And let's be honest. This strategy can be effective in many situations.

Suppose you're engaged in physical combat and you know your reach exceeds that of your opponent. It therefore makes perfect sense to hang back. Stay outside his strike range. Let him tire himself out trying to jab at you with short punches and kicks. Then, when he's finally gassed, you move in fast and go for the kill. That's a great use of exploiting a weakness. Boxers do it all the time.

Or suppose you're playing chess against someone who doesn't know how to properly deploy his knights. One school of advice says to take them out as fast as you can. This increases the power and reach of your minor pieces. Your pawns become much deadlier, more effective in your plans.

Each analogy works in its specific situation. But they fall short when you translate them to the matter of satisfying justice.

You can't have true justice without the truth. And the truth is not something you make up to suit your purposes. That's called a lie.

Mullins's girlfriend and her defense attorney were treating the truth like a game. They thought they'd spotted a weakness in me. Specifically, they thought they could get me to crack and offer concessions. Maybe they judged my character by the false allegations made against me during the trial of Jeff and Barrow. Or maybe they thought I'd be so wary of bad publicity, I'd simply accede to their demands.

There's a third option, of course. Maybe they had no idea what I would do. You know the old saying that rats backed into a corner fight with everything they have? Well, a cornered suspect can be one of the most dangerous things on the planet. I can tell you that from experience.

In my opinion, we had Mullins's girlfriend cold. She was grasping at straws to defend herself on the charges we'd filed against her. That's when she became cornered, when she started throwing everything she had at the walls to see what, if anything, stuck.

In pro football, this is what happens when the quarterback goes for the Hail Mary pass. He's got nothing else to lose, so he whips back his arm, says a prayer, aims downfield, and throws.

But, see, that's exactly why I wrote this book. Right now, cops are under a great deal of strain nationwide. Like I said in this book's introduction, certain events have prejudiced people against the police. Those events are entirely worthy of dissection, consideration, and criticism. But we can't throw the baby out with the bathwater.

At this point, it feels to me like too many people have taken to reflexively distrusting cops. Frankly, that's just as bad as people reflexively being pro-police. The problem is a lack of emotional distance. It's the tendency to ignore the facts, put blinders on, and go with a knee-jerk analysis. All that does in the end is yield garden variety prejudice.

You can't cure bigotry with bigotry. Societies have tried doing that all throughout history and it never works. People need to stop and think for a moment. And when it comes to the police, I'll say it again. You've got to realize we're a population. And like any other population, yeah, we've got bad apples in the barrel, sure. But that doesn't make the whole barrel bad.

If my dander is up on this point, and it is, it's because those false allegations from 2010 have followed me into my personal life.

Recently, I made an appointment with an investment firm. I wanted to speak to a specialist about retirement planning. I'd used the same firm several years before. They knew me and I knew them. Or so I thought.

At this latest meeting, I sat with a financial advisor. Let's call her Janet. Janet looked over my assets and asked what had brought me to see her.

I said, "I've got a little money from my TV work. I'm hoping you and your firm can help me shuttle that money to various funds. I want to treat it wisely. Make it grow as the years go by."

"Sure, sure. That sounds like the right thing to do." Janet tapped her keyboard, taking notes. Then she passed me a form on a clipboard. "If you just sign here, we can start the whole process."

I quickly scanned the form. It authorized Janet and her firm to conduct a background check on me. I said, "Am I reading this right?"

She smiled and tapped more keys. "You are. But it's nothing. Standard procedure these days in the financial services industry. We just need to make sure that nothing in your finances came from illegal means."

"No problem." I signed the form and passed her the clipboard.

Imagine my shock when, the next day, Janet called me. She sounded tense. "Officer Larkin? There seems to be a problem related to your finances."

"What kind of a problem?" I asked.

"Well, you see ... " I could hear her choosing her words very carefully. "We conducted our background check. And it seems your name popped up many times in connection to bribery and corruption charges."

"Ten years ago." I sighed. "Okay, do you have a minute? I'd like to explain this."

"Sure."

I outlined how, basically, I'd been falsely and inappropriately named an unindicted coconspirator, and that charges were never filed on me. I went on to explain that not only were charges not filed on me, but the officers were found not guilty on charges that I allegedly conspired on.

"I see." Her tone grew abundantly cautious. "Could you help us out with something, then?"

"I'll certainly try."

Janet asked if I would provide her office with additional documentation—previous taxes filed at the state and federal levels. Pay stubs. Bank statements. Anything to help validate that my income had been legally obtained.

Dutifully, I gathered all this, and passed it on.

The long story short? Eventually, I was accepted as a client. Janet's firm helped me make the investments I wanted to make, and I was grateful for that. But the hassle of false allegations is a stain that hasn't yet faded. It's now becoming clear to me that it might never go away.

And just so I'm being clear, this is just one little instance where that stain threatened to derail my personal life. There have been others. Many others.

It's infuriating to spend your whole life in the service of justice only to have your integrity questioned. This holds doubly true when you know that the people who've questioned your integrity are themselves deficient in that category. The allegations lodged against me were ridiculous. And yet, because of them, I could have lost my job, or wound up in prison or jail. That's an awful situation.

If there's been any upside to all this, it's been the experience I've earned; experience which I now pass on to my peers. I'm often in a position to train young officers and new supervisors at Tulsa PD.

"This is what you have to watch out for," I tell them. "If you get into trouble of this sort, these are the first things you should do to protect yourself and your family."

And here's another good thing: As a result of this particular corruption investigation, the Tulsa PD changed a few of its key procedures. One of these procedures involves the way investigators handle informants.

Confidentiality rules prohibit me from going into detail. Suffice it to say, it's now more difficult for someone to levy specious charges against an officer and make them stick. Layers of process have been added to make the handler-informant relationship more beneficial to all parties. Both officers and civilians now enjoy increased protections. That's as it should be.

I'll say it again: If justice works for one person, it should work for everyone.

It should especially work for police officers who work honestly and hard to keep us all safe.

CLOSING THIS CASE, MOVING ON TO THE NEXT

So that's my story in a nutshell. I have one final note:

Lady Justice was the first tattoo I got, but she wasn't the last. When José etched her on my bicep in 2010, I had no idea I'd kicked off a lifelong project. Since then, my whole left arm has become a sleeve of tattoos.

Lots of folks tell me how strange they think this is. One daring person even asked me: "Why would an active-duty police officer from Middle America sport an entire sleeve of tattoos?"

I remember smiling when I heard this.

I remember thinking, Man. If you only knew ...

Suffice it to say, there are plenty more stories to tell. Maybe someday I'll get a chance to tell them.

For now, maybe you can see why I wrote this book. I know how it feels to be falsely accused. And it's awful. It's deeply corrosive to our sense of law and order.

Each of the stories I've gathered involves a cop or cops whose lives were challenged or ruined because they wore their badge. Because they were trying to do the right thing.

But don't take my word for it. See for yourself.

PART TWO:
CASE FILES OF OFFICERS FALSELY ACCUSED

CHAPTER SIX:
THE CASE OF THE HONEYBEE KILLER

CASE FILE

Accused officer: Brian Dorian, Lynwood Police Dept.,
 Crete, Illinois

Related parties: Chief of Police Marco Kuyachich

Date of incident: October 8, 2010

Location: Lynwood County, Illinois

It can be frightening when a killer is loose. The danger the killer presents is one thing, the obvious factor to deal with. But the societal damage that fear can cause is another, and often potentially worse.

Even the strongest communities can collapse when weighted by fear and deep-seated mistrust. For this reason, when the virus of a murderer enters a communal body, local law enforcement departments move quickly to neutralize the threat. From long experience, we have learned to apprehend a murderer fast before they can strike again.

Now, as anyone who's worked in law enforcement can tell you, police officers have the greatest chance of successfully capturing a suspect in the first two days following a crime. This short window in which pivotal action takes place is the premise of A&E's popular crime documentary show, *The First 48*.

As of the writing of this book, *The First 48* has been on the air for nineteen years, and with darn good reason. It's consistently one of the highest-rated non-fiction justice series on television. It's even been nominated for a Distinguished Documentary Achievement Award in the Continuing Series category by the International Documentary Association.

The First 48 takes an in-depth look at the work lives of homicide detectives in various cities across the United States. It usually focuses on the work they do in the first forty-eight hours of a murder investigation. Hence the show's title. This format is part of the reason why *The First 48* is successful. Audience members get caught up in the real-life drama of what it takes to catch a killer and shut them down.

Deep down, each of us feels vulnerable. This is part of being human. Another big part is the psychological phenomenon known as projection. Our brains tend to take heightened emotional instances, such as fear for our safety, and project them onto incidents in which, in truth, there is nothing to fear. So if there's a killer on the loose, say, in small-town America, we begin to think there could be killers on the loose anywhere, everywhere all at once.

That's what I meant when I said it's important to catch a killer quick. When this isn't done, people start to act crazy. And crazy, believe me, is nobody's friend.

This notion of catching a criminal within the first forty-eight hours of a crime was very much at work in the autumn of 2010. That's when a suspect whom police dubbed "The Honeybee Killer" gunned down two people in the American Midwest. But in this case, it turned out the local police and a pretty large swath of the public rushed to judgment.

The man they arrested was innocent: Officer Brian Dorian of the Lynwood Police Department in the village of Lynwood, Illinois.

It happened like this:

On October 5, 2010, three construction workers were working a repair job at a burned-out farmhouse outside Beecher, Illinois. They were approached by a middle-aged man who asked them about buying the place. Shortly thereafter, this man got back in his car and drove off. The repairmen went back to work.

But a short time later, the middle-aged man returned. Reportedly, he asked the construction workers about building materials. Then, without any warning, he pulled a revolver out and began shooting.

One of the workers, Rolando Alonso, a father of ten, was killed by the gunman; it was only Alonso's second day working the job. A second construction worker, Joshua Garza, was critically wounded by a gunshot to his right eye. The third victim, whose name I will not disclose, fled the scene.

Later, police officers questioned the surviving members of the construction crew. The cops were hoping to piece together exactly what had happened—why the incident might have occurred and perhaps most importantly, who the suspect might be.

They were stumped. Why would someone pull up to a group of three men, treat them amiably, then return and open fire? It was shocking. It didn't make sense.

But it turned out the horror show didn't stop there.

Later that same day, a farmer named Keith Dahl was shot three times.

Dahl lived in Lowell, Indiana, about fifteen miles from Beecher moving east along local highways. He survived his shooting because, as he later reported, once he got hit, he lay very still. His assailant likely assumed he was dead and the gunman departed without making sure this was so. All in all, this was a very fortunate situation, both for Keith Dahl and the police of Lake County, Indiana.

Dahl later told the authorities that a stranger had approached him and started asking questions about honeybees. This was unusual, but not nearly so odd as how, in the middle of the conversation, apropos of nothing, the man who liked honeybees pulled out a pistol and fired at Dahl three times.

The description Dahl gave of this man matched the one given by the two construction workers who'd survived the Beecher shooting. Once this and other factors were considered, authorities realized they were facing what any law enforcement agency fears: a serial shooting suspect who appeared to randomly target his victims.

Since they had to call the suspect something, police dubbed him "The Honeybee Killer."

They were desperate to capture this suspect. Put yourself in their shoes. A suspect had just committed two random acts of violence whose outcome was one man dead and three others were critically wounded. What, if anything, would stop this man from striking again? And how would the public react if they learned that such random acts of violence were being committed in America's heartland, considered by many to be the safest region of the country?

The officers quickly reviewed their leads. Their biggest clue was the suspect's vehicle. Dauntingly, however, one survivor had described this car as a red pickup truck while another had sworn he'd seen the man driving a common blue sedan.

Knowing that time was of the essence, the police began stopping any car in the region that matched either description. Each vehicle they stopped was searched meticulously and its driver questioned at length as part of a Field Interview Report.

A Field Interview Report, or FIR, is one of the most common and powerful tools in a police officer's peacekeeping arsenal.

An FIR is used to record everything that takes place when an officer stops an individual or vehicle. The officer who conducts the stop uses the FIR to catalog information about the person being interviewed.

Importantly, FIRs do not carry presumption of guilt. Nor is probable cause required at the time the FIR is executed.

The officer conducting a standard FIR merely documents the event. In some cases, this process turns up suspicious behavior that warrants further scrutiny. In other cases, it might clear the vehicle or individual featured in the FIR as free of suspicion. Using the process of elimination, investigators can therefore allocate resources to other inquiries.

Overall, Field Interview Reports are crucial law enforcement tools that have helped solve countless crimes. In some cases, this has even occurred many years after the initial FIR was written.

Now here's where a good cop enters the scene and, sadly, bad things befall him.

As I mentioned, Officer Brian Dorian of the Lynwood Police Department of Lynwood, Illinois, became the primary suspect. But let's wind back a bit and find out why.

To begin with, the village of Lynwood is a suburb of Chicago. You can find it resting comfortably on the big city's southeast outskirts. Drive about ten miles north from Lynwood and you'll hit Lake Michigan. Drive about half a mile east and you'll cross the border into Indiana. Drive about ten miles south by southwest you'll hit Beecher, Illinois. Go the same distance, but this time south by southeast, you'll hit Lowell, Indiana.

In other words, Officer Brian Dorian worked and resided very close to both locations in which the Honeybee Killer had struck.

In October 2010, Officer Dorian had been out of work for approximately one year. Shoulder surgery prohibited him from performing his duties. During this interval, as Dorian himself later explained on the Dr. Oz show, he made himself useful by running various errands for family members and friends.

On October 6, 2010, the day after the Honeybee Killer struck, Officer Dorian was driving to his mother's house. He had offered to sign for some furniture she was having delivered. After that, he was set to have coffee with a friend then pick up some dry food for his dog.

Imagine his surprise when he was stopped by his brethren law enforcement personnel. By sheer coincidence, Officer Dorian's civilian vehicle was a red pickup truck.

Later, Dorian described what happened on his Facebook account:

"Holy crap!! I got pulled over in Schererville [Indiana] and ordered out at gunpoint because I matched this lunatic's description. I definitely [sic] don't like being on the other side of gun barrels being pointed at me!"

While officers held him at gunpoint, Brian Dorian watched other law enforcement personnel search his car. Dorian, of course, had questions about what was going on. The cops from Indiana answered these questions as best they could but, undoubtedly, their minds were on their jobs at the moment. In keeping with FIR policy, they explained why they had stopped Dorian's car and apologized for any inconvenience before allowing him to proceed.

Why would officers stop someone at gun point? Isn't this somewhat aggressive? After all, the police had no idea if Officer Dorian, or anyone else they were stopping, was the murderer.

As a matter of procedure, police officers treat each potential suspect the same. In the case of the Honeybee Killer this means that anyone they stopped who they thought might be the Honeybee Killer was treated as if they were the Honeybee Killer. Until such time, of course, as this seemed inappropriate.

From the cops' point of view, and I concur, every person they stopped to fulfill an FIR might have been an armed murderer. Caution was warranted. It was an officer and public safety issue.

Their first point of business was therefore to get each driver safely out of their vehicle and detain him. Next, they interviewed each of the vehicle's occupants, taking notes on the responses made to their questions, as well as the respondent's general attitude and demeanor while speaking.

While this is going on, it's common for other officers to search the vehicle. Assuming, of course, they have legal grounds to perform such a search. Legal grounds could include the driver's consent to having their vehicle searched (the most common form of legal grounds); probable cause; or a search warrant issued by a local judge or magistrate.

Undoubtedly, some civilians will find this type of car stop upsetting. However, it's important to remember what's really going on. A dangerous individual is loose, and this person may commit violence again at any time, in any place, and for no good reason at all. Law enforcement personnel are trying to make the community as safe as possible for everyone.

Once the police explain things like this, most citizens understand why their car was stopped in the manner it was. And of course, it's common to have officers conducting the FIR apologize sincerely for any inconvenience they've caused.

Officer Dorian had no idea that his troubles were just beginning.

Later that day, on October 6, he'd graduated to become law enforcement's prime suspect in the case of the Honeybee Killer.

Dorian only learned this was so when, a few days later, at some point between 10:30 and 11:30 in the evening, his dog began to growl. Very likely, the faithful pooch had heard or caught wind of the SWAT team which had been dispatched to bring Dorian in. Very quickly, the team penetrated Brian Dorian's home, surrounded him, and arrested him.

Now here again you might be thinking, Really? A SWAT team? Isn't that overkill?

Put yourself in the police officers' position. Yes, it was true; Brian Dorian hadn't resisted at all when having his vehicle searched. Without question, this was a mark in his favor. But consider what was at stake.

An unidentified man had just randomly shot four innocent people. One of these people had already died and more might conceivably perish from their wounds at any time.

For whatever reason, Dorian's name had been moved to the top of the list of suspects. In other words, police were operating on the assumption that he was the Honeybee Killer. They also knew that, as a law enforcement officer, he had training in weapons and tactics. The odds were also dead-on that he had firearms either directly at hand or immediately accessible on his premises.

Finally, since Dorian was at home, he could potentially barricade himself against any force sent to apprehend him. He knew the layout of his home better than anyone. This presents one of the most dangerous situations law enforcement officers can face: a suspect who possesses a deadly edge over peacekeepers sent to address him.

Given all this, a SWAT team seems like the only viable choice. SWAT team members are equipped with the proper tools for this type of scenario, tools that "typical" police officers—patrol duty officers and detectives—don't possess. To my read of this situation, the cops were acting professionally, using the proper degree of caution.

While police slapped the cuffs on Officer Dorian, they explained why they had come to his home. They told him they needed to bring him down to the station for more questioning.

Officer Dorian understood the situation, of course. I have no doubt whatsoever that the FIR he'd participated in at the traffic stop merely days before was fresh in his mind as they led him away.

But I think it's also safe to assume he was baffled. Why was he being detained? After all, he was a police officer. Normally, he was the guy who caught crooks. In other words, why had he moved to the top of the list of suspects? Because he had a red truck and the killer did too? That must have seemed thin.

He must have found the situation confusing. Certainly frustrating. Possibly frightening.

Now this part is pivotal. When he arrived at the police station, Officer Dorian waived his rights to an attorney.

Why would anyone do this, you ask? I can't claim to know what Brian Dorian was thinking.

Perhaps he was trying to show that, as an innocent man, he didn't feel legal protections were necessary. He probably never imagined—not for a moment— that he'd been promoted to the prime suspect in a murder case.

I bet if he'd known that he was, he might have chosen a different course.

Let me address this topic head-on. Personally? If I was arrested for pretty much any reason? I would have an attorney present with me. No question.

Remember what I mentioned back when I started this book? One of the greatest things about the American legal system, something that no one should take for granted, is their Constitutional right to have an attorney present while being questioned by law enforcement.

However, speaking frankly, this right can complicate matters from a procedural point of view.

The moment we have probable cause to arrest, and a suspect "lawyers up"— meaning they request to have an attorney present—police officers will book him or her into jail. The suspect then remains in jail until his or her attorney and the detectives in charge of the case can agree on a time for the suspect to be interviewed.

Here's another law enforcement pro tip: This situation rarely plays out the way we see it depicted on television or in movies. In those cases, a suspect always seems to have an attorney "on tap." Also, to move the plot along, writers just cut to the point where the suspect's lawyer barges in and says something dramatic like, "How dare you speak to my client without me present?"

Uhm. This doesn't happen.

First, most people don't have a personal lawyer. Therefore, it takes them a while to check with family or friends or consult the phone book or whatever before they find someone who will represent them.

Second, attorneys are people, too. Once you contact one and convince them to represent you, they don't just magically appear whenever the suspect snaps his fingers.

All this is my way of saying that, typically, refusing to answer questions before an attorney arrives involves a good deal of waiting. The wheels of justice, as someone once said, turn slowly. Very slowly.

In retrospect, maybe this is the reason why Brian Dorian waived his right to have an attorney present.

But however it happened, the moment he did so, detectives had the right to question him. And this they proceeded to do. For four and a half hours.

I think it's a safe assumption that they grilled Officer Dorian about his life while on leave from the Lynwood Police. Who his associates were. How often he drove his red pickup, and where. His family. His habits. You get the idea.

Without question, they sought to understand Officer Dorian's activities—all his activities, complete with dates, times, and locations—on October 5, the day of the shootings.

To this end, Officer Dorian provided investigators with an alibi for his whereabouts. He claimed this alibi would vindicate him: prove beyond the shadow of a doubt that he hadn't been in Beecher or Lowell when either shooting took place. And therefore, that he couldn't be the Honeybee Killer. Case closed.

And yet.

The Indiana police informed Officer Dorian they were taking him into custody while the investigation continued. By custody, they meant jail. And this is important.

Officials charged Officer Dorian with one count of first-degree murder for allegedly gunning down Rolando Alonso. They also set his bail at $2.5 million. But they didn't tell Officer Dorian this. None of it. All they did was assure him they'd check on his alibi.

But again, the wheels of justice turn very slowly. It took investigators six days to verify everything Brian Dorian told them. Six days that Dorian spent in jail.

And guess what happened? In the end, his alibi held up.

Officer Dorian later commented, "When someone waives their rights to an attorney and talks to you and gives you their alibi and what they were doing, you don't charge somebody with murder without even looking into their alibi."

Maybe so. But here I'll repeat my previous comment. If you happen to find yourself called in for questioning as a suspect—regardless of what the case is about and regardless of whether you feel you're innocent or guilty—my advice is to have an attorney present.

Consider why.

As part of his nearly five-hour interrogation, Officer Dorian was offered a *polygraph test*. Let's pause here to set straight some more misconceptions.

A polygraph, or so-called "lie detector" test, isn't like what we see on TV or in the movies. The truth is, polygraph tests can be so unreliable, many courts refuse to admit them as evidence in legal proceedings.

But again, Officer Dorian accepted the offer. He probably did this thinking that, since he was innocent, the polygraph would prove this and he would be instantly vindicated. But police then admitted they couldn't administer a polygraph until later.

Next, the authorities offered to put Brian Dorian in front of a lineup. Shocked and incredulous, he answered them angrily, "Do you know how many people have been falsely pulled out of a lineup?!"

He's right. According to Locke Bowman, Legal Director of the Roderick MacArthur Justice Center, "Eyewitnesses are overrated as evidence of a person's guilt." During an interview on a local radio station, Mr. Bowman added: "The witness begins to imagine that he saw Officer Dorian at the scene of the crime [for instance]. When he's just actually remembering what he observed in the photo spread."

My own experience bears this out. The human imagination is a miraculous thing. When things go bump in the dark, we imagine monsters under our beds. When things go "wrong" in our lives, we often assume we're responsible—when this isn't always the case. Conversely, when things go "right" in our lives, we may be tempted to think we had something to do with that, too. And sometimes we did. But then again, sometimes we didn't.

It's one of those tricks about living that most people struggle with, I suppose: the ability to weigh certain experiences with the proper degree of proportion. To take credit where credit is due, and responsibility when and where it's warranted. But also not to do this when situations rightfully dictate.

At this point in the proceedings, I imagine that Officer Dorian was losing his patience. That would have been *my* reaction, I think. And I reiterate: This is all the more reason to have an attorney present during these types of proceedings.

Dorian didn't know it at the time, but the odds were stacked against him. Beecher sits in the southeast corner of Will County, Illinois. During Officer Dorian's trials and tribulations, Will County's State Attorney, James Glasgow, said at a news conference, "It's always law enforcement's worst nightmare when someone within the law enforcement community chooses to break the law."

Excuse me? Brian Dorian hadn't broken any laws. He was innocent until proven guilty. That's the American legal standard. To say that Glasgow had leaped to conclusions is an understatement.

At the very least, his statement was injurious and misleading. Especially when we consider that, all circumstantial evidence and false accusations aside, Brian Dorian appeared to be a good cop. His record didn't list any disciplinary issues. His colleagues described him as "low-key." He was a good citizen and proud local resident.

Yes, he drove a red pickup truck. So what? Lots of people drive red pickups. While that factor should have been weighed, police should have also considered the rest of Dorian's profile.

But they didn't. And so, for the next six days, Brian Dorian languished in jail. While he did, law enforcement officials announced the formation of a joint task force. Armed with a composite sketch of the gunman, they began to search for the Honeybee Killer. Which, of course, makes no sense at all. If they thought Dorian was the Honeybee Killer, why would they then go and search for him?

In retrospect, Dorian felt the entire search effort was a sham, bad theater with him starring in the clown role. He became convinced the authorities wanted him to take the fall for what had happened.

"Not once was I told that I was being charged," he recounted angrily on *Dr. Oz*. "Not once was I told that my bond was two-and-a-half million dollars."

"The minute I was brought in, they are announcing [that I was the murder suspect] to the world and getting up in front of the cameras and acting like a fake tough guy."

His accusation carries some weight. Consider this.

After Dorian's arrest, the task force responsible for apprehending Dorian released the following statement:

"Within twenty-four hours, detectives from Will County Sheriff's Office, along with Lake County Sheriff's Office, had developed information and with probable cause, we were able to arrest Brian Dorian. He was arrested after the warrant was issued, signed by Judge Barrett, with a bond of $2.5M dollars. I would like to commend detectives from both departments. The commitment that they also had from the departments themselves in order to develop that information, and finally make an arrest that night."

Without question, this statement is rife with inconsistencies.

In the first place, the officials' timeline is wrong. Reread the press release. It's a grammatical nightmare. For instance, it says the authorities arrested Brian Dorian "within twenty-four hours." Of what? The first shooting in Beecher? The second shooting in Lowell? Did they mean "twenty-four hours from the time Brian Dorian's vehicle was stopped for the FIR"?

If you want my two cents, ambiguities are never a good thing to publish in a press release.

Brian Dorian later stated the SWAT team arrived at his home two days after he was interviewed at the traffic stop. Does that jive with the press release? No, it does not.

Read it again. The impression I get—the impression both departments likely meant to convey—is that they worked lightning fast and with incredible efficiency to pull off a miracle. But clearly, that wasn't the case. Most glaringly because they didn't do it in twenty-four hours. Doubly so since they arrested an innocent man. Triply so since they'd held said innocent man in jail against proper procedure.

Now I'm no legal scholar. But I know there's such a thing as the writ of habeas corpus. Loosely translated, habeas corpus makes it illegal for someone to be imprisoned without cause. It's one of the checks and balances built into our society. It makes it impossible, or punishable, for police to imprison someone against their rights.

Again, this isn't my area of expertise. But I like to think I have common sense. I also have a nose. And the actions taken by these sheriffs in Will County and Lake County ... well, they smell funny to me.

This is all leaving aside the fact that Brian Dorian gave authorities a verifiable alibi during his interrogation. He said he'd been at home when both shootings occurred. Specifically, he'd been surfing the Internet.

Dorian admitted he'd done this frequently while he was out of work. I'm sure many bored people would do the same thing. In fact, sometimes I think this is precisely what the Internet was made for. To while away time.

From a technical perspective, however, this meant that all investigators needed to do was check Dorian's browser history. Had they done that, they could have verified that Dorian had been home, exactly where he said he'd been, when both shootings occurred. But they didn't do this until later. Much later. Nobody seems to know why.

Admittedly, part of the reason Dorian was held so long was because he was detained over Columbus Day weekend. Columbus Day is a federal holiday. Which means that forensic labs and nonessential police forces, including investigative services, enjoy a three-day weekend.

Still, I don't accept this as a proper excuse for why it took six days to check a fellow officer's alibi in a murder case. Frankly, I find that unconscionable.

While Dorian languished in jail, his friends and family rallied for his release. According to "Trial By Media," a locally broadcast TV news special on Dorian's case, the people who knew Dorian best never believed he'd committed murder.

"Why was he arrested?" Brian's father, John Dorian, wondered. "Because he drove a pickup? What other evidence did they have?"

Or consider the words of Dave Palmer, who was Dorian's boss for six years. Mr. Palmer told a local TV news outlet, "What frosted me most was to charge him so quickly on what they had, which was ridiculous. All they had was one witness and a lot of circumstantial evidence. They could have held him while they did some homework. That falls on the prosecutor."

"The most frustrating thing is that everything revolved around him and nothing around the fact that there's someone still running around out there," Dorian's co-worker Jill Aggan told CBS *Chicago*. "Northwest Indiana and Illinois [are] not safe."

Retired Lynwood Sergeant Tim Smith said the entire police force backed Dorian. "I know Brian's character. I know how he is. I know where he was, what he did during the time of the shooting, and he wasn't there."

Dorian later said this of his supporters: "In your life, you are lucky if you have one or two people on one hand to count on. I obviously need more hands ... The biggest thing that concerned me was all the stress all my family and friends and loved ones were put under."

When investigators finally checked Officer Dorian's alibi, he was released from jail. He walked out a free man on the evening of October 13, 2010. As he did so, Brian Dorian's lawyer assured him that both the County Sheriff and District Attorney would explain the reasoning behind his arrest to him in person.

"Every night when I was locked away," Dorian later shared with a local news channel, "I was in that cage thinking these victims had a false sense of security. I am praying for these victims. They got a long road ahead of them. They'll need prayers the rest of their lives."

As fate would have it, the real Honeybee Killer was shot two months later during an attempted armed robbery on December 11, 2010.

Suspect Gary Amaya of Rankin, Illinois, walked into a tanning store in Orland Park, another Chicago suburb. Amaya had a gun. But so did a customer, who opened fire. The wounds Amaya received were critical. He died approximately one hour after the altercation.

How do we know that Amaya was the real Honeybee Killer? Simple. The gun he used while attempting to rob the tanning store precisely matched the bullets fired at the crime scenes in Beecher and Lowell. And this, by the way, is one of those rare cases where TV shows and the movies get things right about police work.

Firearms are very much like human fingerprints. Meaning that each gun leaves an inimitable mark on its cartridge casings. More marks are made on the bullet as it shuttles through the weapon's barrel. This type of evidence, combined with expert witness testimony in court, can and does provide scientific proof that a certain firearm was used in a particular crime.

But there was more.

When authorities arrived at the tanning store, they found that Amaya had items pertinent to another crime in his vehicle. These items were a rope and a set of handcuffs.

As it happened, a local sex worker had claimed she'd been robbed by a man who'd tied her up and cuffed her while he committed the crime. The prostitute's description of this man matched the physical description of Gary Amaya. Forensic examination of the rope and cuffs in Amaya's car later matched them to the prostitute.

The residents of Rankin said they were shocked when they learned that Gary Amaya was the Honeybee Killer. Amaya, they said, was "a loner"—this according to a CBS local affiliate news station.

We all have loners in our lives, I guess. Not everyone likes to be around other people all the time. Still, I suppose I'd find it shocking if one of the loners in my life turned out to be someone who likes to tie up sex workers before robbing them. But that's how society is sometimes. It's full of interesting people.

But get this.

Even after Gary Amaya was found, even after his weapon was matched to that of the Honeybee Killer, Officer Brian Dorian of the Lynwood Police Department of Lynwood, Illinois, was still waiting to hear why he'd been detained as long as he had. He was still expecting his long-awaited explanation from Will County Sheriff

Paul Kaupas and Illinois State Attorney James Glasgow. But when he reached out again through his lawyers, he heard that neither official was willing to talk. Neither official would publicly apologize for accusing, jailing, and charging the wrong man.

"I feel horrible that Brian Dorian went through this and I certainly would apologize for any inconvenience he has suffered," Glasgow later said, once the charges were officially dropped.

To that comment, Dorian responded, "I remember seeing him [Glasgow] tell the world that it was an inconvenience, what I went through. It was an inconvenience, what my family went through, my friends, supporters? That's his definition? What I went through is an inconvenience?"

"A few months later," Dorian recalled, "after the real offender was killed and it was proven [that Amaya had been the Honeybee Killer], I got in touch with my lawyer, Dave Carlson."

That's when they decided to prepare a case.

In the end, it took Brian Dorian four long years to clear his good name. The lawsuit he waged was all-consuming. It put him and his family through needless emotional, not to mention economic, turmoil. But it was important to him. He wanted to restore his reputation. As would any officer who'd been falsely accused.

Dorian's lawsuit was originally filed in October 2011. According to court papers, he sought a jury trial plus $10 million in damages—$5 million in compensatory damages and $5 million in punitive damages—plus attorney and court fees.

The lawsuit charged the state attorney and the Will County sheriff with six counts of misconduct, including false arrest, false imprisonment, conspiracy, and malicious prosecution. It claimed that Brian Dorian suffered emotional and psychological damage as a result of his wrongful arrest.

"As a Police Officer," Dorian explained. "You gather evidence to support your charges. You don't charge and then gather your evidence to support your charges."

He's dead right on that point.

An important part of Dorian's suit was the information about his vehicle had been coerced out of the key witness. Also, as later became apparent, the real Honeybee Killer's truck did not match Brian Dorian's truck at all. The suit went on to contend something shocking: that the coerced eyewitness testimony had been carefully crafted by local authorities to pin the Honeybee Killer's crimes on Dorian.

Why would the sheriff and state attorney have done such a thing? Dorian admitted he didn't know.

Defendants Kaupas and Glasgow denied these allegations. They claimed that Dorian's arrest was part of normal procedure in murder cases. The investigation, they said, had been conducted "to the letter of the law."

In their joint statement, their defense team wrote, "We are confident a court will find the actions of the parties named as defendants in this lawsuit to be justified after all the evidence is presented."

To be clear, this was a civil lawsuit against the alleged misconduct of Will County, Illinois, police officers. But a very important milestone for Brian Dorian, who felt he'd been badly mistreated. Eventually, Will County settled with Dorian, albeit for a significantly lesser amount than what he was seeking. Not that it mattered. Money never seemed to be Dorian's objective in the first place. Exoneration, to him, had more worth.

On Friday, December 4, 2015, the good name of Officer Brian Dorian was cleared by a Will County judge.

Dorian later said, "I had to forgive and I actually publicly forgive [Kaupas and Glasgow]. I will never forget, but I do forgive."

A few weeks after his name was cleared, Brian Dorian had lunch with his former boss, Dave Palmer. It was Palmer's theory, which he shared with Dorian on that occasion, that the experience he'd just endured might make him a better cop.

"He's now stood in the shoes of someone who was wrongly accused. I told him to learn something from that," Palmer later recalled.

I couldn't agree more.

In fact, when I read that quote, it made me think back to exactly why I had Lady Justice tattooed on my arm—and the way I chose to do it.

Think back to my story at the beginning of this book. I know the system isn't 100 percent fair. I've had that experience. And I can verify absolutely that it changed me, too. For the better, I think.

Isn't that ironic? I can't speak for Brian Dorian here but I can say this: When you're wronged in the manner we were—when you're a law enforcement officer falsely accused—it doesn't make you bitter or angry. It makes you more open. It broadens you into a more whole, compassionate, and understanding person.

You don't give up on the system. No, not all. If anything, you commit yourself to making sure the system works even better. And not just for cops who stand falsely accused. But for everyone. Anywhere. And at any time.

I'll say it again: The American system of justice isn't perfect. Nothing is. But it's the best system of justice I know. For this reason alone, I'm 100 percent committed to seeing it work to its best. If not better.

There's an interesting postscript to this story.

Soon after his name was cleared, Brian Dorian went back to active duty police work. It wasn't easy.

Hard, yes.

But worthwhile?

Also, yes.

Brian Dorian says he now tries to treat inmates very differently than he did before. Suspects, criminals, convicts ... they're not some inherent evil, enemies of the state, the scum of the earth, or any of that macho, muscle-flexing bull crap. Frankly, this attitude alone is what produces much of the vast division between law-abiding citizens and those who break the law.

Letting the job get personal is how we get into bad situations. It's one of the ways we reach the status quo which author Tom Robbins once described like this: "Society had a crime problem. It hired cops to attack the crime. Now society has a cop problem."

You can call it a change of heart, I guess. These days, Officer Dorian tries to treat suspects and criminals less like enemies of society, more like individuals going through a particularly hard time in their lives. I applaud this. Too often we view justice as a load of punishments doled out hard. That's not the intent of the system.

It's supposed to rehabilitate people. To show them the errors they made and get them back on their feet so they can become contributing members of society. If we miss that part, we miss everything. If we fail to lift up the people who fall, we're really no better than people who try their best to push people down.

Somewhere it's been written that we should never judge another human being unless we've walked a mile in their shoes. These days, I see a lot of people judging each other without once having stretched their legs.

But look at the example we have in Brian Dorian.

On February 15, 2017, independent TV station WGN9 out of Chicago captured a moment between Officer Bryan Dorian and murder suspect, Joseph Barner. The footage shows Dorian shaking Barner's hand and treating him with compassion.

Earlier that day, Barner was involved in an armed standoff in which one person was killed and three others wounded. For a while, the situation was very dicey, touch-and-go. Barner had done something awful. Would he surrender himself without a fight?

He did, in the end. But why?

We get the answer from footage obtained in the Lynwood booking room. Joseph Barner told officers there that, "Lynwood is the only police department that takes care of their people and they do their job."

It turns out, Barner's mother had requested the department's help. She knew her son needed prescription medication but she'd had trouble getting it to him all week. Evidently, Barner remembered the officers' kindness. He sought to pay it forward, it seems, in the only way he knew how.

That's astonishing to me. It speaks very highly of Officer Brian Dorian and the Lynwood Police Department. But it also goes a long way to explaining why kindness might be the best crime prevention program the human race ever devised. The kinder we are to each other, the more we tend to see that kindness returned and amplified.

When asked directly why he'd treated Joseph Barner so well, Officer Brian Dorian said, "When I'm talking to someone, when I see someone in bracelets or shackles, I see me."

CHAPTER SEVEN:
THE CASE OF THE CRAIGSLIST CATASTROPHE

CASE FILE

Accused officer: John Kivlin, Bellevue, Washington

Date of incident: April 2018

Location: King County, Washington

*Some names and locations have been changed to protect
the involved parties.

John Kivlin and I have a few things in common. We've both worked as cops.
He likes sports and I like sports. His father was in the U.S. Navy. So was mine.

This last part is not an unusual tale.

A lot of kids whose parent or parents served in the U.S. armed forces become
cops. It could be it runs in the blood. Or maybe it isn't nature so much as nurture.

Imagine that you've grown up seeing the people you love the most in life don a uniform every day. As a child, you note the bearing these adults have, their tremendous respect for the law and their fellow human beings, their discipline and love for their work. You're impressed by their dignity and their yearning to help others. It leaves a mark on you.

Serving the public, you think, is cool. I want to do that.

Sure, you might try running away from it for a while. Running away from our destinies is a classic coming-of-age ritual. We all have our ups and downs growing up, our grappling with our sense of self.

And yet.

Through all those gyrations, you sort of always know which star you've always been angling toward.

You want to be just like your role models. A warrior for the good. A peacekeeper. Someone who wears a badge and helps keep order. Helps keep people safe.

John Kivlin and I are the same in that way.

But, of course, we have differences, too.

While I grew up in California, Kivlin grew up in Scotland and Spain; these locations were determined by his father's postings. Later, he attended a small school in West Virginia on a partial soccer scholarship.

Soccer was always a big part of John Kivlin's life. For a while, he made a go at playing professionally in Europe. But when that adventure ended, he moved to the Seattle area, where his father had taken up residence. While living in Washington State, Kivlin tested with several law enforcement agencies because, to hear him tell it, he'd always wanted to be a cop.

But don't take my word for it. Listen to how he describes his inspiration during my recent interview with him.

KIVLIN: ... Before I graduated [college], I was out celebrating with some friends and maybe had a little too much to drink. There was a cop who was an asshole ... My roommate had arranged [my] place to stay and I was just making noise, trying to find him. And instead of the cop trying to help me out, he was just a dick. He decided that he was going to book me for public intoxication, disorderly conduct. As I'm in handcuffs, my roommate came out of an apartment that he had rented to come get me. And instead of just letting me go sleep it off, the cop took me and arrested me for disorderly. So after I was pissed off, I said, "No, there's a better way to treat people." And that's how I decided I wanted to be a cop.

In 2002, Kivlin signed on with the city of Bellevue. Five miles east of Seattle across beautiful Lake Washington, Bellevue lives up to its name. It's a gorgeous place surrounded by woodlands and wetlands iconic to the Pacific Northwest.

With a population of about 150,000, Bellevue's one of those American cities that neatly bridges the gap between small-town life and urban living. From early on, it was a bedroom community for white-collar workers at Microsoft Corporation. Later, however, it welcomed top executives for Facebook and Amazon. A real community started to flourish.

Years passed. The city increased itself in size, as well as diversity. A predominantly white citizenship began to welcome people from all over the world who came to work in the software industry.

While this fostered a burgeoning middle class, Kivlin notes that his department had a hard time keeping up. As Bellevue's population expanded two or three times, its police department only hired a handful of additional police officers.

KIVLIN: Back in the day when I got hired or even right before that, Bellevue was pretty well known throughout the law enforcement community as one of the top tier departments, even though it was smaller. Since then, instead of increasing in value, so to speak, they've decreased. One of the big issues was technology. Being right next to Microsoft, you would think that we would have computers. And actually, that was the running joke when I was in the academy ... The actual fact was, whoever the manager was at the time, didn't want to put computers in the car because he believed the software would be redundant by the time it came out within a few years. So we actually went without computers, probably the first five to seven years I was here at Bellevue.

In many police departments across the country, officers have to be on the job for two to four years before they can look into specializing. Kivlin describes the Bellevue PD as being open to cross-training.

For instance, Bellevue's investigation unit was open to patrol officers who wanted to try detective work, and could when things got slow.

KIVLIN: [Working] patrol, we pretty much did everything and anything we could. If it got too much, we would hand it off to the detectives. I did that for the first three years, I think. And then I tested with a traffic unit and I became a motor cop for three years. Got into some issues with the department, made some mistakes. I had, I would say, a slight drinking problem back then. So I stopped drinking. I went back to patrol, got my stuff together, and probably four or five years after that, maybe four, I tested again with motors and got back into it. Did motors the rest of the time.

By *motors*, Kivlin means that he was a motorcycle cop. Remember this term. You'll hear it again in Chapter Thirteen when we tackle the story of Clyde Ray Spencer.

By "some issues with the department," Kivlin means this:

KIVLIN: I got into a fight and mouthed off about writing a [State Personnel Board] officer a bunch of tickets. They thought that was a bad thing and they removed me, which they were correct. I went back to patrol, did my thing, did my time, tested for motorcycles again, got back in. Did that for, I think a total combined of ten years on motorcycles, maybe a little bit longer, eleven or twelve. At the very end, I had put in for field training officer and collision investigator and I got both of them. And I was just transitioning to collision investigation, when all this crap happened.

By his own estimation, Kivlin had been on the force sixteen years and three months. He'd had his ups and downs like everyone else who calls themselves human.

But then, in the autumn of 2017, something happened that changed the course of his life forever. Something he says he's still trying to figure out to this day.

KIVLIN: I had a wonderful wife and three beautiful kids that basically I walked on water for them. And I decided to throw it away for a badge bunny. Back in the day, Craigslist was still doing the personals. There was a girl on there who advertised she wanted a cop. I answered it. We met briefly while I was on duty, just for coffee. And then it kind of spiraled and went from there.

The woman Kivlin met was of Asian descent. She told him her name was Amy Rouso and said she was twenty-nine years old. She worked as a nurse, she said, and was a resident of Issaquah, a suburb four miles southeast of Bellevue.

She was married without any kids, she said. And she made a point of explaining that her husband didn't mind her engaging in extramarital relationships ... so long as there was no emotional connection between partners.

Kivlin accepted this information. At that point, he felt comfortable enough that he and Rouso met after Kivlin was done with work a week or two later. They began a sexual relationship.

KIVLIN: I met her, we had a relationship or an encounter, I guess. And then it was a couple of weeks before I met her again. And then I went to Miami on a vacation with some friends. Got back and I got really sick. I don't know if it's something in Miami or what it was but I had no energy. I ended up coming to work. My boss said, "Hey, just go get in the car." Because by then it was November. So a lot of the times we would go off of the motorcycles if it was really cold or snowy on the ground. I was using the car and they said, "Look, if you're feeling that bad, either call in sick or go hit a substation and just hang out there until you get a call."

Kivlin was able to take things easy because the motors in his department worked to fulfill quotas. This is a common practice in police departments across the country.

> A quota is either a formal or informal policy that police departments maintain on the number of tickets or arrests they should give out or make in a given time frame.
>
> In a formal policy, a department might come right out and say something like "Each patrol officer is responsible for writing [insert a number] citations per month."
>
> Informal policies turn out to be just as prescriptive. A department might call the number of citations or arrests a target, a benchmark, or a goal. Frankly, it doesn't matter what they call them. It all amounts to the same.
>
> The idea is that a standard's been set and the officers in that department are expected to meet that standard if they want to be considered effective.

In Kivlin' department, once a motor cop's quota was fulfilled, they were more or less free to do as they pleased until the next quota cycle began.

KIVLIN: ... And once we were done with [our quota], we were done. We could do whatever we wanted or we could help out. Or if there was a collision and they needed people to close down streets, that's what we would do.

Kivlin said that he and Rouso didn't meet very often. And during their first few encounters, Rouso had chosen to pay the hotel bills.

He therefore didn't protest when she rented a room in a house in Redmond, a nearby suburb about two miles northeast of Bellevue. The couple began meeting there for their encounters, many of which, Kivlin told me, weren't of a sexual nature.

KIVLIN: A lot of it was just us hanging out. It wasn't anything more than that.

The relationship started to blossom into something more than sex.

Kivlin began taking Rouso on ride-alongs.

Now I've already covered what ride-alongs are in the first chapter of this book. But what you might not know is how common ride-alongs are. Buddies, boyfriends, girlfriends, and spouses ride with officers quite routinely. It's totally normal.

In fact, in Kivlin's department, he said, husbands and wives rode with their officer spouses all the time.

Due to civil and liability concerns, many police departments across the country put limits on the number of times an individual can do a ride-along per year. But the Bellevue PD had no such limits in place. The only official process was to have a supervisor sign off each time a ride-along occurred.

As loose as this policy was, Kivlin admits he only officially signed Rouso out for one ride-along. Unofficially, she rode with him on the job about ten more times.

KIVLIN: On Saturdays, I would come in and usually there was nothing going on. At this point I was in collision investigation. So she would come along and she would jump in the car and ride along with me. I'd go take collisions and that would be it. And then after four hours or so, she'd go, "Okay, I'm going to take off." It was comforting having someone there to talk to.

As the two grew closer, Rouso opened up a bit more. She admitted, that she'd lied about many things the first time they'd met.

For instance, her real name wasn't Amy. It was Kia. She wasn't twenty-nine, she was forty-four. And she did, in fact, have children. One was twenty-one years old and living in Sweden, where Kia once lived. Two others were approximately ages ten and twelve years old. They lived in Issaquah. Each child had a different father, she said.

Was she really a nurse? Kivlin was later told that Kia had worked as a nurse in Sweden. But when she came to the U.S., she either couldn't or wouldn't take the equivalency exams. Instead, she became a medical assistant at one of the local hospitals.

Was she married? Yes, that part was true. It also turned out to be true that her husband was aware of her infidelities. And he was okay with them so long as, just as Amy/Kia had said, no emotional connections developed.

And yet, to hear Kivlin tell it, Rouso began to develop feelings for him.

For instance, at once point, she showed up to meet him with a black eye.

KIVLIN: And I said, "What the hell happened?" She said, "I told Mark," which was her husband, "about you. And he gave me an ultimatum, it's either him or me, and I chose you. So he put my head in the wall and then he beat me the next day as well."

Throughout this ordeal, Rouso would call Kivlin for support.

KIVLIN: ... She called me, locked in her bathroom, crying. I told her to call the police. She refused. Following that, I gave her a [domestic violence] booklet from Bellevue saying, "Here's some good numbers to call that can help you move on with your life, if you want to deal with this. Because, the way he's treating you is not the way it should be."

In retrospect, Rouso was developing emotional attachments. Unfortunately, Kivlin didn't feel the same way toward her.

He liked Kia Rouso as a person and thought they had a good relationship. As friends with benefits, Kivlin thought. But no more than that.

They were people who each had spouses, kids, commitments to other parties.

He thought this was clear. After all, hadn't Rouso been the one to tell him at their very first meeting? No emotional attachments.

But then.

KIVLIN: There was a point in probably early March [2018], maybe late February that she kind of freaked out on me. Because she told me I needed to leave my wife. And I said, "Hey, look, I've been married for almost nineteen, twenty years. I've known you for six months ... So I'm not going to be leaving my wife anytime soon."

Little did Kivlin know, that decision was about to be made for him.

On or about April 9, 2018, Kia's husband, Mark, texted Kivlin's wife. He announced that their spouses had been having an affair.

This caught Kivlin's wife completely by surprise. She didn't know who was sending the text so, naturally, she inquired.

Kia's husband, declined to identify himself. However, he offered Kia's cell phone number so Kivlin's wife could call and verify things for herself. Which she promptly did.

The two women spoke and it all came out.

KIVLIN: So then that was the end of my marriage, and pretty much the next day, I was out of the house.

A cop's life follows the same trajectory as practically everyone else's life on the planet. The person we are at work bears a striking resemblance to the person we are at home. But they're not the same person.

Personal problems become work problems, and vice versa.

Think about it. You could be a doctor, an accountant, an underwater demolition contractor, or a dental hygienist. I don't care what you do for a living. The same dynamic likely holds true.

You and your co-workers show up at work. You do your job, do it well, and try to enjoy it. Then you go home and enter a whole different universe that most of your colleagues never get a chance to see.

And in this particular sphere, the realm of the personal, Kivlin's life was a wreck.

He'd been having an affair. His wife had found out. She wanted a divorce. He was out of the house and away from his kids. He'd gotten himself a tiny apartment near his home in Gig Harbor, a suburb southwest of Seattle.

He was still seeing Kia. And he was confused.

Then, to complicate matters, Kivlin got selected to be a Field Training Officer, or FTO.

In police departments across the country, a Field Training Officer is an experienced employee whom the department selects to help train junior officers.

Like a college or university lecturer, FTOs might offer classroom instruction. But most of the time, an FTO offers more "hands-on" training. The younger officer and an FTO will ride together. During these sessions, the FTO uses his/her experience to help mold the younger officer so they can perform the job on their own. They will teach basic skills such as report writing and traffic enforcement as well as more advanced things such as surveillance, arrest procedures, and interviews.

FTOs are an important asset to any police department. They create a culture of knowledge-sharing and camaraderie within the organization. Also, studies have shown that FTO-led training courses can improve relationships between police departments and the communities they serve.

Some studies even show that FTO-led training initiatives can reduce civil liability complaints and lawsuits against the department. This, in turn, makes it easier for a law enforcement agency to stay within its budget.

Overall, being selected to serve as an FTO is considered an honor. Many law enforcement officers rank it among the highlights of their career.

In late April 2018, Kivlin was set to attend a training session in Wenatchee, a city on the Columbia River about four hours from where he lived. Kia agreed to meet him there. The two planned to share a hotel room. Kivlin would spend his days in class and the two would spend their evenings together. It sounded pretty idyllic.

Kivlin drove out to Wenatchee with one of his coworkers who, as it happened, was also Kivlin's neighbor in Gig Harbor.

This co-worker and Kivlin knew each other well. Even so, the co-worker hadn't a clue about Kivlin's domestic situation. The fact that he and his wife were separated. The fact that he'd been seeing Kia. That fact that Kivlin had gotten himself an apartment.

KIVLIN: No one knew anything about my affair with this woman until we got to Wenatchee and I told him. I said, "Hey, just so you know, this gal is going to come over here so you're not going to see me at night." And he said, "You're an idiot," pretty much. So he kept away from her, he didn't want anything to do with her. I would stay with her at night, I'd go to class in the morning ... So that was, I think, April twenty-first through the twenty-seventh is the class.

That Thursday night in Wenatchee, Kivlin was busy preparing his presentation for the next day. He felt pretty good about it. Late that evening, however, Kia woke him up.

She'd been smoking marijuana all week and doing edibles, she said. Kivlin never partook of such things. They were legal in Washington State, but he wanted no part of them.

KIVLIN: She woke up the Thursday night or woke me up and she said, "I need to go to the hospital." And I said, "Why?" She goes, "You're going to find this funny, but it's not funny." I go, "Okay." She goes, "I can't stop having orgasms." I said, "Okay." She goes, "Call the hospital, make sure they're not too busy." I'm like, "All right." So I called the hospital, ask the charge nurse, and of course, the charge nurse laughed at me. She goes, "Look, if it's that bad, just bring her in." I said, "Okay." Well, [Kia] got pissed off that the charge nurse laughed at her. So she called back up and then yelled at her, and screamed at her, and eventually I fell asleep. When I woke up, she said she was feeling better. I just assumed it had something to do with all the drug use that she was doing and she seemed fine.

That day, Thursday, Kivlin made his presentation. But right in the middle of it, his phone started ringing and ringing.

It was Kia calling. She was still in their hotel room but she insisted that Kivlin had to come get her. As in, immediately.

Kivlin had no idea what was going on. However, given the previous night's behavior, he was concerned. And he wasn't pleased.

He asked his partner if he would accompany him back to the hotel.

KIVLIN: "Can you just go across the street and hang out? Because, something weird is going on." And he said, "Yeah, but I don't want anything to do with this." And I said, "I hear you." I went back, I couldn't find her. So I called my buddy over and finally I found her, but she had earbuds and she wouldn't take the earbuds out. And I'm trying to ask her what's going on, she won't answer me. She's sitting down in the middle of the parking lot.

At this point, Kivlin felt certain he'd made a mistake. One of the biggest errors he'd committed was ignoring what is often a cop's best friend: his gut instincts.

All along, he'd felt that Kia was ... well, a bit off. There were all those lies she'd told in the beginning of their relationship. And her tendency to threaten him when things didn't go her way.

For instance:

At one point a few months before the trip, Rouso and Kivlin had an argument. It was one of Rouso's ongoing beefs that, early in their relationship, Kivlin had run a check on her license plates.

Rouso had taken offense to this. She'd held it over him ever since.

At one point, she'd even sent Kivlin a picture of herself outside the Issaquah Police Department. The message implied by this photo was clear. Rouso was going to go to the police and tell them about "crimes" Kivlin had allegedly committed.

Eventually, they had talked the matter out. Kivlin was shaken by this. Simply put, it wasn't normal behavior. But he let it pass.

Now he was standing over Kia, who'd seated herself in the parking lot of the hotel they'd shared in Wenatchee. She'd been acting strangely all week. But this wasn't strange. It was closer to crazy.

KIVLIN: At one point she screams at me, she's having an anxiety attack. So I said, "Okay, that's fine. Let's get in your car, I'll drive and we'll get to a certain point, and then I'll go with my buddy and you can go home and you'll be fine." She didn't want to do that. She wouldn't answer me, but she wouldn't get in the car. I went to my friend and I said, "Hey, what do you think I should do?" At that point, he goes, "Dude, she's not going to go there ... "

So we called her bluff. I got in the truck with him and we took off. She started texting me, "Say goodbye to your career. Your career is over. You're a fucking asshole," the whole gamut.

The drive to Gig Harbor was long. Kivlin went to his apartment and fell asleep.

At about one in the morning his phone rang. It was his captain down at the Bellevue PD.

KIVLIN: She said, "John, you need to step outside your house. We have to talk to you." And I said, "Well, Carol." Because that was her name. "Carol, I'm actually not at my house anymore." She was, "I know. We're outside your apartment."

Still wiping sleep from his eyes, Kivlin stepped outside his apartment.

His place was on the second floor. Looking down, he saw two figures.

The first was his captain, who'd spoken with him on the phone. The second was a King County Deputy.

This confused him.

Bellevue was in King County. But this was Gig Harbor, in Pierce County.

Why the jump in jurisdictions?

KIVLIN: And then I looked over and I saw a SWAT sniper on the other balcony.

Look, it's always a serious matter when a law enforcement officer stands accused of a crime. Everyone's hackles go up. As I said, the good apples don't want bad apples around. They want them out of the barrel.

Frankly, it's no surprise to me that authorities used snipers and SWAT teams when trying to bring in John Kivlin.

They knew he was armed and trained in the use of weapons and tactics. They were therefore being abundantly cautious. Doubling down on the side of safety.

It turned out, Rouso had lied to police and told them Kivlin assaulted her. As far as the police knew, Kivlin was a violent offender. He had to be treated as such until the matter could be sorted out.

But at that point, Kivlin thought the only thing he was in trouble for was running Rouso's license plates a few month's back.

Technically, this was a gray area. Should he have done it?

While it might not have been in keeping with best practices, there was nothing illegal about it that he was aware of.

But here were his colleagues demanding that he relinquish the keys to the car he'd taken to Wenatchee—a car that belonged to the Bellevue PD—as well as his duty regalia. His badge. His radio. His weapons.

Once he did this, he was placed under arrest. He asked what the charge was. Domestic assault, they told him. Which allegedly took place in King County. Hence the presence of the King County Sheriff's Department.

Kivlin knew right away it was crap.

KIVLIN: I knew she had taken pictures of her face from when her husband had done it. But at that point, I wasn't thinking that. I didn't know what she was saying that I had done. I know for a fact I've never laid hands on her.

Handcuffed, Kivlin was placed in the King County patrol vehicle, and taken to King County jail where he spent the weekend in lockdown. As I mentioned with my own story, this is standard procedure whenever a police officer is incarcerated. My own police officer colleagues were in lockdown once they were arrested to ensure their safety.

It's the law in Washington State, that all cases of domestic violence come with an immediate restraining order. Kivlin was told to steer clear of Amy Rouso/Kia. Meaning, he was to have no contact with her whatsoever, either in person or telephonically.

Kivlin was still confused by what was going on. But he consented.

He thought that would be the end of it.

Boy, was he wrong.

Things were about to get much, much worse.

Released from jail and back to something like normal, Kivlin was soon arrested again. The charge this time? Rouso claimed he had violated his restraining order by texting him.

Kivlin was stunned. All the more so because he'd done no such thing.

Amy Rouso/Kia, it turned out, was not only vengeful and a liar, she was technically savvy.

And so she'd spoofed him.

Spoofing is any act of telephonic communication such as emails, phone calls, texting, websites, and so on that pretends to be from a known or trusted source.

Thanks to modern computing, a hacker can send a text to a known client but do so from somebody else's phone number or sender ID. Very often, spoofed messages will include links to malicious websites. These can initiate automatic malware downloads that can hijack a victim's personal information and exploit it for criminal purposes.

Some marketing companies routinely spoof their phone numbers purely for the sake of convenience. They might replace a longer number with a shorter one, for instance. Or a foreign number with one that's more local.

But hackers use the same technique. By posing as a legitimate person or organization, bad actors can hide their true identity and intent.

Evidently, Amy Rouso/Kia got a new cell phone into which she loaded a previous conversation she and Kivlin had maintained by text. This conversation was clearly related to their relationship. When she sent it again, the old conversation showed up in real time. Meaning, it looked as though Kivlin had reached out to her by text after receiving a restraining order that explicitly forbade him from doing so.

KIVLIN: ... And then she showed [those messages to] the detective for King County, who I hope to God I never ever meet her, because I don't know what I'll say or do to her. But instead of taking the phone as evidence, like you're supposed to, like any cop out of the academy knows ... if there's a violation of an order, you take the phone to be forensically checked ... she took screenshots.

This detail is very important.

Screenshots only presented one side of the story. Essentially, they took Kia's tale at face value. Alone, they made it seem clear that Kivlin had violated his restraining order.

Had the actual phone Rouso used been confiscated and searched, as protocol demanded, it would have been clear that what she'd presented was nothing but a clever ruse.

Lacking this evidence, however, the King County detective whom Rouso spoke with deemed she had probable cause to arrest Kivlin not once, but two more times.

KIVLIN: ... Each subsequent arrest, the SWAT team came out. I was arrested both times in just my underwear. My house or apartment was searched. I got kicked out of my apartment because of the third [arrest] because apparently a little kid said one of the SWAT members pointed a gun at him. Which I don't think he did. But whatever.

To be clear, both of these subsequent incidences were founded in false evidence. Amy Rouso/Kia was claiming that John Kivlin had violated his court-appointed restraining order. When he hadn't.

And all this was on top of false testimony she'd already given that he'd assaulted her.

It boggles the mind.

But it wasn't over.

Not even close.

When all was said and done, Amy Rouso/Kia levelled more than twenty allegations against Officer John Kivlin.

KIVLIN: There were allegations ... of sex in the chief's office, sex in all of the substations, sex in the patrol vehicle, sex on duty. Issaquah borders with Bellevue, and there were two times where I picked her up to get her car looked at, at the garage, and then drove her to her house ... [they] decided those were violations of policy because I didn't get supervisor approval even though it's a common thing, like I was saying, in other things. But the unofficial ride-alongs, she alleged that she didn't sign the official ride-along request, which she did. So they tried to say that I forged signatures.

Kivlin was also accused of tampering with evidence and brandishing his weapon.

Rouso claimed this: At one point, after Kivlin dropped her off after one of their ride-alongs, they got in an argument. Kivlin got pissed, she said, grabbed her by the hair while pulling his sidearm. Brandishing his weapon.

All this, Kivlin maintains, is just more fiction spun from the brain of a very disturbed individual.

As time went on and the inquiries proceeded, Kivlin learned more about the crazy, fantastic stories Rouso had made up about him and told the authorities.

That's when the first inconsistencies popped up.

KIVLIN: She initially came to the department and said that I ran her plate and gave them a big spiel. And then the next day she came in and showed pictures of her face and said, "He assaulted me, and he brandished." Well, to me, it seemed a little odd at the time. When I finally figured out what was going on and I spoke to my attorney about it, I said, "Look, if you just been punched in the face by someone ... or had a gun pointed at you, wouldn't you say, that was why you were going to meet with the police first and not, "He's running my plate?"

When I heard this, I couldn't believe my ears. As a law enforcement officer, this sort of "testimony" from a "victim" wouldn't have passed the smell test.

Obviously, Rouso should have been listened to. Obviously, her claims should have been taken seriously. Assault against anyone and especially a woman should be thoroughly investigated. But what about the rights of her alleged attacker? To my mind, those should have been safeguarded as well.

A woman who claims to have been assaulted but doesn't appear to have been assaulted ... who shows, as proof of her assault, a photo of herself with a black eye that was taken weeks before ... who doesn't explain why she didn't report the claim earlier ... who first claims her cop ex-boyfriend ran her license plates but then, a day later, recalls that he'd beaten her up ...

None of this makes any sense to me.

Frankly, it leaves me wondering how it ever appeared to make sense in the eyes of the detectives who eventually charged Kivlin.

Of course, Kivlin's department placed him on administrative leave. But it turned out he wasn't alone.

KIVLIN: Now, mind you, at this point, the chief had been put on administrative leave, too. Because when [Rouso] went to them and she started making allegations against me, they saw something on her phone that was a conversation with us, where she said that she had basically slept with other officers. And I said, "Who?" So she said, she told me over the phone the detectives name. And then she said, "And your boss." And I said, "Which boss? I've got lots of bosses." And she goes, "You know like the CEO." So then I said, "The chief?" And she said, "Yes." So because of that, the chief had been placed on administrative leave. So now a deputy chief was running the show. This is where it gets a little ... well, the whole thing is odd.

Rouso had alleged that she and the Chief of the Bellevue Police Department had had an affair. Not only that, she claimed that he had raped her.

The chief denied this allegation. Furthermore, he denied that he even knew who Amy Rouso/Kia was.

Investigators looked into this case, as well. Eventually, they determined that, while there was no probable cause to show the police chief committed any crime whatsoever, there was probable cause to believe that, in accusing him, Rouso had committed perjury, tampering with evidence, and making a false statement against a public servant.

Suddenly, what started out as a tiff between two people having an extramarital affair spiraled quickly into a full-blown community crisis.

Imagine John Kivlin's surprise in all this. When he found Rouso's personal ad on Craigslist, he never imagined she'd done this sort of thing before with other cops.

KIVLIN: Later on, I found out that she had met with other cops, different departments. Not necessarily had sex with them or maybe she did, I don't know. But we knew people because of her. There's some officers that I know from playing soccer and just in general, she happened to know. Because they must have responded to her ad as well. Or previous ads ... She would go to different agencies. She ended up dating some Renton cop at some point. She went over to Wenatchee to supposedly just be friends with the sergeant over there. I have no clue how accurate or to what extent their friendship on any of these people were.

Kivlin also later uncovered that, prior to meeting him, Rouso had engaged in at least two rape fantasies involving King County residents. One of these involved a detective from the Bellevue Police Department.

In this case, which took place in April 2017, Rouso alleged the detective had raped her. She even went so far as to check herself into a hospital and have a rape kit done. However, when police investigated, they determined that the relationship hadn't involved actual rape but consensual sex with a rape fantasy element.

Ultimately, prosecutors declined to file charges. They cited insufficient evidence. There were too many contradictions between Rouso's account of what happened and the text messages she and the detective had exchanged.

However, and this is worth noting, court documents showed that Rouso had also met this detective after posting an ad on Craigslist. An ad that specifically said she wished to have sex with police officers.

Why this incident never came up in Kivlin's case remains a mystery.

KIVLIN: ... It didn't make a lot of sense to us, because it was the same County that had done the investigation prior, and now this detective [who met with Rouso], all she had to do was run her name and that would have popped up ... it would have cleared up a lot of things and this one a bit over a lot sooner.

But, as so often happens with people who lie, Rouso's ruses began to unravel. Here I'll quote that line from Sir Walter Scott: "O, what a tangled web we weave when first we practice to deceive."

How did Rouso deal with the stress? Not well, as things turned out.

While the Kivlin case was writhing its way through its various crazy contortions,

Rouso took a trip to Canada and came back with drugs in her car. She was arrested for that and her case turned into an arrest warrant.

But then she went to Portland and stole some merchandise there and was also arrested. That case went to warrant, as well.

KIVLIN: ... Finally, King County, wasn't going to file anything against her because they didn't want it to look like victims can't come forward. But eventually they said, "Yes." So there's four counts of different things about ... basically lying, accusing the chief and myself of these things.

Amy Rouso/Kia exited this strange tale when she jumped on a plane bound for Sweden. You read that right. She fled the country.

Authorities told Kivlin they weren't going to start the extradition process. They said they assumed she'll come back eventually. After all, she has two kids here in the U.S., they said.

Kivlin disagreed with their logic.

KIVLIN: ... I mean, she left her daughter with her parents in Sweden for nineteen years or so ... I don't think she's coming back.

So what's become of John Kivlin?

He resigned from the Bellevue Police Department. The acting chief there closed the internal investigation into his case before it was finished. This left Kivlin in a kind of procedural limbo, which he decided he shouldn't have to tolerate.

KIVLIN: ... The whole reason I resigned, was because of all the false allegations she had made that was going to become open to the public. My family had already been through enough. So I resigned. Otherwise, I'd still be there and fighting it.

Eventually, all charges against him were dismissed. It didn't matter. Once charges are filed, they stay in the system and work against you.

Here's another very important pro tip for law enforcement officers: Expunging false accusations isn't as easy as it sounds.

KIVLIN: Apparently, it'll take five years before I can get [my record] sort of redacted. But anyone who is actually, like, another law enforcement agency, if they want me, they're going to be able to find that no matter what. So even though everything's been tossed and dismissed, I've got paperwork proving it, I can't get a job except shitty jobs.

Now Kivlin drives a bus full-time and does part-time security work. No, it's not his dream job. But it's work. It pays the bills.

He says he'd still love to be a police officer. He loves the job. Loves helping people.

Somewhere deep inside him there's still that kid who had a run-in with a bad apple. And he still wants to fix that.

He still believes there's a right way to treat people. With dignity and respect.

But his outlook has certainly changed, he says.

KIVLIN: My feel for the judicial system has changed greatly. I once thought that you follow the rules, you do everything you're supposed to do, and everything will work out. I mean, in the end, everything did work out. But it took its toll. It took a while … and I know it has changed me.

CHAPTER EIGHT:
THIS "ROUTINE" TRAFFIC STOP WAS FAR FROM ROUTINE

CASE FILE

Accused officer: Sgt. Stephen Floyd, Stone Mountain, GA Police Dept.

Related parties: DeKalb County Fire Captain Terrell Davis; DeKalb County Fire Dept. Educational Specialist, Krystal Cathcart

Date of incident: May 15, 2015

Location: Stone Mountain, Georgia

Police work is bound by procedures which are designed with specific goals in mind. The idea behind any good procedure boils down to two factors: safety and rights. A procedure should protect the safety and rights of both the suspect or suspects and the officer or officers handling them.

Knowing this, police officers rarely deviate from established procedures. We know that, should this happen, even the tiniest kind of infraction can start to get ugly incredibly fast.

Case in point. Consider what happened during this "run-of-the-mill" traffic stop. Yes, it started out strictly routine. But from there, it quickly devolved to where it changed a police officer's life.

Sergeant Stephen Floyd of the Stone Mountain, Georgia Police Department was out on a routine patrol. The date was May 15, 2015. Sergeant Floyd was a member of his agency's traffic unit. This meant that, among other things, he was obligated to pull over vehicles showing clear instances of what we call equipment violations.

Equipment violations are civil infractions against any ordinance, statute, or rule relating to the safe operation of a motor vehicle. What constitutes an equipment violation will vary from state to state. Common examples include driving a car with tinted windows when such windows are forbidden by law. Driving a vehicle with improper or missing license plates. Possession of a radar detection or jamming device. Or improperly loading a vehicle, such as when a driver's jammed so much luggage in their back seat, they can't use their rearview mirror.

Normally, getting stopped for an equipment violation will earn you a traffic ticket. However, some states now issue what's called a fix it ticket.

A fix it ticket formally warns the motorist that their vehicle has incurred a violation. It notes the date and time, and allows the motorist to attend to the problem within a given time span. Failure to do so incurs the violation's full penalty.

Officer Stephen Floyd had spent many years serving other law enforcement agencies, including the Fulton County Sheriff's Department. On the day this incident occurred, he was in his tenth year with Stone Mountain PD.

In other words, he was no cadet fresh out of the police academy. He was a seasoned law enforcement professional who, in the course of his long career, had conducted several hundred car stops. All without incident.

On this late Friday morning, however, Sergeant Floyd observed a car with an expired registration tag. Flashing his rollers and pulsing his siren, he pulled the vehicle over and came to a stop in front of a local school.

I interviewed Sergeant Floyd regarding the details of all that happened that day.

STICKS: I appreciate you taking the time to talk with us.

SGT. FLOYD: Well, I appreciate you acknowledging the situation. It got quite ugly, and I'd like to shed some light on it.

Following procedure, Sergeant Floyd got out of his cruiser and approached the car he'd just pulled over. From his search of the vehicle's tags, he already knew it belonged to a Mr. Terrell Davis. Assuming he found Mr. Davis behind the wheel, Sergeant Floyd intended to alert him that his registration had expired.

Footage later retrieved from Sergeant Floyd's dashboard and body cams shows him conversing with the driver. It was indeed Mr. Davis, who identified himself as the Fire Captain of DeKalb County. Mr. Davis told Sergeant Floyd that he was just about to conduct a presentation on fire safety for the students at the school.

To punctuate this, Mr. Davis showed Sergeant Floyd some coffee and donuts he'd just picked up to bring as refreshments to the meeting.

According to Sergeant Floyd, Mr. Davis immediately began invoking the name of his supervisor, Dr. Cedric Alexander. At the time, Dr. Alexander served as DeKalb County's Public Safety Director. But Sergeant Floyd found this odd.

As he and I discussed, it's common for law enforcement officers to extend certain courtesies to individuals they deem deserving of that privilege.

SGT. FLOYD: I mean, we give courtesy to fire department people all the time. It's just that this individual went too far trying to invoke his authority, like he had some authority. [I was thinking] "You don't have any authority here, sir."

STICKS: Yeah, I mean, [police officers in Tulsa, Oklahoma] give citizens courtesy ... other law enforcements. That's just part of the job. You have that discretion. But I can say when someone's name-dropping, and you feel they try to intimidate you, type of deal ... that doesn't work.

Here's a tip: The biggest reason a police officer will extend or not courtesy is the violator's attitude. A suspect who seems genuinely contrite and offers to cooperate in any way they can isn't deemed harmful to society. Likely, he or she will get a pass that day. So long as the officer feels they're sincere about fixing the matter at hand.

What puzzled Sergeant Floyd in this case was Mr. Davis's assumption that courtesy would be given because of his association with two entities. First: the DeKalb County Fire Department. Second: DeKalb County's Public Safety Director.

Sergeant Floyd found Mr. Davis's demeanor off-putting. So off-putting, in fact, that he decided not to be lenient on this occasion and issue a ticket. He asked Mr. Davis to stay in his vehicle while he went back to his cruiser.

He was in the middle of processing the summons when a woman entered the scene. Krystal Cathcart was an education specialist for the DeKalb County Fire Department and a colleague of Mr. Davis. She had arrived at the school a bit earlier that day to assist Mr. Davis with his presentation to the students.

According to Sergeant Floyd, Ms. Cathcart approached his patrol car and demanded to know what he was doing. Sergeant Floyd was amazed by this behavior.

SGT. FLOYD: When I stopped [Mr. Davis], I saw her coming. I only let her come to the traffic stop because I knew he was going to the school, and he had some donuts and coffee in the car. So I was just going to let her just get the donuts and coffee and go about her business. That's what I was assuming she was going to do.

Ms. Cathcart, however, proceeded to upbraid Sergeant Floyd for stopping Mr. Davis.

SGT. FLOYD: I was like, "Lady, you gotta get away from the traffic stop. I mean, this doesn't have anything to do with you." ... She got bent out of shape because I told her to move away from the traffic stop ... to this day, I wish I knew what possessed her.

Ms. Cathcart refused to leave the scene. Flustered, Sergeant Floyd told her that, if she didn't comply, he'd put her in the back of his cruiser. In retrospect, he says, he would have chosen his words differently. But it should be noted that, as a law enforcement officer who'd requested that a civilian not interfere with his duties—a civilian who denied this request—Sergeant Floyd was within his rights to arrest Ms. Cathcart, if the situation came to that.

STICKS: ... I've watched the video and listened to the body cam [footage]. And I mean, other than you saying, go stand over there or you're going to end up in my car for her interfering with a traffic stop ... we would tell anybody that [who] interferes with a traffic stop. It's a dangerous thing for us. We don't allow that.

SGT. FLOYD: Right.

Repeating Mr. Davis's comment, Ms. Cathcart—to use Sergeant Floyd's words—got "bent out of shape." She kept telling Sergeant Floyd he should call their supervisor, Dr. Alexander. Sergeant Floyd was under no obligation to do so, of course. Besides, by that point any feelings of fellowship he may have had with these two members of the DeKalb County Fire Department had already evaporated.

He continued writing out Mr. Davis's ticket for an expired registration. When finished, he served this ticket to Mr. Davis, got back in his cruiser, pulled away, and continued on his patrol duty.

The situation had left him miffed. It had started out as routine and quickly built toward exasperation. But now it was finished.

Or so he thought.

Sergeant Floyd went about his duties the rest of that morning. Then he broke for lunch. Later that afternoon, his supervisor contacted him with a disturbing story.

Evidently, Ms. Cathcart had been very upset. She'd gone inside the school where a third employee of the DeKalb County Fire Department, a chaplain, had been present. After hearing Ms. Cathcart's description of what she said happened, this fire chaplain apparently got so upset, he encouraged both Cathcart and Davis to file formal written complaints against Sergeant Floyd.

While Davis made a complaint, Cathcart went so far as to write hers out on DeKalb County Fire Department stationery before she submitted it.

In her complaint, Ms. Cathcart stated that Sergeant Floyd had been intimidating. That he'd created a sense of fear at the scene. She stated that Floyd had cussed at her twice. That he'd told her to "back the f*** up." Barring that, he would throw her in the back of his squad car.

Ms. Cathcart went on to describe herself as being traumatized by the incident. Said she felt very threatened. Fire Captain Davis corroborated Cathcart's statements in his own account.

All this triggered an investigation. The matter was brought before Stone Mountain's Internal Affairs review board. And this, says Sergeant Floyd, is where his situation got really frustrating.

As any law enforcement officer knows, it's stressful when formal complaints are filed against you. Doesn't matter if you're guilty or not. The stress will always be there.

If you did something wrong, you're stressed because you know you'll have to face disciplinary action. On the other hand, if you didn't do anything wrong, you're angry and frustrated because you did your job well, but the system seems to be working against you.

Again: that's my whole point of writing this book. There is no more uncomfortable situation I can fathom as a law enforcement officer than to be falsely accused.

As a matter of procedure, Stone Mountain IA reviewed the footage captured on both Sergeant Floyd's dash and body cams. Thank goodness they did. Because the on-scene footage told quite a different story from the accounts offered by Davis and Cathcart.

STICKS: As far as you wearing a body camera, is that something that your agency, as a whole, everybody wears? Because I've spoken with guys that buy them for themselves and things like that. Is that a department-wide policy for your agency there?

SGT. FLOYD: Yeah. We initially got cameras ... let me see. They were digital [ILI] cameras and we got those cameras when digital ILIs first started getting ... manufacturing them. So, we were, like, really testing them out. We started getting those, that version, because of ... actually, we got them because of citizens making false complaints. They usually complain because they're mad because they got a ticket. So, I work in a traffic unit. So, of course, I come in contact with a lot of folks who are upset because they're getting tickets. So, I used to get plenty of complaints all the time ... three [or] four a week ... that's the norm ... the dash cam was sufficient [in this case], but it just wasn't as clear as the body cameras. So, it captured the voice a little bit better because the mic is right there instead of the mic up on your shoulder or on your belt. So, the audio along with the video was absolutely magnificent.

STICKS: Do you know how long you'd been actually wearing [a cam] yourself there? I mean, approximately.

SGT. FLOYD: Let me see. I'm trying to remember when we first got our cameras. It had to be somewhere around [2012]. Somewhere around there.

STICKS: Yeah, you guys were definitely ahead of the curve. I mean now, it's pretty much everybody, as we know, in the last four or five years [has cameras] ... Good for you guys and your agency. And that's exactly it. A lot of old school officers are just apprehensive because it's something different and new. Several guys that I work with and have worked with a long time were kind of that way about it. But once they started wearing [the cams] and seeing ... how it helps both [suspects and police officers] in court, so the officer is not called a liar for what he says happened, and then, even all these complaints like this type of deal. They've been great.

SGT. FLOYD: Well, I understand the reason why the officers ... some of them don't like it because too many people try to remove the human element out of the police officer. Oh, you gotta be professional, you can't curse. I mean, these people are still human. And when stuff hits the fan, everybody's verbiage changes for the most part. So I understand what people are saying, things like that. Like, one time they had a news [story] issued out here about all the officers who were high-fiving each other after they finished arresting somebody or tackling him down. "You did a good job." They're not saying [they were happy they tackled the suspect]. We're saying "High five. Hey man, good job" to each other. I mean, that's what goes on with the camaraderie in the circle that we have.

STICKS: ... I know exactly what you're talking about ... taking out the human element. [For instance], let somebody spit on you and see what your reaction to that is.

SGT. FLOYD: Right. Correct. Right.

STICKS: We don't stand there and go, "Sir, don't spit on me." That's not how it works. That's not real life.

SGT. FLOYD: Right. Correct. Right.

In the video footage, any observer can see that, although Sergeant Floyd was stern with Ms. Cathcart, he remained professional in both his conduct and demeanor. From his point of view, he had every reason to ask her to leave the scene.

For a moment, put yourself in Sergeant Floyd's shoes. From his point of view, Ms. Cathcart had no reason whatsoever to involve herself in events surrounding a routine traffic stop. Sergeant Floyd didn't know what Ms. Cathcart's intentions might be. He had no way of knowing if things between the parties might escalate or become violent. Floyd therefore asked Cathcart to move away from him so he could finish his work.

QUOTING FROM SGT. FLOYD'S BODYCAM:

SGT. FLOYD: You can wait over there.

MS. CATHCART: Why?

SGT. FLOYD: Because I asked you to. This traffic stop had nothing to do ...

MS. CATHCART: I can stand right here.

SGT. FLOYD: No, you cannot stand right there, and it's the last time I'm going to ask you or I'm going to put you in the back of my car.

(Here, in the video, Ms. Cathcart steps aside.)

MS. CATHCART: We'll call Dr. Alexander.

SGT. FLOYD: That's right. Call Dr. Alexander. Thank you very much.

The cam footage showed that Ms. Cathcart indeed seemed very annoyed at being reprimanded by Sergeant Floyd. But she did not appear to be traumatized at the time of this verbal exchange. This evidence defied her later claim.

Floyd's dash cam footage also showed Krystal Cathcart doing something which has become commonplace in our modern era. She filmed the entire incident herself using her smartphone.

Cell phone cameras have become so sophisticated—and cell phones are so ubiquitous these days—it's common for police officers around the country to find themselves being filmed multiple times during an average shift.

STICKS: I mean, how many times ... you've been out on, like I said, a felony car stop or a high-risk car stop or something. And you've got guns pointed down at this car, and you've [got] people that are literally putting themselves out there in the middle of it just because they're [trying to film it] ... and you're yelling at them, "Hey, you need to get back, get back!" [But they respond:] "Don't tell me what to do. You can't tell me..."

SGT. FLOYD: Right.

STICKS: It's just like ... are you kidding me?

SGT. FLOYD: Exactly. I've been on traffic stops and folks come walking down the street. They walk to the middle of the cars. What are you doing?

STICKS: I've had that happen, too. Right between your car and the suspect's car. And you're like, What are you doing? ... You have somebody stopped. He's a 24-year-old young man. Somebody will walk up, "That's my boy you just stopped." I'm like, "Okay, he'll be out of here in just a minute." "Well, that's my son." "He's a man. He will be okay. He's going to talk with me now but he'll be just fine. He will contact you when he's done with this car stop." "You need to tell me why you're stopping him." No, I don't.

SGT. FLOYD: Right. Exactly.

For the record, I personally don't have an issue with civilians filming police work in action. So long as it doesn't interfere with an officer doing his or her job. That last part's important.

In this instance, it quickly became apparent that neither Krystal Cathcart nor Terrell Davis were aware that Sgt. Floyd had a bodycam and dash cam. They didn't seem to understand these instruments were capturing everything that transpired. Nor that, when everything else was said and done, this video footage would vindicate Sergeant Floyd from false accusations. But the story didn't end there.

Sergeant Floyd grew flustered on behalf of his fellow law enforcement officers everywhere. He wanted to show a different side of being a cop: the side where cops get falsely accused, and how common this has become.

He asked his department to be more proactive in telling the truth about what happened. His department, however, declined to do so.

STICKS: ... You're talking with your chain of command. What was the reason that they just kind of wanted to let [the matter] die? Just because it was other first responders [involved in the incident]? Do you have any idea why that is?

SGT. FLOYD: That fire department [where Davis and Cathcart work] is in the county, which encompasses us. So they didn't want to ruin the relationship ... with those people.

STICKS: I gotcha.

Sergeant Floyd wasn't satisfied with his department's response. He asked them to give him a copy of the IA investigation file. With this in hand, he reached out to a local TV reporter and shared what had happened.

The reporter was very impressed. He urged Sergeant Floyd not to contact anyone else about what had happened. Out of consideration for the truth and everyone involved, the reporter wanted to vet everything properly before breaking the story. Which he eventually did.

This occurred in January 2016, seven months after the incident happened.

The effect was practically instant.

Sgt. Floyd's story hit the airwaves and quickly went viral. In no time flat, it attracted more than 400,000 views online.

Highlighted in the inquiry was that fact that the Stone Mountain Police Department's Internal Affairs unit had found Ms. Cathcart and Mr. Davis to have been "less than truthful in their written and recorded statements." This was explosive.

Krystal Cathcart was called in and shown the footage from Sergeant Floyd's body and dash cams. She was no doubt surprised that such existed, and also surprised that her take on things was much different than what actually transpired.

While she still believed that Sergeant Floyd had acted too aggressively, she wrote a retraction, which stated in part: "I recant the error of Sgt. Floyd using profanity."

Once he was shown the dashboard footage, Mr. Davis also recanted his story, saying:

"After a sound night sleep and being thankful that traffic stop didn't escalate to anything more. I cannot honestly say that I remember Officer S. E. Floyd use the word 'Fu**,' but I do believe that I heard disrespectful remarks to Krystal Cathcart during their conversation in the school parking lot with parents dropping off their children at the school."

Both Kathcart and Davis would face consequences, and for good reason. They could have gotten an innocent officer disciplined. And this discipline could have included Sergeant Floyd being terminated from his position, albeit unfairly.

Darnell Fullum was, at that point, Fire Chief of DeKalb County. After personally reviewing the camera footage, he said, "I had the same feelings and thoughts as probably everybody, and that was shock and surprise."

The upshot was that the DeKalb County Fire Department fired Captain Davis. Krystal Cathcart was given a notice of termination. Fullum, however, later accepted her resignation in lieu of termination.

Later, Chief Fullum said that he didn't punish his employees without first giving the issue thorough consideration. "You never want to see anybody lose their job, lose their pay," he said. "But you know—there's times it's warranted, and you have to take action."

Dr. Cedric Alexander was not happy that Crystal Kathcart and Terrell Davis had invoked his name during the incident. He later said, "The conduct of their behavior is certainly unbecoming of any employee ... It was unprofessional, and it certainly did not warrant them using my name, by any regard whatsoever."

For the record, neither Davis nor Cathcart called Dr. Alexander—as each had threatened to—after the alleged incident with Sergeant Floyd.

SGT. FLOYD: She [Ms. Cathcart] ended up getting convicted of [making] false statements.

STICKS: As in criminally convicted for it?

SGT. FLOYD: Yes. Yes.

STICKS: ... Wow. What was the ... I guess the sentence or punishment or fine or anything for that. Do you know?

SGT. FLOYD: ... They gave her first offender [status] because it was the first time for her to be a criminal. She had to write a letter of apology to myself, one to the department. She had to pay a fine, two thousand or a thousand dollars, I can't remember exactly what it is. She had to do some community service. Can't work in any kind of public law enforcement or fire fighter capacities within three years or four years, something like that.

STICKS: So she, too, ended up having to lose her job. And, as far as you know, she's not back into that field of work right now?

SGT. FLOYD: Correct. As far as I know.

After reading about my own harrowing tale, you can probably see why I sympathize with Sergeant Floyd's predicament.

The complaint filed against him was highly improper. Yes, investigators acquitted Sergeant Floyd of any wrongdoing. In the meantime, however, he was viewed with suspicion in the kangaroo court of public opinion. And his department refused to release the information it held that verified his innocence.

These days, when cop videos go viral, it's often because the cops are the ones shown conducting themselves improperly. Here the situation was reversed. The video showed the public how an officer conducted himself professionally to the best of his abilities under very stressful circumstances. It also served the twofold purpose of vindicating him against exaggerated claims made by members of the public.

But consider the double standard at work. Had the IA investigation shown Sergeant Floyd to be in the wrong, he would have been swiftly and harshly punished.

Following the DeKalb County Fire Department's decision to fire both Davis and Catchcart, Musa Ghanayem, the attorney who represented both employees, stated, "Both regret the statements with regard to maybe exaggerating what was said. But they both still felt threatened, they both still felt there was a sense of fear."

Think about this for a moment. Read that quote back to yourself.

"Statements with regard to maybe exaggerating what was said"?

Are you kidding me?

If any police officer were to document an incident and "exaggerate what was said" in their official report, they would be fired. As they should be. If an officer lies, their credibility for the remainder of their career (if they even get to keep their job) is gone.

My own department in Tulsa has adopted a policy we refer to as "you lie, you die." Meaning, if you lie in any way while performing your duties as a police officer, the matter will be investigated. And if it's shown that you did, in fact, lie, you lose your job, no matter how small the lie was. We have zero tolerance for lying.

But here's an interesting note: Captain Terrell Davis appealed his firing and was subsequently rehired by the DeKalb County Fire Department. His lawyer made the case that the ruling against him was unfair because he was such a dedicated firefighter.

As part of the appeal she pursued, Attorney Ghanayem cited how, after he'd slept on the matter, Davis submitted a second letter that clarified his first written statement. This was Davis's admission where he stated that, after getting a good night's sleep, he didn't remember Sergeant Floyd using any foul language. But he did feel that Sergeant Floyd had made "disrespectful remarks."

"[Davis] corrected himself in twenty-four hours," his attorney claimed. She also pointed out that, unlike Ms. Cathcart, Mr. Davis hadn't made a formal complaint.

To which I say, So what?

Now listen. I admire a dedicated firefighter as much as a I admire the dedicated police officers I work with every day. I also know the rules we all live by. Please refer to my previous statement about lying. Again, like my department in Tulsa, I have zero tolerance on this matter.

As it turned out, Michael Caldwell of the Georgia Association of Chiefs of Police had a much different opinion of Captain Davis and what transpired.

"That's ridiculous," Caldwell said in a TV interview. "Whether it's in a formal complaint or an informal report, it doesn't matter. They should tell the truth."

By "they," I can only intuit that Michael Caldwell meant "municipal employees." Public servants. To which I agree.

Mr. Caldwell went on to say that Terrell Davis should not go unpunished after filing a false statement.

"He is a captain, he is a higher-ranking officer. He has greater responsibility. He is very high up in the fire department and he has to lead by example."

STICKS: Okay. Let me ask you this ... What do you think, possibly, would have been the result had you not had a body camera?

SGT. FLOYD: Me, personally? Probably those two ganging up on me. I might have gotten in some trouble.

Here I'm afraid Sergeant Floyd is being a bit too optimistic. If not for the footage from his body cam documenting what actually happened during the traffic stop, Sergeant Floyd could have been reprimanded or otherwise punished. Specifically, this could have happened in any number of ways. Reassignment out of a unit he loved. Suspension without pay. Getting terminated from his job.

Instead, he remains on the force where he continues to professionally serve his community.

STICKS: Do you have any advice for future cops? For any future officer that may read this book? Or any advice you want to pass on for something like that or these type of deals that go on these days?

SGT. FLOYD: My advice to any cop is to don't take it personal. Because people really aren't personally upset with you, they're upset they got caught doing something. And the moment that you interject your personal thoughts and/or feelings into it, it's going to go sideways and ugly. That's why I don't have to curse at these people. You're an officer. You have the final say. You've got three things, three options. You have warning, ticket, jail. You're the one that has the final say. You're in control. So, don't allow somebody to push your buttons and take you out of your control. Self-discipline. That's all it is. All you have to do is articulate what you're doing, end of the conversation.

I don't understand why somebody gets bent up out of shape. Why are you yelling? What are you screaming for? Sometimes you have to talk to some people like that because that's the only thing they understand. But for the majority of them, you don't have to do that. You can sit up there and articulate it and either you're going to get a ticket, you're going to jail, or you're going to let them slide.

STICKS: Alright. Let me flip that, then. How about for the general public? You got any advice for them on ... say traffic stops or just these types of situations? If they do, in fact, have a complaint?

SGT. FLOYD: The same thing I would tell the officers: Stop taking this stuff personal. These officers are human. They're just like you. You wouldn't like it if he yelled at you, so stop yelling at him. And stop thinking, just because he's trained ... they're all still human. You don't know what's happened to him earlier, him or her, earlier in the day. Who knows? The same thing you want him to extend to you, you need to extend to the officer because 99 percent of the time, nothing's going to happen.

To all this, I say, "Amen."

This not-so-routine traffic stop reminds us that officers have to act professionally and courteously in every situation. In the heat of the moment, as people on both sides get angry and frustrated, things can escalate to something much more serious.

Thank goodness that, in this case, Sergeant Floyd had a bodycam and dashcam. Their footage helped corroborate his side of the story: that he was just a police officer trying to do his job as best he can.

Had those instruments not been in place to protect his integrity, the situation would likely have ended very differently.

CHAPTER NINE:
A SEXUAL ASSAULT THE VICTIM DENIED EVER HAPPENED

CASE FILE

Accused officer: Daniel Hubbard, Texas Dept. of Public Safety

Related parties: Sherita Dixon-Cole; her unnamed fiancé; attorney Lee Merritt; activist Shaun King

Date of incident: Sunday, May 20, 2018

Location: Ellis County, Texas

Here's another law enforcement pro tip: When an officer pulls over a driver and approaches their car, the number one thing on their mind is safety. Not writing a ticket. Not whether or not they should offer the driver leniency for an infraction. Safety.

Most civilians don't know this, but safety is drilled into police from the moment our career begins. It's one of the primary focuses taught in police academies around the country. It's a central tenet of field training regardless of what specific skill is being taught. And it's literally job one when it comes to any course of continuing education. By which I mean the ongoing training that law enforcement officers, like attorneys, must engage in if they wish to continue practicing in their fields.

So let's bring this all back to a car stop.

This procedure may look simple and it's certainly very common. But it's actually the result of your local police officer executing dozens of procedures. Every detail of stopping and approaching a vehicle has been drilled into us. If we make it look seamless, and we should, chalk it up to experience and training.

Our procedures dictate how we position our patrol car behind the vehicle we've pulled over. What information we should pull up on the suspect's vehicle using our on-board database resources. How to use that information in assessing possible threats. Which hand we should hold our flashlight in (I'll give you a hint: it's your non-shooting hand). Precisely where we should stand when approaching the suspect's car. Which warning signs our eyes, ears, and noses should be scanning for as we make primary contact.

And really, all this is just the beginning.

I mention this here to put you in the proper frame of mind. I want you to imagine what it was like to be Officer Daniel Hubbard as he pulled over a vehicle at approximately 1:30 a.m. on the morning of Sunday, May 20, 2018 in Ellis County, Texas.

The vehicle in question was a white 2013 Chevy Malibu. Officer Hubbard had observed the vehicle driving erratically. He deemed this sufficient probable cause for him to activate his flashers and sirens, to pursue the vehicle, and to stop it.

But the Malibu didn't respond. With Officer Hubbard's patrol car behind it, flashing its lights—a sight hard to miss—and revving its siren—a sound not to be ignored—the Chevy Malibu did just that. It continued for two full minutes before the driver at last pulled over.

I'll tell you this from my own experiences. It raises concerns when a vehicle fails to heed an officer's lights and siren and stop. Put simply, this isn't normal. Why would a driver not choose to yield?

The possible answers are obvious once you've been trained. A police officer's first suspicion—and biggest concern—is that a driver who won't pull over is trying to hide something. In many cases, this means drugs or alcohol, which are illegal in most jurisdictions while operating a motor vehicle. It could also mean the driver is trying to hide an illegal weapon of some sort.

Weapons are obviously of grave concern to law enforcement personnel since they can potentially hurt us as we seek to perform our duties.

Sometimes the issue is far less dire. For instance, it's common to pull over an elderly person who's confused about what's going on. In some cases, you'll deal with a person who's so intent on listening to the radio, they didn't see you back there.

But sometimes the issue is dire, indeed. In my day, I've pulled over a few people who were so intoxicated, they didn't seem to realize what was happening to them.

The bottom line for each of these cases is the same. When a driver fails to pull over after being signaled to do so, a police officer's senses become heightened. For this reason, I urge anyone who's driving a motor vehicle: If you hear a siren and see flashing lights, it's always best to pull over as soon as it's safe for you to do so.

When the white Chevy Malibu finally came to a halt, Officer Hubbard got out of his own vehicle and cautiously approached. With his flashlight in hand, he addressed the driver, who turned out to be a woman—one Sherita Dixon-Cole. As Officer Hubbard tried to make contact, Ms. Dixon-Cole was talking on her cell phone. This raised another issue entirely.

Law enforcement officers do not appreciate it when civilians talk on their phone during an interview. This is just common sense.

Personally, I find it rude when anyone is in the presence of another human being and won't put their phone down. Call me old fashioned, but that's how I feel.

But put yourself in the shoes of a cop who's just pulled somebody over. You didn't do it for fun. You did it because you have cause to think that someone is breaking the law. By breaking the law, they're making the community less safe, both for themselves and their fellow citizens. To have them talk on the phone while you're trying to correct this imbalance comes across as disrespectful and glib.

Law enforcement officers will ask any driver they've stopped to stay off their phone once contact's been made. For professional reasons, we insist that a driver focus on what's going on. If a driver can't focus on a simple conversation, how can they handle the mental demands of operating a motor vehicle? Again, we're not just pulling you over for kicks; the chances are pretty darn good that you've committed a violation. And we hope that you're concerned about this, as any responsible citizen should be.

Also, from a practical standpoint, we need to exchange information with you. For instance, we need you to verify your identity. Who owns the car you're driving. Whether its paperwork is in place. Importantly, we also need to inform you why we pulled you over in the first place. And none of these things will go smoothly when you're talking to your kids or playing a round of Angry Birds.

But there's another important reason why cell phones can be a nuisance to cops. It often happens that someone who's being pulled over will call for "backup." Meaning they want a friend or relative to show up at the car stop and offer some kind of assistance.

This is inappropriate. Go back to the story you just read in Chapter Eight. At best, having additional parties appear at a car stop becomes annoying. At worst, it becomes an officer safety issue.

We have no idea who you might be summoning or what their intentions might be. The analogy I like to use is that you've gotten into an argument with your spouse. Normally, this is bad enough, an uncomfortable situation. Now imagine that suddenly, some person you don't even know and who has no bearing whatsoever on your relationship, shows up to offer opinions. How would that feel?

Exactly. We've just gone from bad to worse. And why? For no good reason at all.

Somewhat gruffly, though still well within the confines of professionalism, Officer Hubbard reminded Ms. Dixon-Cole that stopping for police officers who flash their vehicle lights and use their sirens is normal behavior in a civil society. He asked her to put down her phone. Then, according to procedure, he asked her to provide her driver's license and vehicle registration.

Ms. Dixon-Cole began gathering her paperwork. She did not put down her phone. She explained that she had been talking to her fiancé who'd just moved to the area three days prior. She didn't know his address, she said. She'd been discussing the matter with him and was still doing so.

Officer Hubbard observed that this answer was not relevant to being pulled over. He also couldn't help notice that Ms. Dixon-Cole was slow to gather her paperwork and slow to respond to his questions. Also that, while speaking, she occasionally slurred her words. At this point, any police officer's instincts would have been piqued.

As we saw in the previous chapter, it's common for police officers to use their discretion as to whether or not an offense should be given leniency or a summons. Take this hypothetical case:

After checking a driver's documentation, the police officer finds they have a clean safety record. The issue of erratic driving might have been explained by the fact that Ms. Dixon-Cole was indeed looking for her fiancé's house. Erratic driving is never a condonable situation, though it's sometimes understandable. In this case (again: hypothetically), an officer might alert the driver to the fact that she was driving erratically. Then, after issuing this verbal warning, he might help her find the address she was looking for.

But Officer Hubbard felt something was amiss. Why had Ms. Dixon-Cole taken so long to pull over? And why was she behaving like she'd been drinking? Why was Ms. Dixon-Cole taking a relatively long time to answer his questions? Why was she taking longer than expected to gather her paperwork?

To a trained police officer, these are all red flags.

I myself have witnessed intoxicated drivers search for their license or insurance and not be able to find them. In a couple of cases, they were already holding their documentation in their hands. In other instances, I've seen intoxicated suspects hand officers credit cards, bus passes, and other items they thought were their driver's licenses.

Ms. Dixon-Cole's behavior troubled Officer Hubbard. He thought he might be dealing with a potential case of DWI, or Driving While Intoxicated. In the state of Texas, this infraction is defined by a person twenty-one years of age or older who operates a motor vehicle with a .08 blood alcohol concentration and/or while under the influence of drugs.

To decide whether or not this was indeed the case, Officer Hubbard engaged in small talk.

Now don't laugh. When I mention the subject of small talk, a lot of civilians shake their heads and snicker. Their attitude seems to be, "Really? Small talk? That's a law enforcement technique?"

Why, yes. It surely is.

I know it's become very common—very modern, I guess you could say—to only trust information we read in print or see on videos. Ideally, these printed articles and videos are posted on the Internet. Somewhat inexplicably, this is the only scenario that seems to validate information in many peoples' minds.

But make no mistake. Small talk—conversation—is one of the oldest and, as it turns out, most reliable ways for law enforcement personnel to gather information.

I've used the small talk technique frequently throughout my entire 24 years as a police officer. Why? Because it's natural. Human beings like to talk to each other, don't we?

For instance, when I approach someone's car, I don't want to be perceived as some robotic figure standing there, doing a paint-by-numbers protocol. Do this in Situation A. Do that in Situation B. That could be very off-putting.

On the other hand, I don't want to come across as too lenient, too loose, too chummy.

No, in the end, a cop is just like a doctor, a lawyer, a dentist, or a plumber. Meaning that, in any professional situation, there are limits to how much of our personalities we can and should present while we attempt to fulfill our role.

Again, the point I'm trying to make here is that cops are human, like everyone else. We're there to help, not hinder. Making small talk eases everyone's nerves. It's a great way to gather information in a friendly, non-threatening way.

Officer Hubbard had observed Ms. Dixon-Cole's erratic driving and the fact that she refused to initially pull over. Coupled with this, she presented herself as someone who might be impaired by drugs or alcohol. So Officer Hubbard asked Ms. Dixon-Cole if she'd been drinking that night. And if so, how much she'd had to drink.

Sherita Dixon-Cole replied that she'd taken one drink about two hours prior to being pulled over. Had this indeed been the case, she would have been under the legal limit. But her story didn't corroborate Officer Hubbard's observations. The erratic driving. Failure to pull over. Resistance to putting her phone down. Slurred speech. Impaired behavior.

As he continued his conversation, Officer Hubbard spotted some groceries in the backseat of Ms. Dixon-Cole's Chevy Malibu. These groceries clearly included perishables. He saw eggs in a carton. He also saw two bottles of vodka and these bottles were not full.

In the course of the conversation that followed, Ms. Dixon-Cole offered a few stories which contained inconsistencies. For instance, when Officer Hubbard asked how the alcohol came to be in her car, she first reported it came from the grocery store. Later, however, she mentioned the vodka had come from her house.

At another point, she said that she'd picked up the groceries three days before. When Officer Hubbard asked why she hadn't unloaded them, Ms. Dixon-Cole said she "had to go out."

"That's not safe to [eat] anymore," said Officer Hubbard. Meaning the eggs.

Clearly, none of this made much sense. Officer Hubbard decided to begin a field sobriety test. This decision was well within his purview. Likely, he felt certain enough that Ms. Dixon-Cole was a danger both to herself and other motorists that a sobriety test should be administered soonest.

Following protocol, Hubbard used his radio to inform his dispatch he'd be conducting multiple sobriety tests on the motorist he'd pulled over. Once dispatch acknowledged his message, Officer Hubbard informed Ms. Dixon-Cole as to what he'd decided to do. She put up no argument. She complied willingly. Officer Hubbard offered to have her change her high-heeled shoes to flats. That way she could more easily execute the famous heel-to-toe walking test.

Ms. Dixon-Cole completed all the sobriety tests she was given without incident. But Officer Hubbard remained unconvinced. The truth is, many people can pass a roadside sobriety test because they're experienced drinkers. Fearing this might be a factor, and being conscious not only of Ms. Dixon-Cole's safety but the safety of other drivers, Officer Hubbard chose to arrest her for driving while intoxicated.

Let's follow Officer Hubbard's logic. The evidence against Ms. Dixon-Cole was clear. Erratic driving. Failure to pull over. Resistance to putting her phone down. Slurred speech. Impaired behavior. Inconsistent narrative.

On top of all this, Officer Hubbard understood something crucial. An arrest is not a conviction. If Ms. Dixon-Cole was truly innocent, she would have ample opportunity to prove it in court. Meanwhile, Officer Hubbard had a responsibility to keep everyone in his jurisdiction safe. I can only imagine this was a tough call for him. In the end, however, I believe it was the right call to make.

Officer Hubbard read Ms. Dixon-Cole her Miranda warning. She then asked if she could call her father, whom she identified as a judge in the city of Dallas.

Officer Hubbard told her that Dallas was too far away to come to the scene. He let her call her fiancé instead, since he was apparently much closer. He then used handcuffs to secure Ms. Dixon-Cole and had her sit in the front of his squad car where he told her to wait while he searched her vehicle.

> Across the country, many police departments, including my own in Tulsa, place suspects in the front seat of their patrol cars for transport. This is a normal, everyday practice.
>
> Personally, I prefer to have the suspect in the front seat. It allows me to have a conversation with them while driving. As noted, conversation is one of the best ways to gather information.
>
> I also prefer to see the suspect at all times. This alerts me if they start moving around or possibly trying to remove contraband from their person or even retrieving a weapon that wasn't discovered during my initial search.

What was Officer Hubbard looking for in the suspect's vehicle? Any evidence that might have corroborated his worst fear: that Ms. Dixon-Cole had been driving while intoxicated. While searching her Chevy Malibu, Hubbard noted a strong smell of alcohol coming from a container in her front-seat cupholder. He searched the entire car and ended up removing the alcohol containers, which he would document as evidence. He also searched more thoroughly through Ms. Dixon-Cole's purse.

Not long after the call was placed, Mr. Dixon-Cole's fiancé arrived. Officer Hubbard spoke with this gentleman briefly. He explained the reasons why he was taking Ms. Dixon-Cole to be booked. He also allowed the soon-to-be-marrieds to talk while he assented to recovering Ms. Dixon-Cole's wallet and a few personal items from her car. During this interval, Officer Hubbard even allowed Ms. Dixon-Cole to get out of the police vehicle while speaking with her fiancé.

Sherita Dixon-Cole told her fiancé she thought Officer Hubbard was arresting her merely because he was angry she'd been talking on her cell phone when Hubbard was speaking to her.

When Officer Hubbard returned to the pair, the fiancé tried to press him for more information. Officer Hubbard refused to supply this. The matter boiled down to privacy.

"This is something that happened to her," he explained. "It's not my place to tell you. She can tell you if she wishes."

Officer Hubbard said this exchange of information could take place when Ms. Dixon-Cole got out of jail. He assured the fiancé that event should occur at some point that very day, meaning that Ms. Dixon-Cole probably wouldn't have to stay in jail overnight.

At this point, the tow truck arrived to transport Ms. Dixon-Cole's car. This essentially ended the back and forth. The fiancé departed. Officer Hubbard drove Ms. Dixon-Cole to jail.

Everything I've outlined above took place within fifty minutes or so from the moment Officer Hubbard chose to pull over Ms. Dixon-Hubbard's 2013 white Chevy Malibu.

Please bear all this in mind. Because, from this point, the story gets crazy.

The family of Sherita Dixon-Cole posted her bail bond at 3 p.m. on Sunday, May 20, 2018. Six hours later, Ms. Dixon-Cole was picked up from the Waco County Jail. Almost immediately upon her release, Ms. Dixon-Cole claimed that Officer Hubbard had sexually assaulted her and tried to pressure her into performing sexual favors in exchange for her release at headquarters. She also alleged she'd requested a rape test but had been denied. The police, she said, hadn't taken her accusation seriously enough to open an investigation.

A civil rights attorney, Lee Merritt, got wind of Sherita Dixon-Cole's story. He later said this story came from Ms. Dixon-Cole herself. Regardless, the spurious allegations were soon picked up and telegraphed by civil rights activist Shaun King.

King is an influential writer on the platform, *Medium.* On that platform, he posted that Sherita Dixon-Cole had been "raped" and "kidnapped" by Officer Daniel Hubbard. His cited source to corroborate these allegations? Lee Merritt.

Published merely hours after the alleged incident had taken place, Mr. King's account went out to each of his followers. And since *Medium* is essentially an open platform, it was soon available to millions of readers.

But that wasn't the end. It was just the beginning. Mr. Merritt also notified several news outlets of Ms. Dixon-Cole's allegations. Very quickly, Tarana Burke, the prominent founder of the #MeToo movement, contributed to spreading the story. Other media and online influencers followed suit, including *The Root*, a prominent webzine that specializes in African-American themes.

Each of these sources amplified Ms. Dixon-Cole's allegations. Then there was *Black America Web*, a news site focused on racial justice issues. It was also among the first publications to break the story. An article posted on *Black America Web* claimed that, while Sherita Dixon-Cole had passed a sobriety test, she had nonetheless been placed under arrest for having a "bad attitude."

Sadly, this claim only inflamed readers more. Perhaps it was designed to. Why? Because having a "bad attitude" had been at the heart of another claim involving an African-American woman who'd been pulled over. I'm speaking here of the high-profile Sandra Bland case that took place three years earlier in Hempstead, Texas.

Briefly, this case involved a twenty-eight-year-old African-American woman, Sandra Bland, whom a Texas State Trooper, Officer Brian Encinia, pulled over on Friday July 10, 2015.

The reason? A minor traffic violation.

Officer Encinia stopped Ms. Bland for failing to make a traffic signal. However, as was later corroborated by partial footage from Encinia's dashcam, this exchange escalated to the point where Officer Encinia arrested Ms. Bland on the charges of assaulting a police officer. Her bail was set at $5,000.

Three days later, the body of Ms. Bland was found hanged by the neck in her jail cell. Footage from a motion-activated camera showed no one entering or leaving the cell. Her death was therefore ruled a suicide.

Toxicology reports later stated that Ms. Bland had "a remarkably high concentration" of THC in her blood. THC is the active psychoactive ingredient in marijuana. The toxicology report therefore suggested that Ms. Bland had somehow gained access to marijuana while in jail. This, of course, is unlikely.

Another, more probable explanation, is this. She'd been a user of marijuana, and her consumption was such that that her body was fairly saturated with THC.

A toxicologist for the Tarrant County medical examiner's office stated that

"I have never seen a report in the [medical] literature or from any other source [citing] residual THC that high [as Sandra Bland's] three days after someone stops using the drug."

The Texas Department of Public Safety maintains that Sandra Bland died by suicide. But activists cite doctored or missing footage to indicate that police may have murdered her while she was in custody. According to *The Guardian*, Bland's family eventually settled for $1.9 million with the Texas Department of Safety.

I mention all this for a few reasons.

ONE: to make you aware. The Sandra Bland case sparked national outrage over racial injustice. If you don't know this case, I urge you to read up on it. Apart from being a tragedy, there are many inconsistencies that warrant consideration.

TWO: to reiterate that, as a law enforcement officer and a fundamentally decent human being, I will defend anyone—anyone at all—against racial injustice to my dying breath.

THREE: to demonstrate how easily the Dixon-Cole case found seed in the national psyche. The Bland case was still fresh in everyone's minds. The fact that the Bland and Dixon-Cole cases both took place in Texas seemed to throw fuel on a very hot fire.

And lots of people knew this.

Consider this excerpt from the *Black America Web* article:

"Bad attitudes are not illegal. [The case of Sherita Dixon-Cole] is basically the same thing a Texas officer chose to arrest Sandra Bland for. In that case the cop claimed to pull Sandra over because she failed to put on her turn signal, which was a fabrication, so he needed some other excuse to drag Sandra out of the car, assault, and arrest her."

Or how about this, from the same article:

"The fiancé also confirmed for me that Sherita was handcuffed and strangely placed in the front seat of the police car—which confirmed another part of Sherita's story."

Statements like this show how ignorance of police procedures can inflate to conspiracy theories. As we covered a few pages back in this chapter (see the sidebar), it's not strange to have a suspect sit up front in a patrol car during transport to jail. It's valid law enforcement technique—hardly corroboration that something was amiss.

Still, very quickly, the incident that took place between Officer Hubbard and Ms. Dixon-Cole was packaged and broadcast as a crime, and specifically one where a member of law enforcement had abused his power. Officer Hubbard was portrayed as a bad cop for breaking the law, a misogynist for assaulting a woman, and a racist who'd assaulted an African-American.

Taking place as it did on the heels of the Sandra Bland case and the #MeToo explosion, the story of Sherita Dixon-Cole caught like wildfire over the Internet. To say it went viral would be an understatement. Too many accounts to list garnered multiple retweets, Facebook shares, blog posts, you name it. People were out for blood.

There was only one problem. Sherita Dixon-Cole's accusations turned out to be utterly and completely false.

How do we know this? I bet you've probably guessed by now.

Footage from both Officer Hubbard's bodycam and his patrol vehicle's dashcam capture the entire two-plus hours that Officer Hubbard and Ms. Dixon-Cole interacted.

Picture this footage in your mind. Or, if you'd rather, look it up on the Internet. It's posted there for all to see.

It starts when Officer Hubbard elects to pursue Ms. Dixon-Cole's erratically driven vehicle. It shows how he activates his flashers and sirens. How those sirens continue to blare for two full minutes before Ms. Dixon-Cole pulls over.

It shows Officer Hubbard getting out of his vehicle and approaching the white Chevy Malibu. Admittedly, it shows him gruffly remonstrating Ms. Dixon-Cole for talking so long to pull over. He also gruffly requests that she put down her phone while speaking to him. But these are the only times in the tapes that viewers might sense that Hubbard expressed any hint of emotion. Also, as I mentioned, Hubbard's annoyance was both justified and within his purview as a professional police officer.

The footage shows the entire exchange that took place between Officer Hubbard and Ms. Dixon-Cole. Any professional law enforcement officer who views the footage can see an arrest is coming. Throughout the conversation, Ms. Dixon-Cole isn't paying attention. She's slow to respond to questions and commands. Also, at points when she's talking, her speech is slurred. She's contradicting herself. These are all tell-tale signs that she's impaired.

The tape shows Hubbard explaining to Dixon-Cole that he's arresting her for suspicion of intoxication. Legally, he had grounds for this. Her behavior certainly implied inebriation. She had alcohol in the car and her story of how it got there didn't make sense.

The footage also shows the arrival of Ms. Dixon-Cole's fiancé. You can actually hear them talking though we never see the fiancé in the camera's frame. Only his vehicle.

Throughout all this, it's clear to any observer that all appropriate procedures were followed. There was no blocking of the camera, no edits, and no interruptions. Officer Hubbard kept his hands visible at all times while he entered his report into the system. There's no sexual assault. Nor does the tape show anything untoward during his entire interaction with Ms. Dixon-Cole's fiancé, through multiple trips to and from his vehicle, and all the way through the ride to jail.

Now, I've heard some armchair critics question Officer Hubbard's decision to make the arrest. If Ms. Dixon-Cole's case was borderline, they say, why didn't Hubbard show her leniency?

The answer is likely simple: Officer Hubbard was probably doing his best to ensure the safety both of Ms. Dixon-Cole and other citizens. What if he'd let her drive off and she crashed and injured herself, or someone else?

Another factor that might have come into play was the suspect's behavior.

As I mentioned in Chapter Eight, a major factor that can affect the outcome of any traffic stops is the suspect's attitude. Had Ms. Dixon-Cole shown respect for Officer Hubbard's position, not to mention the rules of the road, things might have gone differently. Sadly, it seems, she did not.

In the footage, Ms. Dixon-Cole's initial tone seems composed but annoyed. Trust me when I say this is a less than stellar attitude with which to greet a law enforcement officer who's putting his or her own life on the line to stop a car for driving recklessly in the middle of the night. It only adds to the officer's assessment that they did the right thing in pulling this person over to check their sobriety.

No one can deny that driving while intoxicated is a serious offense. Beyond putting the driver at risk, it endangers everyone who shares the road with them. Apart from the loss or injury of human life, property damage can occur. This is why police officers are so vigilant about catching individuals who drink and drive. Doing so is the logical equivalent of snuffing out a lit fuse before the flame reaches a keg of TNT.

It all boils down to that old piece of advice Ben Franklin wrote in his newspaper, The Pennsylvania Gazette, back in 1734. "An Ounce of Prevention is truly worth a Pound of Cure."

We do well to remember that law enforcement officers aren't always there to catch crooks. A big part of our job is prophylactic. We're there to make sure that crooks with a clearly malicious intent don't get a chance to do evil in the first place. That accidents stop before they can happen. And that safety, health, and happiness rule the day in our communities.

Notwithstanding all this, a national outrage was building. The assumptions broadcast by Lee Merritt, Shaun King, and so many others found fertile ground in the public's imagination. People were in uproar. And let me clarify: I sympathize.

Suppose the situation had gone down the way Ms. Dixon-Cole claimed it had. Guess what? I would have been leading the charge to have Officer Hubbard expunged from the rosters of law enforcement and prosecuted to the fullest extent of the law.

But things didn't go down that way. Far from it, in fact.

It was all a pack of lies.

To nip this issue in the bud, the Texas Department of Public Safety released the footage from Officer Hubbard's body and dashcams in their entirely. As I mentioned, this footage clearly shows a routine traffic stop and an officer—Daniel Hubbard—following standard DWI procedures. Also, as mentioned, the tapes show that no untoward behavior took place during the entire two-hour incident. As in zero. Meaning none.

During a local television interview several weeks after the incident, Ms. Dixon-Cole stated that she'd never authorized anyone to speak publicly about her DWI stop.

Moreover, she adamantly denied that she'd ever hired Lee Merritt as her attorney. She said that she'd only spoken to Mr. Merritt after she'd posted bail. And by this point the social media firestorm had already erupted.

Mr. Merritt later contended that Ms. Dixon-Cole's fiancé had authorized him to represent her. He said that detailed allegations of the supposed assault only came from Ms. Dixon-Cole herself. "Those are things she told me directly," he stated. Meaning the lies about sexual assault. About the rape kit. All of it.

What was that line from Sir Walter Scott? "O, what a tangled web we weave when first we practice to deceive."

So we're left to wonder. Did Ms. Dixon-Cole make the whole thing up? Or did Lee Merritt? Or the fiancé? Who would have motive to do such a thing? Who on earth thought it wise, that they might profit by heaping such vile aspersions on law enforcement officers? And who, quite frankly, could be stupid enough to think they'd get away with it?

In the end, I suppose, we'll never be sure.

In addition to supplying the body and dashcam footage, the Texas Department of Public Safety released a written statement about what had occurred. This statement ran widely over various social media. It also accompanied a posting of the footage on YouTube.

I quote the statement here, in part, to give you, the reader, an idea of how the department handled the matter:

"Sherita Dixon-Cole, 37, from Grapevine, was arrested and transported to the Ellis County Jail, where she was charged with DWI. Following the arrest, spurious and false accusations related to this traffic stop were made against the Texas Trooper. Upon learning of those allegations, the Texas Department of Public Safety immediately took action to review the video in connection with this traffic stop and arrest. The video shows absolutely no evidence to support the egregious and unsubstantiated accusations against the Trooper during the DWI arrest of the suspect. The Department is appalled that anyone would make such a despicable, slanderous, and false accusation against a peace officer who willingly risks his life every day to protect and serve the public. At the department's request, the Ellis County District Attorney's Office has reviewed video of the traffic stop and arrest, and authorized the release of the video. The department today proactively and publicly released the video captured by the Trooper's body camera (which is posted here). (Note: Certain sections of the video have been blurred or rendered in audible to protect information that is confidential by state statute, including Cole's personally identifiable information.)"

Why did the post offer the note it did at the end? The one that states certain parts of the video have been blurred or rendered inaudible?

So that no one could jump to conclusions.

Apart from protecting Ms. Dixon-Cole's personal information and that of her fiancé, these steps protected a spot in the video where Officer Hubbard took a call related to another case he was working on. One that had nothing to do with pulling over the white Chevy Malibu.

In any event, the intent was verification. The Texas Department of Public Safety was stating that none of the video footage has been altered to hide Officer Hubbard's incriminating behavior. Because there was none.

Once the Texas Department of Safety released Officer Hubbard's video footage, public opinion turned around completely, and practically overnight. Lee Merritt, Ms. Dixon-Cole's attorney, released an apology in the following a public statement:

"It is deeply troubling when innocent parties are falsely accused, and I am truly sorry for any trouble these claims may have caused ... I take full responsibility for amplifying these claims to the point of national concern. This office regularly receives hundreds of complaints of abuse from across the nation and we are obligated to filter these messages thoroughly before relaying them to our powerful allies. Our office takes claims of abuse—particularly by law enforcement officers— very seriously. It is our responsibility to call for swift, transparent and thorough investigation into any such accusation. Our calls for professionalism and adherence to protocol, however, should not be misconstrued as a rush to judgment. To the contrary, our goal in presenting claims of misconduct is to arrive as quickly and accurately as possible to the truth. We are thankful to the members of the community willing to echo our demands for transparency and justice. However, in this matter it seems your righteous vigilance was abused."

Shaun King also retracted his first article. While walking back his statements and issuing a public apology, he stated he'd looked over the video footage three times to ensure it hadn't been doctored.

"I viewed it with an editing expert," King wrote. "They agree. Nothing horrible took place there. Nothing criminal has been edited out of this video."

He went on:

"I can't even begin to make sense of why someone would concoct such an awful story. It does a tremendous disservice to actual victims when something horrible like this is fabricated. It provides an unfair spotlight to a good cop and undeserved cover for the bad ones who will try to use an incident like this as false proof of their innocence."

According to ABC, on May 23, the district attorney floated the possibility of charging Dixon-Cole with the crime of falsifying information. Ultimately, this was not done, however.

From an article in *Blue Lives Matter*, according to District Attorney Patrick Wilson, "In order to be charged with filing a false report, Dixon Cole would have needed to make a false complaint to a sworn peace officer."

However, weeks after the incident, Sherita Dixon-Cole claimed in an interview that she was avoiding using her cell phone, looking at social media, or going out in public. Why? Because people were vehemently calling her a liar.

She maintained that the story took on a life of its own. That she was in jail when a "narrative" of what supposedly occurred began to develop online. She claimed that she never used the words "rape" or "kidnapping" when talking to her boyfriend, though he was the only person she spoke with while in jail.

"Looking back, I was an instrument," she said.

"I feel like I definitely have to take accountability for my actions," Sherita Dixon-Cole said in her interview with a local TV station.

During this interview, she also apologized to family and friends for any worry or concern caused by the very public way in which the entire incident played out.

Yet notably to my mind, at least—she stopped short of directly apologizing to Officer Daniel Hubbard. And therein lies the rub, as they say.

We can be tempted to think of this incident as an essentially victimless crime. It wasn't. Not by a long shot.

The local police force of Ellis County, Texas, was maligned. So were police officers all over the country. Frankly, the malicious allegations tarred anyone wearing a badge with the same foul brush. An undeserved stain.

The lies, of course, also directly affected Officer Daniel Hubbard.

But they also, as fate decided, affected another cop. Also named Hubbard.

In his original blog post, Shaun King didn't include Officer Hubbard's first name. Similarly, Lee Merritt's initial false statements only referred to Hubbard by his last name.

In some ways, this turned out to be good. Daniel Hubbard was not initially targeted for false accusations against him.

But someone else was.

As it happened, there was another member of the Texas Department of Public Safety whose last name was Hubbard. This was Texas State Trooper Jarrod Hubbard, who began getting death threats on his personal phone and Facebook account.

Clearly, people had mistaken Jarrod Hubbard with Daniel Hubbard. Assuming that Jarrod Hubbard had been the officer who'd pulled over Ms. Dixon-Cole, social media users posted the names and birth dates of Jarrod Hubbard and his family members in the sick hope that people would harass them.

Threats on the Hubbard family's life escalated to the point where Jarrod Hubbard had to shut down his social media profile and turn off his phone. It didn't help. Within twenty-four hours of the alleged incident, Jarrod Hubbard's picture and information had been shared thousands of times on social media.

This practice is known as doxing.

> Doxing is when someone uses the Internet to expose personal information about another person in retribution over something they allegedly did. Doxing frequently happens in chat rooms, forums, or during agitator-produced videos. You'll also find it on Facebook, Twitter, and Instagram.
>
> On July 21, 2015, then-presidential candidate Donald J. Trump gave out the cell phone number of South Carolina Senator

> Lindsey Graham. Why? They were competing against one another for the Republican nomination. Trump didn't like that Graham had criticized him. And one thing led to another.
>
> But doxing is dangerous. For one thing, it doesn't really level the scales of justice. It merely escalates incidents of stalking, death threats, intrusions on personal privacy, and/or assault.
>
> For another thing, doxing often places innocent people in jeopardy. Exactly like Trooper Jarrod Hubbard and his family.

The risks to the Hubbard family's personal safety was ample. Small wonder that Jarrod Hubbard is suing both Shaun King and Lee Merritt for not clarifying their statements and putting his life, plus the lives of his family at risk.

None of the above should imply that Sherita Dixon-Cole get off scot-free. She most certainly did not.

Ultimately, she lost her job as a human resource specialist. Also, since "the Internet is forever," as many people like to say, partisans on both sides of the police-abuse-of-power issue continue to post opinions about her case.

In truth, it remains a mystery as to who exactly concocted the story that Officer Daniel Hubbard sexually assaulted Sherita Dixon-Cole. Also in truth, however, the point seems moot. The damage is done. And that damage was shocking.

Here's my personal summary of this case.

While this story spread over social media, I argue it probably would have spread without it. The medium wasn't to blame so much as the dynamic embraced by the people involved.

Sadly, Daniel Hubbard's accusers went to the press rather than wait for a complete raft of evidence to sail forward. And, while everyone assumed the accusations against Officer Hubbard were real, in reality these accusations were based on assumptions—plus news related to past cases.

Without the dash and bodycam footage, this case could have dragged on for months. Maybe years. Imagine what that would have been like for everyone involved.

But know this. In any questionable arrest, the suspect would have had her day in court. She could get the charges against her dropped and the arrest record expunged. If she felt the arrest was unwarranted due to racial bias, she could have filed a civil rights lawsuit or filed a formal complaint with the Texas Department of Public Safety.

Put simply, there was no need for anyone to lie about what had happened.

Lying about a sexual assault case is a foul and sickening thing. It's already a nightmare scenario when women (or men, for that matter) have to come forward and publicly attest they've been physically taken advantage of. Therefore, lies of the sort perpetrated here potentially discourage any victims of sexual assault who now or in the future might be attempting to rally the courage to step from the shadows and face their attackers.

But the damage done to police departments is obvious. Whether it be on an individual or institutional basis, the lies told in the case of Sherita Dixon-Cole malign the reputations of good police departments and good cops.

The bottom line is this: the case of Sherita Dixon-Cole hurt everyone involved. It hurt Ms. Dixon-Cole. It hurt the two Officer Hubbards, plus their families. It hurt the law enforcement community. It hurt victims of actual sexual assault and actual police brutality. And it hurt the broader community.

Whether you see that community as being on a local, state, or national scale, we all suffer when trust in our institutions is undermined.

To me, that's purely unacceptable.

CHAPTER TEN:
JAILED FOR SIX YEARS—
UNTIL THE REAL KILLER CONFESSED

CASE FILE

Accused officer: Detective Jeffrey Scott Hornoff, Warwick
Police Dept., Warwick, Rhode Island

Related parties: Victoria Cushman; Todd Barry

Date of incident: August 10, 1989

Location: Warwick, Rhode Island

"My name's Jeffrey Scott Hornoff and I'm a police officer. I was convicted of first-degree murder and sentenced to life in prison. Every step of the judicial system failed me and my family. And if not for the guilt and remorse of the true killer, I'd still be in prison."

This is how Scott Hornoff begins the lecture he presents on college campuses and community venues around the country.

Hornoff always knew he wanted to be a cop. He recalls getting hooked on police work at the age of twelve when he saw his brother, Todd, get accepted into the Rhode Island Police Academy.

"The job really appealed to me," Hornoff recalls. "For one thing, you're not behind a desk all day. You're out on the streets. You're pretty much your own boss until you call for a sergeant when you make an arrest and you're helping people. I really was attracted to that."

Hornoff became a detective for the Warwick Police Department in Warwick, Rhode Island. Like many New England towns, Warwick is small and frankly idyllic. Picture low-slung Cape Cod-style homes on water, surrounded by ancient trees. The community is twelve miles south of downtown Providence. With a population of just over 80,000, it's Rhode Island's third largest town.

By all accounts, Scott Hornoff was a good cop, and an active one. For instance, when a local boy drowned, Hornoff became instrumental in founding the Warwick PD's dive team.

"It was another way to give back to the community, too," he said. "So in order to pay for the dive gear, I sold my motorcycle. I went through the training, which was at Alpine Ski and Sports in Warwick, and I loved it. It was really a great experience. And as I said, you know, you're giving back to the community, you're helping, and you're trying to make a small difference."

While training at Alpine Ski and Sports, Hornoff met Victoria Cushman. "Vicky," as she was known to family and friends, worked in the sports shop's shipping and receiving department.

During one visit to the store, Scott realized he had to order some special equipment. Vicky Cushman helped him place the order. The two developed a friendship which evolved into something more.

Now when all this started to happen, Detective Hornoff was married with an infant child. This quickly set up some conflicts within him. A few weeks after their affair began, he broke things off with Vicky Cushman. She did not take the news very well.

Apparently, she'd invested more in the relationship than Hornoff had. For instance, as was later revealed, Cushman told some of her co-workers over at Alpine Ski and Sports that Hornoff was going to leave his wife for her. Not true, said Hornoff later. As far as he was concerned, his affair with Cushman had been a mistake that lasted two weeks. Then he shut the thing down.

What was the truth?

Later, this is precisely what investigators struggled to figure out when Victoria Cushman turned up dead, the victim of murder in her own home.

On August 10, 1989, Scott Hornoff attended a party at the home of an acquaintance. A lot of his fellow officers were also guests. The affair was lively.

As Hornoff later admitted: "There was a lot of drinking, a lot of food, loud music. The police were called a couple of times for noise complaints."

Scott Hornoff's brother, Todd, drove him home. But Hornoff soon realized he'd forgotten his cooler and cassette tapes back at the party. So he drove right back and arrived at the house a little after 11 p.m.

"The alcohol really hit me," he later said, "and I don't remember much about being back at the party."

The next morning, August 11, Vicky Cushman didn't show up for work. This was very unlike her, particularly since she lived right next door to the dive shop. Co-worker Gary Anderson offered to check on her.

As Anderson climbed up her stairs, he noticed that Cushman's bedroom door was ajar and her cat was making weird noises. Taking care not to disturb anything, Anderson pushed the door open with his elbow.

As he later admitted during an interview on A&E's show, *American Justice*, "I entered the room and there she was, lying on the floor, a large pool of blood around her head. It was obvious that she was dead."

From the very beginning, even Gary Anderson, untrained as he was in investigatory techniques, felt something was deeply amiss.

Anderson later recounted, "After the first officer arrived, it just seemed like group after group of non-uniformed personnel came in. To the point where there had to be eight, ten, maybe twelve people up in a very, very tiny apartment. And you could hear an awful lot of shuffling around. Doors opening, drawers opening. It just seemed unusual."

Officers who arrived at the scene collected Vicky Cushman's rolodex and other personal items. They also turned their attention to a sealed, unmailed letter they found on the coffee table. This letter was addressed to Scott Hornoff.

When detectives opened the envelope and read the letter, it became very clear that Vicky Cushman and Scott Hornoff were more than mere acquaintances who'd met at the dive shop. They were lovers.

Among other things, Vicky had written, "My day doesn't feel complete until I see you. I'm hooked on you."

Later that same afternoon, Scott Hornoff arrived for his shift at the Warwick PD. Right away, he knew something was up. His friends and colleagues were acting strange. Then someone mentioned that Vicky Cushman had been found murdered.

Astonished, Hornoff went to the area of the department where detectives normally convened to discuss investigations.

As Hornoff later recalled:

"Detective Sergeant Richard Santos met me at the door and put his hands up and said, 'We'll be with you in a minute.' And right then, you know, bells went off. I just figured I would be questioned because I was on the dive team and Vicky worked at the dive shop. Because of my intimacy, they really thought I was a serious suspect in this."

Hornoff also later shared this:

"Being a police officer and being questioned for a murder was an indescribable feeling."

In his interview on *American Justice*, Hornoff recalled, "They shut the door behind me and I started to get nervous, and they basically read me my rights. That I was a suspect in the murder of Victoria Cushman. My head was spinning. My stomach was doing flip-flops."

Detective Hornoff's interview with his colleagues was short and, curiously, it wasn't recorded. During his interview, Hornoff later said he admitted that he and Cushman were friends but did not elaborate further. As far as his whereabouts for the previous evening, he told his fellow detectives what he remembered. He'd been at the party, he said. A few of them had seen them there. Then he offered to take a polygraph, hoping that this would help clear him quickly of any suspicion that he was the killer.

Hornoff's superior, Captain Carter, accepted his offer. Carter moved immediately to set up the lie detector equipment, which would be administered by one of the officers from Hornoff's department.

"I was especially nervous," Hornoff later recalled, "because I had just written [Carter's] son a ticket for causing a traffic accident. But I took the polygraph and he said I was telling the truth, and that he believed I had no involvement."

Here's something especially worth noting. During his polygraph session, Hornoff came clean about his brief relationship with Vicky.

"I just wanted to be 100 percent cooperative so they would eliminate me as a suspect and move on," he said.

At the end of this process, Detective Hornoff was told he was cleared of all suspicion. That other officers who'd also been present at the party verified his story. And that he should take the night off.

Hornoff later said, "I was relieved. I thought it was all over. I thought now they can look for the guy responsible."

But he also said he had an uncomfortable feeling that everything happened too quickly.

"They didn't come to my house and seize my clothing or take me to headquarters. They didn't treat me like a suspect. And looking back, I really wish they had."

In hindsight, Hornoff was saying, a more thorough investigation, had it been conducted, would have ultimately cleared him. I agree with his assessment. But then, we all know what people say about hindsight.

The next day was August 12. Detective Hornoff returned to his regular routine. The investigation into Vicky Cushman's murder continued. Unfortunately, it wasn't solved quickly.

Then, about eight to ten days later, the city of Warwick experienced a triple murder. The case made national headlines. Every detective was put on the case.

Footprints had been left at the scene of the latest crime. In short order, Scott Hornoff found himself going door-to-door in the neighborhood. His job was to photograph shoes of all the males who lived in the houses. He also outlined the shoe soles on pieces of paper for later comparison by investigators.

Eventually, police arrested a suspect in the triple murder case. Hornoff's department felt good about that. But the murder of Victoria Cushman remained unsolved. Even worse, it had languished for days.

Reporter Jim Hummel of WLNE-TV covered the story. "I remember her father, Robinson Cushman, coming to us," Hummel said. "Coming to the media, going to the Warwick Police. Look—please don't lose track of my daughter."

As fate would have it, Scott Hornoff was frequently assigned to speak with Mr. Cushman when he stopped by at the Warwick Police Department for an update.

"I remember guys in Major Crimes saying, No, you go talk to him. No, you tell him something," Hornoff recalled. "And it was heartbreaking. I mean, Vicky was a friend of mine. And Major Crimes didn't say too much to everybody else. But it was frustrating because we didn't know what they were doing."

Hornoff said he focused on doing his job and getting on with his life.

"My partners and I would sometimes talk about Vicky's murder and we felt really bad that there was no progress in it."

A couple of years went by.

At this point in the drama, enter Detective Paul Ainsworth. He joined the Warwick PD's detective unit in 1991. As one of his first assignments, he was handed Vicky Cushman's file.

As Ainsworth later told *American Justice*, "There were a lot of names of people that had been interviewed, and none of them had any leads. It came back to— we have to talk to Scott Hornoff and get a statement from him."

From Ainsworth's point of view, no clear reason had ever been given as to why talking to Hornoff was off limits.

"If he is a suspect, fine," Ainsworth reasoned. "If he's not, we'll rule him out. But we don't have any information from him. Nobody in that unit was able to talk to him. And that was wrong."

From my own, albeit limited point of view, I can think of two key reasons why Hornoff may have been cleared by his fellow detectives.

First, many of them were part of Hornoff's alibi. A lot of cops had convened at that party the night before Vicky Cushman was killed. Scott Hornoff had been seen there by many people, including his peers on the force. In a lot of people's minds, that might have been good enough to remove his name from the suspect list.

Second, I wouldn't rule out the idea that some of Hornoff's associates were trying to save him from embarrassment. Hornoff's relationship with Cushman was an infidelity. The more someone, anyone, started probing around what had happened, the more likely it would have gone public that the two had been sleeping together.

Is this a good reason not to investigate someone as a likely murder suspect? No. But like I've already said, Lady Justice isn't completely blind. Nor are the scales of justice totally balanced. In other words, cops are people, too. In this case, they may have inadvertently been trying to protect one of their own from embarrassment, not murder charges.

In the fall of 1991, Warwick's frustrated detectives brought the Cushman case to the attention of their state attorney general, who in October of that year, recommended that it be turned over to state police.

"It was kind of a relief," Ainsworth later revealed. "Let the state police handle it. Nobody's gonna tell them they can't interview certain people."

But the efforts of the Rhode Island State Police didn't bring them any closer to solving the case. They also hit a procedural wall in the form of botched forensics, specifically the polluted crime scene described earlier by Gary Anderson, the employee of Alpine Ski and Sports.

Attorney Kevin Bristow, who later reviewed the case for the City of Warwick, described this situation when he was interviewed on *American Justice.* "Something that became incredibly apparent immediately was that there were severe problems with how the initial investigation was conducted at the crime scene."

Yes. The crime scene had been compromised by having so many people trample through it. But that was just the beginning. The evidence that police had collected was then mishandled. And other evidence was ignored.

For instance, blood samples found on the window screen in the bedroom of Cushman's apartment were never sent for analysis. The same was true of the clothing Vicky Cushman was wearing when her body was discovered.

The upshot? Botched opportunities. Closed-off avenues. Wasted time.

Here's how Kevin Bristow described it. "There was a latent fingerprint that had been found. And the Warwick police, in their investigation, spent a lot of time having different people come in, and having their print compared to this print. And they never compared it to the deceased. And it was hers."

Hornoff later agreed with Bristow's assessment. "It was just ridiculous how the police handled the investigation from the very beginning," he said.

Another glaring mistake: Instead of looking closely at every contact on Vicky Cushman's rolodex, police brought the focus back around to Hornoff. They had the unmailed letter from Vicky to Scott, so they knew the two had had an affair. They also knew that Hornoff was at the party the night of the murder. That his brother had driven him home, but that he'd returned to the party an hour or so later. In the minds of many investigators, this was ample time for Hornoff to have committed the murder.

In an interview on *American Justice*, Detective Ainsworth of the Warwick PD said, "He [Hornoff] was a different person when he came back [to the party]. And he never talked about where he was."

"I really don't know why they just focused on me," Hornoff said later. "I know that members of our department didn't like my brother, and I inherited his friends as well as the ones who didn't like him. I don't know why they put on the blinders, but they had already made up their mind that I was guilty. They didn't go into it with an open mind, and I really wish they had."

On November 13, 1992, after the State of Rhode Island had been investigating the case for a year, Detective Scott Hornoff was formally interviewed by investigators for the first time.

According to Warwick City Councilman Carlo Pisturo: "By then it was almost [considered] common knowledge that Scott had killed the girl. All indications were that he was guilty and that the cops had covered for him."

Hornoff's attorney, Joel Chase, was unable to make that meeting with state investigators. As Chase later revealed, "He [Hornoff] said I'm gonna go on my own then, because I didn't do anything wrong and I'm simply gonna tell the truth. Major mistake."

As far as what he was thinking, Detective Hornoff offered this commentary:

"'I want to go down and talk to them,'" Hornoff said he told Chase. "'I'm innocent. I want them to see I'm innocent. I want to tell them what I remember … I want them to solve this.' Looking back, it was one of the biggest mistakes of my life. Going down to headquarters to answer questions without an attorney, or actually going at all. But I did. I wanted to cooperate. I should've known better."

> The Sixth Amendment of the United States Constitution reads as follows:
>
> "In all criminal prosecutions, the accused shall enjoy the right to a speedy and public trial, by an impartial jury of the state and district wherein the crime shall have been committed, which district shall have been previously ascertained by law, and to be informed of the nature and cause of the accusation; to be confronted with the witnesses against him; to have compulsory process for obtaining witnesses in his favor, and to have the assistance of counsel for his defense.
>
> I'll say this again. In my opinion, exercising the right to have an attorney present when questioned is the strongest possible choice a suspect can make.
>
> And yet, realistically speaking, there are incidents where having an attorney present simply isn't necessary. Because it won't help. Not in the least.
>
> For instance, sometimes people get caught red-handed. This includes being videoed in the commission of a crime, a modern and increasingly common phenomenon. When this happens, the evidence tells all, and it's firmly stacked against

the suspect. So, in this case, having an attorney present typically doesn't matter. In my experience, the best lawyer in the world won't be able to help someone who's been incriminated by concrete evidence.

Bear in mind, I'm not advocating the use of attorneys as some tacit way of saying, "Lie to the police." You should never lie to police. It shows a lack of integrity on your part and a lack of faith that professional peacekeepers can do their jobs properly to protect the community.

But a good attorney will know which of the questions you're being asked are germane to the case at hand and which are not. In the long run, this prevents slipshod investigations from building a case against you on specious grounds.

As we're about to see, this is exactly what spelled disaster for Detective Scott Hornoff.

During his interview—again, without counsel present—Detective Scott Hornoff had no problem revealing the duration and nature of his relationship with Vicky Cushman. But when it came to discussing his timeline surrounding the party of August 10, 1989, he got confused. As he'd already stated time and again, his memory of that night was not very clear.

"They told me to take my best guesses when I didn't remember something," Hornoff told *American Justice*. "And even though I was familiar with being a cop and with investigations, I went along with it and I took my best guesses."

"That was another huge mistake," he admitted. "Taking best guesses is not a good idea when you're being investigated for a murder. But again, being innocent, you know, I told them, I'll take another polygraph. I'll take sodium pentothal, voice, stress analysis, hypnosis, whatever you want to do to me."

"They took head, hair, and pubic hair, and blood samples. I knew I hadn't been at Vicky's apartment, at the crime scene. I knew they weren't going to find anything. They took them from my brother, too. But there was no evidence linking me to the crime because I wasn't there. And that's why I just kept cooperating."

After eight hours of questioning, investigators released Detective Hornoff on his own recognizance. Right then, he wasn't aware that his "best guess" at where he'd been and when on the night the murder took place didn't match the information supplied to police by other witnesses. In fact, it turned out that even Hornoff's wife, Ronda, gave information that contradicted him.

Four months later, Scott Hornoff was asked to come back in for another interview. Investigators wanted him to clear up some inconsistencies.

In the time between his first and second interviews, Hornoff had spoken with Ronda at length.

"I had no idea what was ahead of me, but I knew it wasn't going to be good," he later recalled. "I went to my wife's work and I called her out of her office and I said, I'm going to lose one of two ways. Either I'm gonna be convicted of something I didn't do or you're gonna leave me because I was unfaithful to you. And she said, 'We'll get through the investigation and then we'll get through the other.' And she was really strong about it."

"I still had faith that the state police were gonna eliminate me as a suspect," he told *American Justice*. "I just took it for granted that they were gonna see that I was innocent and that I wasn't a suspect. Or at least not a good, viable suspect. I regret a lot of my choices back then as far as going down there without an attorney. I regret going at all."

Rhode Island Attorney General Sheldon Whitehouse later said, "Scott Hornoff had small secrets that he wanted to protect. Protecting those small secrets made him look like he was protecting the big secret that he had murdered Victoria Cushman."

Rob Warden, Director of the Center on Wrongful Convictions at the Northwestern University School of Law, said: "The criminal justice system is simply unforgiving when people do things that are quite natural. When somebody asks if you're having an affair, it's quite natural to lie. [But] then you're a liar. When you start telling the truth, you're changing your story. That's two strikes as far as a jury's concerned."

Nevertheless, the state investigation continued another two years. During that time, after so much additional work, it wound up right back where it started: with Detective Scott Hornoff as the only viable suspect investigators had.

For this reason, in December 1994, more than five years after the crime had occurred, Detective Jeffrey Scott Hornoff was indicted for the first-degree murder of Victoria Cushman.

Now when someone gets indicted, it doesn't make them guilty of the crime. An indictment simply means that the grand jury has heard enough testimony to warrant charges being filed against a person.

But the truth is, it isn't that difficult to get a grand jury indictment. Prosecutors do it all the time, in large part because they have the ability to put evidence and testimony in front of a grand jury while the accused isn't there to defend themselves. For this reason, there's an old saying in legal circles: "You can get a grand jury to indict a ham sandwich."

My own experience bears this out. Let's just say I've seen grand juries hand down in indictments I would call questionable at best.

The upshot? On May 15, 1996, in Providence, Rhode Island, Detective Scott Hornoff stood trial for the murder of Victoria Cushman. But not before he was offered a plea deal.

"I was offered a guilty plea," he later recalled, "and I said, Hell, no."

Hornoff's wife, Ronda, had made the decision to stick by her husband. She believed he was innocent and was willing to look past his indiscretions.

But would a jury do the same?

With no physical evidence linking Hornoff to the murder, prosecutors built their case almost exclusively on witness recollections. This included Scott Hornoff's cloudy memories of his own doings on the evening of August 10, 1989.

Keep in mind that, by this point, more than seven years had passed since the discovery of Vicky Cushman's body.

Gerald Coyne, Deputy Attorney General of Rhode Island admitted, "The long passage of time makes a case harder to prosecute because people's memories just aren't as good."

Local reporter, Jim Hummel, later recalled, "They got into excruciating detail, rightly so, about the events that happened that night, the night of the murder. That [Hornoff] went to the party, he came back, he looked dazed."

Complicating matters, friends, colleagues, and even Scott Hornoff's wife could not corroborate his timeline.

In an interview on the *American Justice* show, a juror in the trial, Dianna Welch, said, "Very conflictual type of testimony from a lot of different sources. It did sort of bring a turning point to that trial for me."

"It took two grand juries to get an indictment on me," Hornoff recalled. "The first grand jury, I was told, was leaning towards a no true bill, which would mean I wasn't going to be charged. And from what I learned afterwards, that grand jury was dismissed and a second one was convened. I requested to testify before the first grand jury, and that was denied. I was granted permission to testify before the second grand jury, which wasn't held at a court hall courthouse. There was no formal setting. No sense of professional conduct. It was held at a National Guard armory. It was right before Christmas. All of the jurors brought in plates of food. They were on a first name basis with the state police. It was a party atmosphere. They were very hostile to me."

The use of grand juries varies across the country. I can say that, in Tulsa, Oklahoma, we use grand juries almost exclusively in the federal courts.

Most of the criminal cases are filed at the state level and with the office of the Tulsa County District Attorney. This is done by a law enforcement officer filing a report and affidavit listing the probable cause for charges to be filed. These documents are then reviewed by a Tulsa County Assistant District Attorney.

If an assistant DA believes there's probable cause to charge the suspect or suspects with the commission of crimes, they sign off on it, and the process continues through the system.

As a law enforcement officer, I have testified many times before federal grand juries. The last time I did, I was also a potential suspect in the case. That situation was particularly nerve-wracking. I had no idea what the grand jury had been told about me. As far as I knew, prosecutors had told them lurid stories maligning my history and character. Stuff that doesn't have any basis in reality.

Believe me, it's a weird feeling to sit in front of a group of people whom you have to assume have been told negative things about you and the people you work with. People who, to serve the prosecutors' needs, have been painted a dark picture of police officers and their nature.

To put it lightly, a grand jury is a one-sided argument. Remember, grand jurors do not take part in the eventual trial process where a suspect's guilt or innocence gets decided. So they never get to hear, for instance, a defense attorney question the prosecution's assertions. They don't get to hear the rebuttals or refutations of testimony and evidence.

To this day, I feel certain there are people who were part of the grand jury I sat in front of who still think I'm a dirty cop. Why? Because of the one-sided testimony they heard. Because no one was present to contradict assertions made against me.

While standing trial for the murder of Vicky Cushman, Detective Scott Hornoff faced the full force of his state's legal system.

"When they say 'The State of Rhode Island vs. Scott Hornoff' or 'The State of North Carolina versus you,' they're not kidding," he later recalled. "They have unlimited resources. And the State of Rhode Island used those resources against me."

These resources included a raft of expert witnesses. Among them was the legendary forensics expert Dr. Henry Lee. Dr. Lee was asked to render his opinions on blood splatter even though he'd never been present at the crime scene.

In his grand jury testimony, which was entered as evidence at his jury trial, Detective Hornoff stated: "I'd had affairs before [Vicky Cushman] and after her. It was just one of those things."

His attorney, Joel Chase, told *American Justice*: "I made it very clear to [the jury] that [Hornoff] was married and had certain affairs and relationships with other women during his marriage, and that they [the jury] weren't gonna like him very much because of that. But they were obligated to find him guilty or not guilty based strictly on the evidence."

"The prosecution did a really good job of getting the jury to dislike me," Hornoff later said. "Basically, to the point where they took a leap that if I could be unfaithful to my wife, I could commit murder. As I said, there was no physical evidence. There were no witnesses. There was nothing linking me to the crime except for this suspicion."

Hornoff's trial was a roller coaster ride of emotions for him. He later recalled that, early on, he had hope of being vindicated. But that hope was soon dashed.

Right before his trial started, it was discovered in an autopsy that Vicky Cushman's body was found with a Braxton Hicks dental guard in its mouth. This type of equipment is typically used to keep a person from grinding their teeth while they sleep.

About this, Hornoff said: "The prosecution's whole case was that I went [to Vicky Cushman's apartment], we got into an argument ... Well, I don't know if any of you have ever worn one of those mouth guards but you can't talk with that. And if she had a crush on me, I'm pretty sure she would have taken it out of her mouth [to talk]. So we felt pretty good going into deliberations. But at the same time, you know, I really had this feeling that things weren't going to go our way. And I was right ... I kept going back and forth with the feeling each day in court. One day I was feeling pretty good when I found out about the dental mouth guard. I thought, there's no way [I can be convicted] if this jury's paying attention. Same as in the grand jury when one of the jurors, he kept falling asleep. And I wanted to stand up on the table and yell, 'Wake up!' And my defense attorney said, 'Oh, no, that's in our favor.' But I guess it wasn't."

Hornoff's attorney, Joel Chase, felt that the state's evidence simply didn't add up. He thought the prosecution didn't have enough to convict. And he strongly recommended that Hornoff not take the stand in his own defense.

Some jurors, however, were troubled by this decision.

For instance, Dianna Welch later said, "I just would have liked to have heard him, what his side of the story was."

After closing arguments, Hornoff's case went before the jury on June 17, 1996.

Reporter Jim Hummel had his own opinions about the verdict. "Could he have done it? Yeah. Could he have not done it? Possibly. But having sat through six weeks of that trial, I came away with a growing feeling that they didn't prove their case."

After three days of deliberation, the jury took a vote.

"You could hear a pin drop in that room," recalled Dianna Welch. "Then one by one: Guilty, first-degree. Guilty, first-degree. And we got all around the table. My God, this is our decision."

To this day, Hornoff speculates that the timing of his trial could not have been worse.

"There were a couple other things that were going on at that time that went against me. One was O.J. Simpson. His trial was going on and I think it had just ended. And most of the people thought that he had gotten away with murder ... people thought you were guilty because people think that cops cover for each other, which isn't true. But in Rhode Island, you know, there was this feeling that, you know, if you're accused of something, you got to be guilty. And sure enough, I was found guilty of first-degree murder and sentenced to life in prison."

In his *American Justice* interview, Hornoff speculated, "Normally, if it's a not guilty verdict, the sheriff won't stay right next to you. There's no reason to. But he wouldn't leave my side. So that wasn't a good sign."

After the guilty verdict was read, juror Dianna Welch recalled, "All hell broke loose. People were screaming, people were yelling. I remember looking over at Scott and I think he was just blank."

Keep in mind, there was very little real evidence against Scott Hornoff. There were no fingerprints. No concrete blood evidence. No DNA matches of any kind: hair, sperm, skin cells. No clothing fibers that matched Hornoff's wardrobe. Again, the prosecution's case boiled down to conflicting eyewitness testimonies. Speculation and innuendoes.

Yes, Vicky Cushman's letter to Hornoff came up. It had to. It was one of the few pieces of physical evidence linking Hornoff to Cushman. But Hornoff's defense pointed out that the letter had been found sealed. Therefore, Hornoff had not read it.

This, they felt, was important.

Listen to Hornoff tell us why. "I'm pretty sure if I had gone to Vicky's apartment that night, that she probably would have given [the letter] to me and stood there while I read it."

The website Truthinjustice.org, later posted that: "[Hornoff] was jailed as a result of making the purely coincidental choice of having an affair with a woman who was murdered."

I couldn't have said that better myself.

At his sentencing, Detective Scott Hornoff told the court, "Am I guilty of something? Yes, I am. I broke my sacred wedding vows, and for that I will never forgive myself."

But as for the murder of Victoria Cushman, Scott Hornoff continued to insist that he was completely innocent.

Hornoff recalls that, after he was found guilty: "I was led downstairs to the courthouse cellblock. They took my tie, my belt, my shoelaces. Strip-searched me. It was pretty humiliating. And I was in shock."

Detective Hornoff was then placed in protective custody. This practice is common when the convicted are also police officers, prison guards, juveniles, and child molesters. People of this sort present various problems when prisons lump them in with the general population.

As Hornoff later recalled: "Quite a few of the guys in there, me or my brother, had a hand in putting me in prison."

Unlike popular depictions of cops in prison, Hornoff didn't have to do much fighting while he was incarcerated.

"Most of the guys that were in protective custody, they were kind of cowards. If you stand up and show that you're not going to take anything from them ... I melded in, kind of I kept to myself. I did talk to a couple of the other police officers that were in there."

From the moment he heard the word "guilty," Hornoff began planning his appeal and retrial. According to his attorney, this process would take maybe a year.

"I don't know if I can do a year," Hornoff later recalled saying.

He wrote a screenplay while in prison. He wrote poetry. Took up drawing. Wrote thousands of letters. He read hundreds of books.

Then, while watching an episode of *Dateline* on NBC, he saw a profile of a group called the National Police Defense Foundation. This organization investigates claims of innocence by police officers who are in prison. Detective Hornoff wrote to this organization and, after certain discussions were held, the NPDF offered to take his case.

First, they did their own investigation of the crime scene. This included deducing what size shoe the murderer must have worn. Interestingly, NPDF investigators concluded the murderer must have had much larger feet than Scott Hornoff's.

Now remember back at the beginning of this story? I mentioned that a triple murder happened in Warwick a short time after Vicky Cushman's body was found. Turns out a man had been convicted for that murder.

While in prison, this man began bragging that he'd also killed Vicky Cushman. And it turned out this convicted murderer's shoe size matched the shoe size of Vicky's murderer.

Spurred by this, Hornoff's team filed a motion for a fresh trial based on newly discovered evidence.

Hornoff recalls his excitement. "I was feeling really good ... thinking I was going to get a new trial. This was awesome. And we filed a motion before my trial judge, Robert Krause ... He denied the motion without even having the hearing, without even hearing the evidence. He just denied it. And I didn't know he could do it, but he did it. After that, I fell into a very heavy depression."

Being falsely accused takes a massive psychological toll on anyone (including officers), plus their friends and families.

I don't mean to equate my own case with Scott Hornoff's. That would be wrong on too many levels. For one thing, I never stood falsely accused of murder. For another, I was never convicted and incarcerated, nor did I have to fight to regain my freedom, as Hornoff did.

Still, I resonate with the level of frustration he felt. I'll tell you point-blank, it bothered me to no end that I and my fellow officers were having our names dragged through the mud in the public. That this indignity was predicated by little more than flat-out lies. And that we had no recourse. There was no way to put a stop to it. We could only ride things out.

> After the trial in Tulsa, I felt good about clearing my name. Remember, my department's Internal Affairs division had done a very thorough investigation into all the allegations against me. And not guilty verdicts were returned on all the charges I was alleged to be associated with.
>
> Furthermore, once I was cleared by Internal Affairs, my Chief's office sent a letter to the U.S. Attorney's office in Tulsa asking them to clear my name. The U.S. Attorney's office stated, that since the investigation was handled by the U.S. Attorney's office in Arkansas, my request would have to be handled by them.
>
> The Chief's letter was then sent to Arkansas. To this day, they have yet to reply.

"I just didn't see any way out," Scott Hornoff later commented. "I knew I had a state appeal [left to me], but those were hardly ever won. And then I saw a profile of the Innocence Project. And I wrote to the New York Innocence Project and Barry Scheck wrote me back, which I thought was a really big deal."

Barry Scheck was an attorney who'd gained national prominence by serving on O.J. Simpson's Dream Team.

"And [Barry Scheck] said, we think your case has merit. The New England Innocence Project has just started up as a satellite. Please write to them. I'm also going to let them know to expect your letter."

The New England Innocence Project looked at Hornoff's case. They examined the crime scene photos with care and they said they wanted to conduct some new DNA tests, particularly on some blood stains, which had been found on a set of rubber dishwashing gloves that were clearly depicted in crime scene photos.

The Innocence Project investigators speculated that maybe the DNA found on the bloody gloves would match the blood of the convicted triple murderer. The same man who'd openly bragged that he had also killed Vicky Cushman.

Hornoff's team filed to have this DNA testing done. It was a gamble. They knew that, given the passage of time, some of the crime scene materials had either been lost or destroyed. Fortunately, however, the gloves had been preserved. They were sent to a lab in California, but the testing results returned were inconclusive. Back to square one.

Right around this time, exactly as he had feared, Scott Hornoff's state appeal was denied.

"I had thought I was going to be released somehow but, by this point, every step of the judicial system that was put in place to protect the innocent, it was failing me and my loved ones. And I was starting to lose hope," he said.

Also, at around this time, the authorities transferred Hornoff to a high-security setting that was much more restrictive. He filed a federal civil suit against the prison, the warden, and the director. Up until that point, Hornoff had mostly been confined to a single cell, meaning a cell that accommodates one person. But this new facility bunked him with some of the worst guys in the penitentiary. This was especially dangerous given that Scott Hornoff had been a cop.

He kept this suit going, filing paperwork week after week, in search of relief.

"I was filing grievances and I guess I was just lashing out the only way I knew how."

Hornoff kept fighting, kept appealing, kept maintaining his innocence, but no one with any power seemed to be listening.

"I was told in the facility I was at for five and a half years, their job was to break everybody, to break their spirit. It wasn't rehabilitation. There weren't really any opportunities for people to turn themselves around or to prepare themselves for reintegration."

Undoubtedly, Detective Scott Hornoff felt abandoned. The laws he had once worked hard to serve and his true mistress, Lady Justice, had failed him. Truth had kicked his butt to the side of the road. Falsely accused, he stood alone in the existential torment of paying the price for another man's crimes. He'd run out of strings to pull that would make his predicament bearable, let alone to regain his good reputation and freedom.

Personally? I consider myself a reasonably strong human being. Strong in body, yes, but more importantly, strong in spirit. Strong in faith. But whenever I think of this case, it makes me shudder.

How Scott Hornoff bucked himself up under these incredibly trying circumstances remains a mystery to me.

But to every darkness, there is a dawn.

Scott Hornoff's luck was about to change.

☆ ☆ ☆

On October 28, 2002, more than six years after Hornoff went to prison, a local Warwick carpenter named Todd Barry reached a momentous decision. Early that morning, he dialed a family friend, attorney Bill Devereaux.

"Seven o'clock on a Monday morning I got a call at my home, and it was Todd," Devereaux told *American Justice*. "And he explained to me that he had something he wanted to get off his chest and that he seemed to be very upset."

Mr. Barry told attorney Devereaux he wanted to confess to a crime he'd committed thirteen years before.

"It was basically a deep sense of remorse," Devereaux recalled. "And it was almost volcanic when it just kept building and building and it finally came out, and he just made the decision that he was gonna right this situation."

After hearing Mr. Barry's story, Mr. Devereaux contacted the attorney general's office. Soon after that, prosecutors set up a meeting with Barry and his attorneys. At this meeting, Todd Barry basically confessed to the murder of Victoria Cushman.

Mr. Barry revealed that he and Ms. Cushman had dated but had stopped seeing each other months prior to her death. On the night Ms. Cushman was killed, Barry said he'd been drinking heavily and smoking marijuana. He stopped by her apartment to see her. He said she discussed her relationship with Scott Hornoff and repeated what she'd told her colleagues at Alpine Ski and Sports. That Hornoff loved her so much, he was going to leave his family for her.

On his confession tape, Todd Barry said, "It got a little tense because I was like, 'Vicky, you're gonna ruin this guy's life ...'"

At that point, Barry said, Vicky's cat suddenly climbed out the second-floor window, and Vicky threatened to sue him if something were to happen to the animal.

Barry said he "lost it" then. He started to strangle Ms. Cushman.

"And then I whack her on the head with something that was on the coffee table or it was close by," he said.

At first, the police were incredulous. They simply didn't believe Mr. Barry's account. Why would anyone come forward and admit to the crime of murder after thirteen years had passed? They thought he was crazy. They thought he was seeking attention.

But there was one piece of testimony Barry supplied that detectives couldn't deny.

Todd Barry said he'd hit Vicky Cushman over the head with a very particular object. He wasn't precisely sure what it was but when he was asked to describe it as best he could, the investigators knew that Barry had to be the real killer.

Here's why.

Vicky Cushman had been hit on the head with her jewelry box. Detectives knew this, of course. The forensic reports had confirmed it. But they never released this information. Whenever they spoke to the media, they said that a fire extinguisher had been used to bludgeon Ms. Cushman to death.

This is a common tactic law enforcement officers use when trying to catch a criminal. The alteration of key details keeps the public informed in a way that is proper to any civil society while maintaining a screen behind which only the real criminal, in this case a killer, can eventually come to justice.

Consider these words from Gerald Coyne, Deputy Attorney General of Rhode Island: "It [the fire extinguisher] had never been viewed as the actual murder weapon. It was a jewelry box. And he [Barry] discussed that in great detail and actually how he used [the box] to strike her. And that was the kind of graphic detail that convinced us that he really was the person that killed her."

In retrospect, Todd Barry's name and number were in Vicky's rolodex. Yet no member of any investigatory team had called him to ask who he was, his relation to Vicky Cushman, and what, if anything, he knew about her untimely death. And that's sad. Because, in his confession, Todd Barry stated how surprised he was that nobody from law enforcement had come to talk to him. If they had, he might have confessed.

Barry even mentioned how he'd tried to get the authorities' attentions.

Listen to how Scott Hornoff later described this. "The day I was found guilty, he [Barry] actually called the *Warwick Beacon* [a local newspaper] and he said they got the wrong guy. 'Scott Hornoff didn't do it. You need to look into this.' He was never questioned by the Warwick police or the state police. And he said if there had been a knock at his door, he would have confessed."

In case you're curious, Barry never detailed any reason for his actions, only remorse for them.

"I'm not 100 percent certain of all the things that went on that night. Except I was whacked out of my mind. I did a horrible thing to this poor girl. She didn't deserve to die. Whatever possessed me to do something like that, I have no idea."

It was guilt, Barry said, that had made him come forward.

"Hiding all these years and then this guy's in jail," Barry said. "And there's no freakin' way I can have this guy in jail and me outside. No way, no how."

On this point, Barry's attorney, Bill Devereaux, stated his opinion like this: "You had somebody who almost seemed more at peace in his own mind after he went through the process and basically surrendered himself to the state police."

At this point, Deputy Attorney General Gerald Coyne said, "... we had to do what we could to get [Scott Hornoff] out of jail as quickly as we could."

On November 2, 2002, Scott Hornoff's attorney, Joel Chase, got a call from the prosecutor in the Vicky Cushman murder case.

"He said something significant has happened over the weekend. He said I really can't talk about it over the phone. [I said,] 'At least tell me if it's a good significant or a bad significant.' 'For you and Scott, I think it's a good significant.'"

Later that morning, Jeffrey Scott Hornoff was taken from his cell to a windowless conference room.

"When I walked into the room, there was my trial attorney," he said. "But right next to him was an assistant attorney general, two state police detectives, and somebody else. And I stopped and I thought to myself, what are they going to accuse me of? Now, I had heard that they were looking at me for two other murders. It's really easy to clear crimes when you already have somebody in custody. And that's what I thought was going to happen. Instead, they told me to have a seat. And eventually they said, do you know anybody by the last name of Barry? That's

Todd Barry, and I said, well, I know Tim, Tom, and John, they grew up on my street. And they said, no. Do you know Todd Barry? I never heard of him."

Once Hornoff gave officials this information, they relayed Barry's story to him.

"Turned out Todd Barry was Vicky's on-again, off-again boyfriend," Hornoff recalled." And he had come forward a few days earlier and told them that he had killed Vicky."

The authorities told Hornoff they believed Todd Barry's story. They told Hornoff he was going to be released.

Hornoff couldn't believe it. "Here I am fighting for my life, and here this guy comes out of the blue."

Jim Hummel offered this commentary: "Some people have no conscience at all, but obviously Todd Barry does. The irony is, if you look at all of that, that he was getting engaged just as Hornoff was getting indicted. He was having his kids, just as Hornoff was going off to jail. And it has to nag on him every single day."

Scott Hornoff was brought to the courthouse the very next day. Everyone there was fine with releasing him—all except the Honorable Judge Krause, the judge who'd presided over his murder trial.

Judge Krause said he had a problem with the wording of Hornoff's release papers. So they sent him back to prison. He ended up staying there two more days since the following day was election day and the courts, by law, were closed.

Not that this mattered so much to Scott Hornoff. As far as he was concerned, a miracle had happened. An angel of sorts had stepped forward and the truth had literally set him free. Or at any rate, it was about to.

Elated, he proceeded to give his possessions away to his fellow inmates. To celebrate, one of the guards brought Hornoff a bacon double cheeseburger.

"Guard after guard came in and shook my hand," Scott Hornoff said. "Even the ones who said 'I thought you did it.' They shook my hand and said, 'I don't know how you got through this.' That felt really good."

On the *American Justice* show, Hornoff admitted the whole thing shocked him at first.

"I was skeptical and a little taken aback. It was just another episode in *The Twilight Zone* of a very long-running series."

On November 6, Scott Hornoff was once again brought to the court house.

"Walking in there with shackles and handcuffs was pretty tough," he said. "But I knew it was the last time I was ever gonna wear 'em."

Throughout his time in prison, his biggest fear was that his mother wasn't going to live to see him released. For this reason, and for so many others, his trip to the courthouse was a very powerful moment.

But there was a dark side to it, as well.

"There was no apology from the judge, the prosecutor, the attorney general. Actually, I think they were upset at me for being innocent."

Even though Todd Barry completely confessed, the authorities still wanted Hornoff to admit he had gone to Vicky Cushman's apartment, witnessed the result of her murder, and done nothing. Scott Hornoff would do no such thing. He'd insisted on August 11, 1986 that he'd never gone to Cushman's apartment that evening, and he continued to stand firm on that point. He would not confess to something he didn't do.

In Hornoff's opinion: "There is still the idea that if you've been arrested, you did something here. He must have done something really bad because he's a policeman and the police arrest him. And that that was something you were never, ever going to get over."

Later, on the steps of the superior courthouse, Scott Hornoff made his first statements as a free man.

"My thoughts go out to Vicky's loved ones and to Mr. Barry's loved ones and to the thousands of other innocent people still wrongfully imprisoned across the United States."

Here's an interesting note.

Victoria Cushman's family still thinks Scott Hornoff was somehow involved in her murder.

Soon after Hornoff walked free, Patricia Cushman, Victoria's mother, said "I'm stunned. We're all stunned ... I don't have enough to make a decision. There isn't enough information for me to change my mind."

"If they were interested, I would happily talk to them," Hornoff said. Though he admitted: "I'm not really sure what I would say."

Now consider this sobering thought offered by Rob Warden, Director of the Center on Wrongful Convictions at the Northwestern University School of Law: "We probably don't have more than a dozen examples nationally of cases in which a voluntary confession has led to an exoneration ... If this had happened in another state that had the death penalty, Hornoff would almost certainly be dead."

Juror Dianna Welch stated, "Of course you go back and you say, 'Oh my gosh! What did I miss? What could I have seen?' However, I would still come to the same conclusion today, if given what was given to me as a juror at that time."

After he was released, Detective Hornoff wanted to go back to work. But he had to fight with the city of Warwick to gain reinstatement. City officials argued he'd been correctly terminated and didn't deserve to get his job back.

"A lot of guys in the department turned their backs on me," Hornoff said. "When you're a police officer, you're lied to every day. Some people become jaded to it and you start thinking everybody's guilty. A lot of guys in my department thought I was guilty. After I got out, they threw a fundraiser for me, a steak fry. And guys actually came up with tears in their eyes saying, you know, I'm sorry, I thought you did it. I didn't hold anything against them."

Eventually, a judge ruled in Detective Hornoff's favor. He was reinstated to the Warwick Police Department, whereupon he immediately retired. As part of his agreement, he received $650,000 in backpay. Of that, his attorneys received $200,000 and his ex-wife, Ronda, received the rest.

"I didn't see a dime of it," he later recalled. "I told my wife that I thought I was going to be released someday, but I didn't know how long it was going to take and I wanted a divorce because I didn't want her stuck in there also. It started off amicably, but, you know, it kind of went sour. I have no hard feelings against my ex-wife. She went through hell raising three boys on her own. But I'm glad she got the money. Now, my boys have a house."

Hornoff struggled to find work after his reinstatement. It didn't matter that he'd been exonerated or that his record had been expunged. No one seemed to want to employ him.

Eventually, he found work overseas. He wound up in Afghanistan for about four years where he trained the Afghan police and later protected members of the U.S. Army Corps of Engineers who were stationed in Kabul.

It was rewarding work, he later reported. Doing something constructive helped him regain his sense of self-confidence not to mention his sense of purpose.

"There I was. You know, people were trusting me with their lives. I was trusting them with mine," he said. "We were focused on a mission. It was really great being a part of something like that and just trying to help the people there... [it] actually turned out to be a good thing because it gave me back a sense of self-worth. You know, me relying on other people, trusting them with my life and vice versa."

Still, when it comes to Warwick, Rhode Island, Scott Hornoff admits to feeling out of place at times.

"This was my city, and a lot of times I feel like a foreigner. I feel out of place, but it's like ... God. I miss those days and I miss being a part of that."

In January 2003, Todd Barry was sentenced to thirty years in prison after pleading guilty to second-degree murder.

Scott Hornoff wrote to him. He wanted to talk.

"I'd like to know what happened that night, why he did it," Hornoff says. "He said he went to a club in Providence and somebody slipped something in his drink. And he also smoked a joint with a couple guys. And then he has like flashes of memory of driving on the highway and then climbing up the conduit pipe and climbing in through Vicky's window. And Vicky yelling at him for her cat getting out the window. I still don't know how she yelled at him if she had that mouth guard in her mouth. I think he's lying. I don't know why he wasn't totally forthcoming. And so I wrote him a letter and he wrote me back and said, I'm open to meeting with you, but I'm not the center of attention anymore. And if you come in and meet with me, I will be. So I kind of just left it alone."

It's hard for Scott Hornoff not to get philosophical, to not have opinions about what he went through.

"I have a hard time with the death penalty," he said. "I've talked to a lot of death penalty classes at universities and I'm still up in the air on how I feel about it ... I've gone back and forth myself with, you know, whether I believe in it or not. I think in certain instances, like the Boston Marathon bombing, when you have somebody who you know is guilty. Or Osama bin Laden."

He goes on: "I feel like there's enough bitter people in the world, and I'm not gonna be one of them. Sure, I could let this experience consume me, and if it did, it would be like a cancer and it would eat me up. I'm still pro law enforcement. I'm still pro cop. I'm a cop in my heart and I always will be. But I want to see the right person caught. I want to see the guilty held accountable."

Indeed. That's something we all want to see.

Hornoff's case checks a number of difficult boxes for me. Obviously, his is a tale where a law enforcement officer was falsely convicted. Yes, that's what this book's all about. But there's more to what happened to him. Much more.

The case of Scott Hornoff highlights the limbo falsely accused people occupy. If convicted of crimes they didn't commit, they pay for somebody else's misdeeds, and often pay with their lives since, due to their sentence, they might die in prison.

But suppose they're that one in a thousand case where exoneration arrives. Often, the falsely accused will seek to quietly reintegrate themselves with society. They try and try, but they're likely to fail. Why? Because, in many cases, they find that, despite having gone through hell, they can't find a place in the world anymore.

"When an exoneree gets out, there is nothing," Hornoff says. "It's basically there's the door. When somebody makes parole, you have a lot of services offered to you. Actually, you're required to take advantage of them. Some states do have wrongful compensation laws. Rhode Island doesn't, unfortunately. Actually, Texas, the death penalty capital of the world, has one of the best wrongful comp statutes."

With no place to go that felt like home. Hornoff committed his life to helping others wrongly accused.

He points out: "If you [get out of prison and you] don't have a strong support system, it's really easy to feel like you have to commit a crime to survive."

"I thank God and I thank my family and my friends, both old and new, for supporting me and fighting for me and never giving up on me, even in the darkest times when I thought of giving up myself. My thoughts go out to the thousands of other innocent people still wrongfully imprisoned across the United States, and the thousands more facing unjust and unfair prison sentences. And I hope to help change that ... I hope to help at least one other innocent [person] see freedom."

"As far as changing me," he ruminates. "Yeah, I guess I appreciate little things more. I didn't touch a blade of grass for six and a half years. And after I got out I wouldn't walk on a sidewalk. I'd rather walk in the grass."

After all he's endured, Hornoff offers the following bits of advice.

FIRST:

"If you get a call from a police investigator saying, could you please come down to answer some questions, go down with an attorney. Lawyering up is not a bad thing. You want somebody who is knowledgeable to protect your rights. It doesn't mean that you're guilty. If you're innocent and you want to go down there and tell your story, by all means, go. But go with counsel."

AND SECOND:

"I want you to know that if this can happen to a white, educated, middle-class cop, it can happen to anybody. And it does."

CHAPTER ELEVEN:
CONVICTED ON FACEBOOK

CASE FILE

Accused officer: Chief Jonathon Horton,
Rainbow City, Alabama

Related parties: Johnathan Dawon Davis;
unnamed driver; Samantha West

Date of incident: July 13, 2017

Location: Etowah County, Alabama

People don't believe me when I say this but I never engaged in any form of social media until mid-2016. That's when I finally set up an Instagram account. The only reason I did so was to keep up with (read this as: "spy on") my daughter when she went to college.

Lots of parents do this, I guess. We want to connect quickly with our children, so we create a Facebook account. It makes a certain kind of sense.

Personally, I remember typewriters, hi-fi sets, and rotary phones. But kids today think that's stuff from the Stone Age. They can't remember a day when smartphones weren't glued to everyone's palms. Because all that stuff came about before they were born, or thereabouts.

Anyway, I've maintained my Instagram account ever since. Also, back in 2017, I bit the bullet and started a Twitter account. That also made sense. By then I'd started working on *Live PD*. Interacting with the viewers in real time through Twitter was one of the many things that made that show so special. And I have to say, Twitter's a powerful tool for getting concise messages out to a wide audience—fast!

Notwithstanding all this, I have yet to start up a Facebook page. Yes, I know: Facebook sits at the top of the food chain when it comes to social media. Recently, I read somewhere that something like 2.5 billion people use Facebook every month. I don't know about you but I find that staggering!

Small wonder the platform's become like a double-edged sword.

On one hand, Facebook allows any person to instantly share practically any media they wish with their friends and followers who might be anywhere in the world. All it takes is the click of a mouse or a tap on a piece of touch-sensitive glass. Boom! It's done.

On the other hand, few people bother to verify whether or not the information being shared is truthful. Whether it's been embellished in any way, great or small. Or whether it even makes sense.

Consider how this played out in the following case:

On July 14, 2017, a woman named Samantha West shared a chilling Facebook post. Images West had purportedly taken the night before showed a man who appeared to be close to death. He lay in a hospital bed, his body swaddled in an immobilizing brace, his eyes nearly shut, his mouth bloodied. All his teeth appeared to have been knocked out. Frankly, the picture was gruesome.

The text that accompanied the post said the photos showed a man whom members of the Rainbow City Police Department of Rainbow City, Alabama, had "beat half to death." Allegedly this happened after the cops had pulled the man over. The post further alleged that, after beating the man, officers tased him and pushed him off a bridge.

About the man in her post, Ms. West wrote this:

"[He is] trying to talk but his whole front row of teeth are knocked out, he had to have his tongue sewed back together and his femur bone is broken he has to have surgery on it. He can't sit up or take his neck brace off til they clear him of neck injuries."

The quote went on to express disgust at police brutality:

"We will NOT back down or be quite [sic] this abuse NEEDS to stop! ... This is so wrong and we won't stop until these power obsessed animals pay for their cruelty ... The people who are supposed to serve and protect."

As you may well imagine, this Facebook post went viral almost instantly once it was published. In a matter of hours, it had garnered nearly 29,000 shares. Many people who commented on it did so by venting their outrage. Also, as one might expect, the vast majority of consumers stated their disgust and disapproval over what the police officers of Rainbow City had done to this poor man.

Allegedly.

That's the key here. The word "allegedly."

Because, as we're about to see, no one bothered to stop and consider if the images and information they were consuming were factual or contrived.

"We'd received more than a hundred messages threatening to do all sorts of things—rape and kill our wives and children and launch an all-out war on police," said Chief Jonathon Horton of the Rainbow City, Alabama Police Department later in an interview. "It was pretty crazy stuff."

Crazy indeed. But do you want to know the crazy part?

Yes, of course this post was completely untrue. That's not what I'm talking about.

No, the crazy part is that, while the gentleman shown in the picture had indeed suffered grave injuries, all his wounds were self-inflicted.

They were the result not of police brutality, but of his own actions.

The incident in question took place at about 8:40 pm on July 13, 2017. A Rainbow City squad car conducted a routine traffic stop on a vehicle heading down the Black Creek Parkway. The cop pulled the driver over because their car was missing a tail light.

For this particular story, the officer in question has chosen to remain anonymous. All information about what occurred comes to us through Chief Jonathan Horton of the Rainbow City Police Department.

To hear Chief Horton tell it, the officer got out of his car and approached the driver's vehicle. He was ready to issue a warning about the tail light, nothing more.

The driver, he discovered, was female. This individual will also remain unnamed. However, while interacting with the driver, the officer in question noticed a male sitting beside her in the front passenger seat. And this passenger looked nervous. Very nervous.

Following a hunch, the police officer asked to see the passenger's identification. This is valid police procedure. The fact is that, once a vehicle is pulled over, a police officer has the responsibility to make sure everyone in the vehicle is safe ... as well as everyone else on the road. This can include checking the identification of a vehicle's passengers.

It's not a big deal. Think of it this way: If you've done nothing wrong, why wouldn't you hand an officer your identification?

In this case, however, the male passenger in the stopped vehicle told the Rainbow City officer that he didn't have an Alabama driver's license. In lieu of that, the officer asked for the passenger's name and date of birth. The passenger supplied this data. However, when asked to supply his social security number, the passenger reported he didn't know it.

Fair enough. By which I mean: such things happen. Not often. But yes, they happen from time to time.

The officer then asked the driver and passenger to wait in their vehicle. Returning to his patrol car, he attempted to look up the passenger's information. The system returned nothing. Now the officer was really suspicious.

Let's look at why.

First, it's considered normal for a legal U.S. citizen to carry some form of identification at all times. When someone tells a police officer they forgot their ID at home or whatever, it's forgivable but suspicious. Call this strike one for the vehicle's passenger.

Second, the officer knew that most responsible adults memorize their social security number. It's one of those things that helps you get by in life. Obviously, this isn't a law. But it certainly makes a person seem suspicious when they can't supply their social security number and they claim they're not carrying ID. Call this strike two for the vehicle's passenger.

This was strike three. The officer had requested the passenger's name and date of birth. This information should have been enough to find some record of the passenger in any number of online resources.

By the time they reach adulthood, most U.S. citizens have somehow registered with local authorities. That registration could take any number of forms. Typically, however, it means a valid state driver's license or state identification card.

Most people carry these types of identification out of practicality. Obviously, you can't operate a motor vehicle without a valid driver's license. However, since not everyone drives, a state ID is the minimum requirement to secure employment, buy a pack of cigarettes, or purchase alcoholic beverages.

I would venture to say that 99 percent of the people I've dealt with in the course of my career have been issued one of these two forms of state identification.

So here's another pro tip: When someone tells a law enforcement officer that they don't have identification, they forgot their social security number, and the name and birthdate they supplied don't yield any search results ... well, that person is probably lying about his or her identity.

Now, of course, the question becomes: Why?

Commonly, this happens when a suspect has warrants outstanding for his or her arrest. Believing this might be the case, the Rainbow City officer returned to the vehicle he'd pulled over. Again, he asked the nervous passenger if he could supply some form of identification.

To hear Chief Horton tell it, the passenger then produced an Alabama driver's license. Of course, the officer thought this was odd. Why hadn't the passenger supplied his license in the first place?

Carefully, the Rainbow City officer scrutinized the card he'd been given. Right away, he noticed that the license's photo looked nothing like the man sitting in the passenger seat. He mentioned this fact to the passenger. The passenger explained that he'd recently been in prison where he had lost a lot of weight.

The officer wasn't buying it. Neither would I or any experienced officer, by the way.

At this point, in accordance with proven police procedures, the officer separated the nervous passenger from the female driver. He wished to interview them separately. There are many reasons for doing this.

For instance, if the driver was in some kind of trouble, she could convey this when safely removed from the passenger's presence. However, if the two were up to no good, separate interviews might expose inconsistencies in their stories which could then inform the officer as to what foul play was afoot.

Once she was separated from her companion, the female driver gave up her companion's real name. The passenger was Johnathan Dawon Davis.

Mr. Davis had had his probation revoked. He also had two felony warrants out on him related to dangerous drugs and misdemeanor traffic warrants.

In other words, the officer's suspicions had proven correct.

At one time or another, every law enforcement officer's been in this situation. Faster than you can roll a pair of dice, a routine traffic stop becomes anything but routine. Suddenly, you're facing a known criminal who, for all you know, might be armed and dangerous.

So what do you do?

As it turned out, very little. Because, in this case, Mr. Davis took all the action himself. And that's what got him injured.

But don't take my word for it. Just watch the video.

Yes, of course there was video. But I'm getting ahead of myself.

Once it began to receive threats, the Rainbow City Police Department backtracked these overtures to Samantha West's bogus Facebook post. At that point, they understood why the public misperceived them as being at fault. And so, just as the Texas Department of Public Safety had done in the case of Sherita Dixon-Cole, the Rainbow City Police Department released footage from the officer's bodycam. They were hoping to set things straight.

The video posted to YouTube lasts approximately thirty minutes. As you've likely already imagined, it tells a completely different story than the one described in Samantha West's Facebook post.

Imagine this being shown, and all from the officer's point of view:

The police officer has discovered the true identity of Mr. Johnathan Dawon Davis. He knows about Mr. Davis's criminal past and he knows about the warrants currently pending in federal court. Therefore, upon returning to the stopped vehicle, the officer informs Mr. Davis that he will be taken into custody.

For a moment, Mr. Davis seems calm. Then he bolts from the scene, crosses two lanes of oncoming traffic, and flings himself over the edge of a highway overpass. The officer runs after him but stops at the edge of the bridge. Leaning over, he peers down the nineteen-foot drop to see what happened to his suspect.

Well, you can probably guess what happened. The hospital photo says it all. But it doesn't say this:

Though he'd suffered severe injuries, Mr. Davis continued to run from the law. When backup arrived and officers descended to the scene below, Mr. Davis tried to hide in some bushes. He also took off his pants before trying to jump in the river and swim away. Though cornered and spotlit by flashlight beams, Mr. Davis refused to be handled. He had to be tased before Rainbow City officers were able to subdue him.

Only then did the officers note the true extent of Mr. Davis's injuries. Medics were quickly called to the scene. A helicopter arrived and Mr. Davis was airlifted to University of Alabama at Birmingham Hospital.

Chief Horton describes Mr. Davis actions as captured by the bodycam video like this:

"He jumped off the bridge. There wasn't any physical contact [between him and the officer] other than him being tased."

In addition to releasing the bodycam footage, Chief Horton wrote the following post for his department's Facebook page. It clearly responds to the earlier and erroneous post that vilified his department.

"In response to the 'Social Media Craze' and false allegations that Rainbow City Police Officers would mistreat any citizen (Law abiding or Suspect) I have uploaded this video to discredit the horrendous allegations that on July 13, 2017 the Rainbow City Police threw anyone from a bridge on Black Creek Parkway or in any way did anything other than carry out our duties to the extent of rendering what aid we could to a fleeing suspect. In this video, you will clearly see a man flee from police ... Prior to confronting this subject, he had stated that, 'He had never obtained an Alabama Driver's License and did not know his Social Security Number.' He gave officers a false name and then recanted the fact he had no driver's license and gave police another person's driver's license that he found within the vehicle. After the other occupant of the vehicle help[ed] reveal his identity, you can clearly see him run across two lanes of traffic and leap over a concrete bridge barrier, falling approximately 19 feet to the ground ... Next you will notice that not only did police NOT throw him from the bridge that the police actually rendered him aid as well as they could until medics arrived. Just because it's on Facebook does not mean it is true. We regret that this subject had self-inflicted injuries, as it's our intention to protect all lives and be concerned with all the community's safety as a whole."

Before moving on, I'd like to interject a quick word on the important role that cameras play in modern police work.

I'm sure you noticed how cameras play pivotal roles in the stories I've already told. Small wonder. Again, camera technology has become widespread with the advent of smartphones. Police officers now consider them pivotal tools in protecting both our own rights and the rights of the suspects we deal with on a daily basis.

Still, I know that activists on both sides of law enforcement claim cameras do more harm than good. I disagree with this notion. So, for that matter, does Chief Jonathon Horton.

Chief Horton says that body and dashcam videos not only protect his officers in Rainbow City but law enforcement personnel all over the country. In the case of this fraudulent Facebook post, release of the body cam video cleared the reputation of the arresting officer. But it also cleared the institutional reputation of Rainbow City PD.

To hear Chief Horton tell it, camera technology may also save the lives of other officers and their families who might face vendettas from overzealous activists.

"I'd hate for some guy to get radicalized [from reading these fraudulent claims about police brutality] and think it was true and take it out on some poor cop somewhere else," Horton said.

When he said this, I thought about Officer Jarrod Hubbard. How a simple case of mistaken identity could get blown way out of a proportion. And who suffers? Not an innocent cop—in this case Officer Daniel Hubbard. But a doubly innocent bystander. Another badge-wearing peacekeeper who just so happened to have the same surname.

Chief Horton recalled a situation where this happened about a year earlier in Dallas, Texas. He said that false information which claimed police had brutalized a suspect led to 14 cops getting shot. Five of these officers subsequently died. That's horrific and unacceptable.

Let's put this into perspective. How did I begin this book? I began it by stating what anyone who's been paying attention already knows: that recent events have strained the relationship between police forces nationwide and the general public. At times, this tension has become so great, our country feels like a pressure cooker, waiting to explode.

And explode it does. In terrible ways.

For this reason, I argue it's more important than ever not to exacerbate these tensions. Frankly, I urge you to be suspicious of anyone who does so. Why are they trying to prey on your fears? What are they hoping to provoke? What are they trying to get you to feel? To think? To do?

Personally, I consider it incredibly dangerous to report inaccurate information of any kind on social media. Especially when people's lives are directly at stake.

I hope you concur that we, as a society, don't want to see innocent people (both those in the public and those in law enforcement) getting hurt over something that never actually happened. Isn't life challenging enough without having to deal with this sort of nonsense?

Character assassinations, slander, and libel have no place in a decent society. Aren't we better than that? I say that we are.

This is America, land of the free and home of the brave. I love it. I hope you do, too. But how can we can take pride in our country if we don't behave with fellowship, charity, and goodwill toward each other? Answer: We can't.

Our greatness doesn't begin with our flag, who we vote for, or what channel we get our news from. It begins with you and me. With us. The way we carry ourselves as individuals. That's where greatness lies.

If America is truly great—and mark my words, I tell you it is—it can only be so because of the way we treat one another: as equals. Black or white or brown—doesn't matter. Respect and courage and dignity. These are the only things that matter.

The moment, we treat someone—anyone—poorly, we actually impoverish ourselves.

So by now, you're probably wondering: Who's this person who created the misleading Facebook post?

I already told you her name is Samantha West. Later, when she was approached by authorities and the media, Ms. West described herself as the mother of Mr. Davis's children.

Now, again. As anyone who's bothered to view the bodycam footage could tell you, Ms. West was not present at the scene of the attempted arrest nor the accident that followed. She was therefore not an eyewitness. Therefore, her indictment via social media rode on the back of hearsay, nothing more.

In this manner, it reminds me eerily of the situation with Sherita Dixon-Cole. A legitimate cause, such as police brutality, sadly got blown all out of proportion. And who gets damaged? Police officers, yes. Police departments. Sure, that's also true. But also: legitimate victims of actual crimes, both current and future.

To be clear, the media Ms. West chose to post only showed the results of Mr. Davis's jump. In other words, it showed his injuries. Tellingly, it did not show

Mr. Davis jumping off the bridge. And it certainly did not show, as Ms. West alleged, him being pushed off the bridge.

Ms. West later explained her actions. She said the account of the "beating" Mr. Davis supposedly received at the hands of the Rainbow City police had been relayed to her by people she trusted. That's essentially the same defense attorney Lee Merritt gave in the case of Sherita Dixon-Cole. And it doesn't wash.

Samantha West later removed her false post. Tellingly, however, she offered this bit of commentary on her Facebook page:

"I deleted my posts. But I was not lying. I was going by the only info I received. Police nor medical staff contacted anyone ever all we had to go off of was our loved ones word ... Until the body cam was released. I truly believed he was done wrong and we needed help. Excuse me for being human. But he's not my man he's my ex. Have a good night and god bless."

I find this an underwhelming response. Ms. West seems completely oblivious to all the potential harm her post might have done.

"Excuse me for being human," she says. But did she bother to turn that lens around? Did she ever stop to consider that police officers, peacekeepers, and law enforcement personnel nationwide are human beings, too?

Don't we deserve the same courtesy? The same right to life, liberty, and the pursuit of happiness? Don't we have the right to keep our spotless reputations and professionalism from being sullied?

I think you know the answer to this.

Stealing a person or institution's reputation is on the same level as stealing money from them. Except that, in this case, the bank in question holds the wealth of one's credibility.

Remember what I told you at the beginning of this chapter? Social media is a double-edged sword. Without question, it's a powerful tool. The trick is to balance the edges, as Lady Justice must balance her scales.

Recently, I attended an event at Carnegie Hall in New York City. This event featured various speakers. One of them was the legendary former news anchor and broadcast journalist, Ted Koppel.

Koppel was someone I admired growing up. I watched him my whole life, primarily on his late-night news program, *Nightline*, which aired on ABC. Koppel covered everything on his program: economics, education, politics, science, and breaking news. I wish we had more programs like this right now.

Just hearing Koppel's slow, even, and considerate voice brought back so many memories. Like Walter Cronkite to the generation before mine, Koppel had brought me the world and explained it in detail, using simple terms. In 1987, he held town hall meetings between Israeli and Palestinian factions. In the summer of 1990, he held another town hall with Nelson Mandela, who'd just been released from prison.

There was also that incredible time in 2004 when Koppel slowly and carefully spent an entire episode reading the names of every member of the U.S. armed forces who'd been killed since the Iraq War began the previous year. Here was a man who put integrity first. Whose journalistic chops were some of the best our country has ever benefitted from. And I got to hear him speak!

As part of the event's proceedings, Koppel was asked what, in his opinion, has changed with today's news environment. I thought he hit the nail on the head when he said, quite bluntly, the news became a business, as well as the Internet and social media.

Koppel went on to acknowledge that, these days, anyone with a smartphone or laptop can call themselves a journalist. Literally anyone has the ability to type something on to their device, hit enter or send, and that's it—that information is out there. Anyone can read it. Consume it. It can change people's minds. And who really cares if it's true? (I do. And honestly, I hope you do, too.)

The point is that now, thanks to modern technology, anyone can find information to support or contradict just about anything they believe in. The category of knowledge doesn't matter. It could be religion, politics, gun ownership, and so on. Nothing you post has to be vetted or fact checked. It can all be just your opinion. But once it hits the web, it's free game, and the more controversial the better. As any fool knows, controversy spreads the quickest.

That's exactly the dynamic we saw at play with this incident in Rainbow City, Alabama.

It's also the same dynamic we see too often in national politics.

So what happened to Johnathan Dawon Davis?

Approximately two weeks after officers attempted to arrest him, Mr. Davis was released from UAB Hospital and taken into custody. Police said Mr. Davis was booked for prior active warrants including one for felony probation revocation and a "failure to appear" warrant for driving in Rainbow City while his license was revoked.

But additional charges were filed, all stemming from the incident this chapter describes. Those charges included providing false identification to obstruct justice, attempting to elude law enforcement, and resisting arrest.

Mr. Davis was held in the Etowah County Detention Center. As of this moment, I'm not certain of his whereabouts. But I wish him all the best.

Like Chief Jonathon Horton, I feel badly for the injuries Mr. Davis sustained. But, at bottom, these were self-inflicted wounds. In the final assessment, he lied to police and fled on foot in his attempt to escape apprehension.

No one pushed him off that overpass. He jumped. And honestly? After falling nineteen feet, I'd say he's lucky to be alive.

In fact, one wonders what flashed through his mind as he jumped off that overpass. I guess we'll never know.

The moral of this story appears to be this: Don't believe everything you see or hear. Especially if what you see or hear is posted on the Internet.

Remember to take everything you read with a grain of salt. That nobody has all the answers. And challenge yourself to dig deeper. Do this especially with information you know you really want to be true.

The likelihood is increasingly great that the data you're consuming is either falsified or "enhanced."

Like Johnathan Dawon Davis, perhaps we would all be much better off if we paused and strove to get all the facts before we consented to make our conclusions.

CHAPTER TWELVE:
DRUMMED UP CHARGES LEAD TO A LIFE BEHIND BARS

CASE FILE

Accused officer: Clyde Ray Spencer, Vancouver, Washington Police Department

Related parties: Matt Spencer; Katie Spencer; Sharon Krause

Date of incident: 1984

Location: Vancouver, Washington

I want to be fair with you, reader, so listen up.

What you're about to read may strike you as absurd. In fact, at various points, you might feel tempted to say, "No way. That's impossible! This couldn't happen! You're making it up!"

Sadly, I'm not.

There's a reason I saved this story for last. It's the most harrowing tale I could find of a cop who was falsely accused and suffered immensely because of it.

Let it serve as a lesson to all of us who live in our modern, judgmental times.

The brave men and women who protect and serve their communities, who wear their badges with honor each day and strive to make us all safe ... I think they deserve a second look before we pronounce too harsh of a sentence.

Imagine this. It's 1984. You're in the city of Vancouver in Clark County, Washington. Wide lapels are in style. Bell bottoms are still making the rounds. Each Friday night, people tune their TVs to a hit new show called *Miami Vice*.

Whenever you turn on the radio, David Lee Roth and Van Halen are screaming you might as well "Jump." Either that or Kenny Loggins is telling you you're burning and yearning, maybe it's time we should all get '"Footloose."

The story I'm about to tell you starts here, but ends decades later.

Now picture Clyde Ray Spencer. He's in his mid to late-30s, a handsome cop with longish, side-parted disco hair and a Douglas Fairbanks moustache.

Spencer worked at Vancouver PD in the motorcycle patrol. He liked his job a lot. The big bikes suited his style.

He only been on the force for six years but that didn't make him a rookie. Prior to pinning a badge to his tunic, Spencer had served in the U.S. Air Force, which trained him to work in air traffic control. He spent part of his tenure with the USAF on the tiny island of Guam in the northern Pacific, a thousand miles north of New Guinea and the same distance east of the Philippines. Then, after an honorable discharge, Spencer worked for the Federal Aviation Administration. While working for FAA, he underwent training and joined the sky marshals.

You've probably heard of the sky marshals. They're the covert counter-terrorism agents who board commercial aircraft posing as passengers. Should hijackers pop from their seats and start shouting, the marshals are present to act as deterrents.

Most regular passengers never suspect that an armed law enforcement officer is sitting right beside them as they fly across the country. Hopefully, the marshals are never called upon to act. But whenever they're needed the most, they're there.

Spencer's experience with the sky marshals led him to work in other forms of federal law enforcement. He recently detailed all this during an interview I conducted with him:

SPENCER: I was based as a sky marshal out of Chicago. Flew out of New York, and later transferred back to Los Angeles, and went into federal narcotics with U.S. Customs. Worked the borders, cartels, a marine detail up and down the West Coast. Unmarked boats and drugs coming up north. Cartel found out who I was. I had threats against my family, so I ended up resigning that position and went up to Vancouver, Washington ... My sister lived up in the area, and [I] went to work on their department. I had eight years with the Feds, and then six years [with Vancouver PD] when all of this started to come about.

STICKS: Were you a detective or anything in particular at the time in Vancouver?

SPENCER: No, I was working patrol. I was the assistant SWAT team commander. I enjoyed working the streets. I know there were a lot of officers that were kind of concerned when I came in there with my bachelor's degree in criminology and the feds experience. But in reality, I never wanted to leave the streets. I didn't really want to sit behind a desk.

By now, it may not surprise you to hear that this resonated with me. I know exactly how Clyde Ray Spencer feels. I've never wanted to spend my life behind a desk. I love being out on the street with my guys, interacting with the community, and all the amazing people in Tulsa.

At first blush, Spencer had a solid law enforcement CV. He'd trained in the military. He had a college degree. He'd worked for the feds. And during that time, he'd ventured into those deep, dark places that most cops only wish they could get into ...

Fighting drugs while working with U.S. Customs and Border Protection.

Going undercover in an outlaw biker gang.

Having his cover blown on more than one occasion.

This was the stuff that movies are made of.

Clyde Ray Spencer was one of those rare police officers who's been there, done it, and come back again. Who's entered the criminal underworld where the laws of reality flip upside down. Where light becomes dark, where good becomes evil, and criminals live by their own code of ethics. A code that can often turn deadly.

But here I should say something bluntly. Clyde Ray Spencer wasn't an angel. His biggest flaw was that he loved women. In particular, he loved full-figured blondes.

This might not have been such a problem for anyone else. But Clyde Ray Spencer was married. He and his wife, DeAnne, had two little kids, Matt and Katie. To Spencer, they were the loves of his life.

SPENCER: I have to be perfectly honest with you. My ex-wife was very bitter over the divorce. I wasn't faithful in the marriage, especially when I was flying sky marshal. I'm flying all over the world, staying with the flight crews, and they were some pretty hard partying people. I take full responsibility for not honoring my marriage vows, but she never got over it, and she still hasn't gotten over it.

Later, on an episode of ABC's *20/20* that aired in November 2010, DeAnne told her side of the story like this:

"There were many times that there were other women ... It's not so much the rage and anger that I had [over Spencer's infidelities], but I don't believe anything that was ever said to me was the truth."

The couple divorced in 1981. DeAnne took their kids—Matt, who was five years old and his sister, little Katie, who was two—and started a new life nearly 600 miles away in Sacramento, California.

As part of the deal he worked out with DeAnne, Spencer got to see his kids for six weeks in the summer and one week every other Christmas. It was a hard way to live, being separated from Matt and Katie. I know a bit about this. Many parents find the worst part of divorce is living away from their kids.

"I always wanted to be the father that I never had," Spencer later told *20/20*. "They were my world."

Although they were very young during this interval, Matt and Katie still remember the special times they shared with their Dad.

"I remember fishing. And I remember picking blackberries," Katie recalled on *20/20*. She was thirty-one years old by then. "Those were the kinds of happy things that we did."

Matt offered this comment while sitting beside her. "He [Spencer] taught me how to fish, he taught me how to shoot. It was like we were just about to get to that point where we were going to really bond as father and son. And then, all of a sudden, he was just gone."

Two years later, in 1983, Spencer remarried. His new wife was named Shirley Hansen. Shirley had a three-year-old son of her own who was also named Matt. The family nicknamed her boy "Little Matt" to distinguish him from Spencer's son.

It was a happy moment for Spencer. He thought he'd found love once again. And for a while there, all went well. But then, a year later, it started to crumble.

To hear Spencer tell it, little Katie put her hands between Shirley's legs and told her stepmother, "My brother does this, my mom does this, my dad does this."

At the time, Spencer assumed that, by "Daddy," Katie meant a boyfriend her mom was seeing. Deeply concerned, he called the authorities.

SPENCER: I immediately called [California] Child Protective Services because the kids had already left that morning. And I called my department. I called the sheriff's department, since I lived out in their area. That's what started the whole investigation.

Simultaneous investigations began, one in California through the Sacramento Sheriff's Department and another in Washington State through the Clark County Sheriff's Department.

Members of both teams came out to interview Spencer's kids. In the course of their detective work, the California detectives found there was no basis for what Spencer feared had happened. The kids' statements, they said, were too inconsistent to predicate further investigation.

Pursuing the truth can be one of the most challenging aspects of working with very small children. Their take on reality is more fluid than that of adults. They don't observe the same boundaries we do with respect to fact versus fiction. Nor do they typically command the language skills—a mature vocabulary and facility with metaphor—that lets them describe to adults precisely what happened to them in the course of their young lives.

From personal experience, I can also say this. Working a crime that involves a child is never easy from a psychological perspective. It takes a toll on everyone involved: the officers, the detectives, the parents, the children themselves.

The thought of an adult harming, let alone sexually abusing a child, is horrific. My blood boils just thinking about it. It makes me furious. But young children can have robust imaginations. Detectives have to be careful when combining this miraculous power with a child's inherent desire to please adults. If not handled carefully, a child can be led to tell stories simply to make a detective smile.

Knowing this, most law enforcement agencies now have officers on staff who are specifically trained to work with sex crimes—and with sexual assaults on children in particular. These officers have attended accredited schools that teach proven techniques for interviewing and investigating crimes where children are the victims.

Kudos to all of these child crisis detectives in the country who deal with these types of cases on a daily basis. I know that I couldn't do it.

Having found nothing wrong with Spencer's kids, the Sacramento detectives terminated their investigation. But the two detectives in Clark County followed a much different protocol.

SPENCER: There's a lot of things that took place that unfortunately I didn't know about until after the fact. One of the detectives, Sergeant Michael Davidson, started an affair with my wife ... during the investigation. His partner was a little bit strange, too. She was a waitress, and then the department hired her in without any experience in the sexual assault department ...

The female detective's name was Sharon Krause. She was fresh from the police academy when she got promoted to detective.

I remember being aghast when Spencer told me this.

STICKS: That's insane! I mean, just thinking about that as a cop right now, that's literally insane. With no investigative background like that?

SPENCER: Right. Yeah. She had quite the history, just a side note, of fabricating cases, and had been caught at it by the courts and a number of other people that it came out afterwards that this was not her first rodeo as far as fabricating evidence.

Clearly, Sharon Krause was not aware of the proper procedures for handling sexual abuse cases. Or how to question children. This would be the charitable approach to assessing what eventually happened.

There are less charitable views available.

Consider this:

Twenty-five years later, it became clear that Detectives Krause and Davidson performed what we on the Tulsa PD call a SANE, or Sexual Assault Exam. These exams produced no evidence whatsoever that Spencer's children were victims of foul play. But Krause and Davidson buried these test results and proceeded under the assumption that a crime had been committed.

Krause, in particular, made several trips to Sacramento where she personally questioned Ray's two children. Separately, she took Katie and Matt to her hotel room, where she questioned them. On these occasions, Krause said she took handwritten notes of the interviews. However, even back then, it was an accepted law enforcement procedure to make either video or audio recordings of such pivotal interviews.

SPENCER: My department put me on administrative leave. I was ordered to remain in my residence at all times. I couldn't travel anywhere. I couldn't leave the state. This went on for, like, six months. Sharon Krause would go to Sacramento and she would take [my] children individually out for candy, toys, and then take them back to her hotel room. Did not video, did no audio. As a matter of fact, took no notes that we could ever find ...

By this point, Matt and Katie were ages eight and five. Matt initially denied that any abuse had taken place. But Krause kept working on him.

In the 2010 episode of *20/20*, Matt recalled how the questioning process seemed to go on "for months." He later told *Esquire* magazine that he remembered how, one afternoon, Sharon Krause picked him up at home. Matt was a little scared about climbing into a stranger's car. But Krause, he said, bought him a hot chocolate and a Matchbox car at the 7-Eleven before taking him to her room at the Holiday Inn.

> As a professional investigator, this behavior horrifies me. It seems to show quite clearly how a detective with an agenda tried to manipulate children to say what she wanted them to say. At very least, it leads me to doubt Sharon Krause's professionalism.
>
> Keep in mind, too, that most kids have limited attention spans. They get scared and bored very quickly, very easily. Especially if they're being questioned for extended periods of time. If you give them candy and presents and tell them they'll be done with something soon, you can probably get them to say anything. Especially if you couch what you want them to repeat in a manner that makes them think they're helping their parents.
>
> Most kids love their parents so much, they'd do anything for them. It's a beautiful impulse, born out of love. But in this case, someone seems to have twisted it into something truly perverse: falsely accusing an innocent man.

According to Krause—who again offered no physical evidence whatsoever to back this up—Katie began giving lurid accounts of being raped. Shockingly—and again, per Detective Krause, without any evidence—little Katie pointed the finger at her own father, Clyde Ray Spencer. He had been her assailant, Krause said.

Krause also insisted that Katie had told her other cops were involved with her rape. That they'd even gone so far as to take pictures of her in sexually suggestive poses.

STICKS: Just to clarify. When the allegations happened, Sacramento County basically looked into it and said, "There's not enough there." Or, "There's nothing there."

SPENCER: Correct.

STICKS: Then Clark County continued their investigation. And the male detective, during the course of this investigation, ends up having an affair with your then wife.

SPENCER: Correct.

STICKS: Wow! So then, a sexual assault exam—the term we use is a SANE exam is done on the children at the time. And not only is there no evidence found. They then basically hid these examinations ...

SPENCER: That's correct.

But the final nail in the coffin was about to slam home.

Eight months into the questioning process, eight-year-old Matt Spencer changed his story to mimic his sister's. Yes, he said. Their father had raped him.

And so, in January 1985—again, without a shred of physical evidence to back up the claim—Clyde Ray Spencer was charged with the crime of raping his own daughter.

Spencer later recalled his reaction. He told his superiors: "'You must be crazy, I'm the one who reported this.' I was thinking, this just can't be happening."

But it was.

And things were about to get worse.

Much worse.

Spencer was released on his own recognizance. Meaning: Although he'd been charged with a crime, he was released from jail without posting a bond. He signed paperwork promising he would show up for court.

But, as unthinkable as his situation was, the horror was just beginning.

First, he lost his job.

SPENCER: My department didn't want anything to do with me. Friends that I thought were my friends ... you get a whole new perspective of what a friend is when you run into things like this. One in particular that ... I was on the SWAT team with him. We rode motors. We were in some seriously tight situations. We hunted together. He couldn't get away from me quick enough.

Next, Spencer got separated from his second wife, Shirley Hansen. With no place else to go, he began living in a motel.

However, shortly after their separation, in February 1985, Shirley Hansen asked Spencer if her son, Little Matt, could spend a night with him in his motel room.

SPENCER: One morning ... the separated wife shows up at the motel with her five-year-old son and said, "Well, he wants to spend the day with you." I said, "Okay." I've had plenty of people ask me, "Why in the hell would you do that?" Well, if you didn't do anything [meaning: you're innocent], you don't even think about it. I was the one that took care of him most of the time. So I said, "Okay, where's his pajamas? Where's his toys?" Things like that. She goes, "Oh, well he just asked me on the way over here."

I think we went to a movie, and that night I stuck him in the tub, and put one of my t-shirts on him, and put him in bed. About three days later, I get arrested for supposedly molesting him. But my feelings are: this was a setup. They knew that their case was going to tank ... They needed some additional information, because once that charge came about, everybody turned their back on me.

At this point, as far as the courts were concerned, three children had accused Clyde Ray Spencer of molesting them.

His mental health began to deteriorate. The situation was unthinkable. The stress, unbearable. He contemplated suicide.

"I was starting at that point to question my own sanity," he told *20/20*.

He later told *Esquire* magazine that, one day, things got too much to bear. He pulled out his .357 and sat there looking at it. But then:

"I remember a little voice in the back of my head saying, 'Hey, maybe for your children's sake, you should get some help.'"

Spencer called a suicide hotline and was soon whisked off to Oregon Health Science University Hospital.

"They found me holed up in the corner, crying. I don't remember much of it other than the attendants rushing in."

Clyde Ray Spencer spent two weeks in a psyche ward. The physicians there diagnosed him with severe clinical depression. Later, he could never be sure what had triggered his attack. Was it because he knew he was innocent and no one on earth believed him? Or because he'd begun to wonder if what everyone accused him of was true?

"I would have rather been charged with murder than [molesting my own kids]," he later admitted.

Meanwhile, Detectives Davidson and Krause continued building a case against Spencer. Despite being emotionally and mentally devastated, Spencer felt certain the two were making up evidence to justify their accusations.

SPENCER: Sharon Krause claimed that after one of these instances where my daughter supposedly kept elaborating [on her alleged molestation], that she actually confirmed this with a child psychologist a couple days later. When this all came out many years later, the child psychologist gave us sworn statements that my daughter never implicated me ... That there was no basis for any of this.

STICKS: This was the same child psychologist that allegedly confirmed what Sharon Krause was saying, basically?

SPENCER: Sharon Krause was claiming that my daughter had said this at an interview in her hotel room, and that she had confirmed this with a child psychologist two days later. But the child psychologist said she never ever said this happened.

STICKS: Wow.

SPENCER: Of course, they hid all of that too.

Picture Clyde Ray Spencer living in hell. He'd been charged with eleven felony counts of statutory rape and complicity to rape his own children. And though he maintained his innocence, he was starting to lean toward the notion that he must be lying to himself. He must have molested his children and somehow buried the memory of it. What else could explain the situation he was?

"I'm thinking, if you did this to your own children, you deserve to be locked up," he recalled.

Desperate to know the truth, and with his trial date fast approaching, Spencer agreed to undergo hypnosis and a session with truth serum. It was the spring of 1985.

"They took me so deep that they put me into a self-induced coma," Ray revealed on *20/20*. "The findings from the doctor said I can't find anything here that would lead me to believe that these charges are factual."

The doctors' findings eased Spencer's mind. Finally, he felt certain that he wasn't crazy and he hadn't molested his kids. Now he just had to deal with the fact that he found himself embroiled in what could only be called a catastrophe.

The prosecutors in Clark County, Washington, didn't seem to care what Spencer's doctors had found. They were convinced of Spencer's guilt. And so his trial proceeded apace.

Defense attorney Peter Camiel worked with Spencer and his case many years later. As Camiel told *20/20*: "With these kinds of cases, when you start having multiple victims, they become very hard to defend."

Spencer was worried. He knew it would be difficult for him to win a court battle between himself and his three children. Likely, a jury would tear him to shreds based solely on the heinousness of the allegations. They also might overlook the fact that no concrete proof whatsoever existed to prove that Spencer molested his kids.

With this as his primary reason, Clyde Ray Spencer decided to enter an Alford plea on all eleven charges made against him.

An Alford plea is a little-known and seldom used legal doctrine. By entering an Alford plea, a defendant admits that the evidence against him or her is overwhelming. It will likely convince both a judge and jury they're guilty. But by using an Alford plea, the defendant enters a guilty plea while nonetheless maintaining his or her innocence.

The name of this plea comes from the 1970 case of *North Carolina v. Alford*. Henry Alford, a man charged with first-degree murder, pleaded guilty to committing that crime. But only because the evidence stacked against him was so formidable. At that time, under North Carolina law, a conviction of first-degree murder carried a death sentence. Alford pleaded guilty to avoid execution. The whole time, however, he maintained that he was innocent.

"I just pleaded guilty because they said if I didn't they would gas me," Alford wrote.

After various appeals, the case graduated to the U.S. Supreme Court where the justices decided that Alford's plea was a legitimate legal vehicle. Supreme Court Justice Byron White wrote the majority decision upholding the use of an Alford plea.

The rules pertaining to Alford pleas vary widely from state to state. Some states view the Alford plea as another form of nolo contendere, or a plea of "no contest." Others see the Alford plea as a guilty plea as far as all practical matters are concerned.

In some cases, the defendant's use of an Alford plea allows the judge to move directly to sentencing. This is what happened in Spencer's case.

As Peter Camiel told *20/20*, not admitting his guilt cost Spencer dearly when he was sentenced.

"Those that don't admit with this kind of crime get the maximum," Camiel said. "And that's what [the judge] gave Ray. He gave him every day he could get ... There wasn't one more day he could have thrown on."

In the final assessment, Judge Thomas Lodge sentenced Clyde Ray Spencer to multiple life sentences, plus fourteen years.

When Spencer heard his sentence, his knees gave out. The guards to either side of him had to fight to hold him up. His body had simply collapsed and he was nothing but dead weight dragging them down.

We all know the old saying about hindsight. And it's true. The text of our lives looks clearer whenever we turn the page of years and check them again wearing the reading glasses of experience.

Given this perspective, Clyde Ray Spencer now thinks he might have been doomed from the start with Judge Tom Lodge.

The two men had a history. The year before Spencer stood trial, as fate would have it, he pulled over Lodge's daughter. He wanted to charge her for street racing. But when he'd tried to pull her over, Lodge's daughter nearly ran him off the road.

SPENCER: So I stop her, and stop the other guy she was racing. I see her last name and I said, "Is your dad Thomas Lodge?" And she said, "Yeah." Well I'd been in front of Judge Lodge dozens of times. I actually had a lot of respect for him. So, I cut her loose, and I call him that night at home, thinking he should be aware of it and maybe have a talk with her for a father, for the kids type thing. I said, "Look, Judge Lodge. This is what happened today. Your daughter was racing a guy and nearly ran, T-boned the car I was in. I let her go with a warning, but you might want to have a talk with her." He said, "What right do you have to stop my daughter?" I said, "Excuse me?" He said, "What right do you have to stop my daughter?" I said, "Well, I just told you what my right was." I said, "She was endangering the public along with myself." I said, "And I thought you would appreciate a call letting you know what actually happened today, so you could have a talk with her." He said, "I want to know what right you think you have to stop my daughter." I said, "You know what, Judge Lodge? This is what's going to happen. The next time that I stop your daughter for something like this, I'm going to arrest her. I'm going to book her, and you can come down and get her out of the county jail." So he slams the phone down, and a year later I'm standing in front of this man, and he gave me the harshest sentence that he could, that was ever handed out in that county. Two hundred and twelve years.

Now if you're like me, you seriously question why Clyde Ray Spencer chose an Alford plea in the first place. He admitted that, at the time of his court appearance, his head was clouded by medication prescribed for him by his doctors. Also, he was tired.

As he later told *20/20*, "It's three days before trial and I'm saying, I can't go any further. I just cannot ... I don't have the strength."

There was also this: Spencer had originally hired a local attorney. But when he realized this lawyer wasn't doing much to defend him, he decided to hire a better attorney.

To afford this second attorney, Spencer withdrew money from his retirement fund. But the check was sent to his residence while he was in jail. His wife cashed it. Now the money was gone. It literally disappeared. He later reported that his wife also cashed a check that was sent to him by the IRS, a refund after an overtime audit.

I remind you, reader, this is the same wife, Shirley Hansen, who was now embroiled in an extramarital affair with the detective supervising the investigation into Spencer's alleged molestation of his kids.

All told, Clyde Ray Spencer lost between $12,000 and $15,000 of his own money. Money he could have used to hire a different attorney who might have defended him properly.

But perhaps the biggest irony is this: Had Spencer simply admitted his guilt, he might have shortened his prison sentence to approximately two years. Spencer, however, insisted he was innocent. Evidently, the stance he chose destroyed any chance of leniency with Judge Thomas Lodge.

Not that he would have done anything differently. Spencer thought there was more at stake than his sentence. There was the truth to consider.

As he later told a reporter, "If you did this to your own children, you deserve to be locked away. But I didn't do it and I wasn't going to admit it."

In 1985, Clyde Ray Spencer was sent to the Washington State maximum-security prison. His children, Matt and Katie, were never told where he'd gone or what happened to him. By court order, Ray was forbidden to communicate with his children. Therefore, as far as they knew, their father had vanished. For many years, they remained in the dark about his whereabouts and situation.

As Matt Spencer told *20/20*, "We didn't understand the magnitude of these charges. We had no idea that our father was going to be taken away because we were just getting news through our mom."

Their mother, DeAnne, chose to tell Matt and Katie their father was sick.

As DeAnne later put it, "I just would pretty much focus [with them] on the fact that [their dad] needs to get some help and he needs to get healthy."

Spencer says he thought of his kids every day. He wondered what went on in their lives. What they looked like. What trials they were enduring as they grew up. He wondered if they'd ever forgive him for disappearing from their lives. Or if they remembered him at all.

"It's very difficult because you wonder about those firsts," he later recalled. "The first baseball game. The first date. Graduation. Those are the things that haunt you in a prison cell at three in the morning."

Soon after he went to prison, Spencer's second wife, Shirley Hansen, filed for divorce.

"I received divorce papers shortly after I went to prison," Ray told Katie Couric in 2014 on her talk show, *Katie*. "And the divorce attorney from Clark County—I knew her. So when I contact her and asked her to handle the divorce, she said, 'Ray, it's all over the city. Shirley ... was having an affair with Sergeant Michael Davidson from the Clark County sheriff.'"

It was an awful to thing to hear but maybe the worst part of all was it didn't matter one bit. Spencer's fate had been sealed. The sentence Judge Thomas Lodge had passed was clear and undeniable. Spencer would spend the rest of his life in a maximum-security prison.

And in that kind of environment, the only thing a man has is his will to survive.

In prison, Spencer had two very big strikes against him. First, he was a cop. Second, he was a convicted sex offender whose victims were children.

The cop part shouldn't be hard to understand. It should come as no surprise that convicts don't like cops very much. When you lock up an ex-cop in a prison, it makes for a hairy situation.

Some convicts pride themselves on assaulting ex-cops who live on their cell block. This can lead to injuries and even deaths. For this reason, most ex-police officers are usually kept out of the general population. Most prisons put them in some type of protective housing unit, both for their own safety and that of the other inmates. If you recall, we saw this happen in the case of Detective Scott Hornoff.

But the part about child molesters might bear explanation.

As it happens, those people convicted of child molestation might be the most reviled class of prisoner anywhere in the world. They're the bottom of the barrel. Even murderers and rapists despise them.

In the U.S., fellow inmates often call these convicts "chomos" —slang for child molesters. Chomos often get targeted for acts of violence. Many prisons won't let them mix with their general population. Again, for their safety as well as the safety of other inmates, chomos also frequently kept in protective housing units.

In the eyes of his fellow inmates, Clyde Ray Spencer was both a chomo and an ex-cop. He knew this better than anyone. And he knew he had to watch his back or it might start sprouting shivs.

SPENCER: ... Judge Lodge did say that I should be transferred out of state and my identity changed. But when I went to prison into reception in the State of Washington, they stuck me in maximum security lockdown, and basically I guess they were just going to leave me there, I guess until I died. You're locked down twenty-three hours a day. One night, a guard came to my cell about 3:00 a.m. He whispered to me, through the door: "Look, this went through the law enforcement community like wildfire. You were set up. I'm going to go to the FBI, but you can't tell anybody or I'll lose my job. I can't advocate for an inmate, but I can't just sit back and let a fellow law enforcement officer you know have to go through this."

At this point, Spencer had only been in prison nine months.

The guard who approached him made good on his word. He and another corrections officer took Spencer's case to the FBI.

SPENCER: ... the FBI, instead of using a little discretion, they came in and said, "Okay, we were contacted by two prison guards about this situation, and we want to interview the guy."

It was the worst approach the feds could have taken. The overtness of their actions called unwanted attention to Spencer. They pulled him out of his cell for an interview that lasted an hour or so. Every minute of which turned out to be wasted time.

In the end, the FBI chose not to pursue Spencer's case. But the damage they'd done was already telling. Their visit had alerted the penal system that two corrections officers had advocated for Spencer.

SPENCER: ... this captain calls me in and he said, "I want to know who these officers were that went to the FBI on your behalf." I said, "I'm not telling you." He said, "You will tell me." I said, "What are you going to do, captain? I've got two life sentences and 171 months. What else are you going to do? And I'm sitting in maximum security." He tells the other guard to take me back to my cell. An hour later, the sergeant in charge of that unit calls me down, and I'm in waist chains, ankle chains, and this guy is just spitting mad, because he knows two of his officers went behind his back . . . He said, "I want to know who these officers were." I said, "I'm not telling you." He said, "You will tell me," he said, "Or I'll beat it out of you." I said, "Why don't you take these chains off, sergeant. We'll decide that one." ... He tells the guard to take me back to my cell ... And I would sit at night and I would just listen. I never slept soundly. I would always listen to what was going on, and there was always something going on in those type of units. I heard it go from one cell to another. "The guy in Cell Fifteen is a cop." And pretty soon, you've got a hundred inmates banging on the door saying, "Let's kill the cop."

Spencer later stated that the sergeant he'd just denied snitched him out to the other inmates. It was payback for Spencer not ratting on the two guards who'd tried to help him.

Things got so bad that it forced the hand of the Washington State Department of Corrections. They had no choice but to move Clyde Ray Spencer to some other location lest some kind of altercation break out.

SPENCER: They had their tactical unit come in and escort me out. They stuck me in their mental health ward because they didn't know where the hell to put me. So, they had had an agreement, an interstate compact with Idaho. So they ended up transferring me to Idaho. I thought, "You know, I'm not going to live to see daylight, but I sure as hell can't live locked down twenty-three hours a day." So I told them, "I'll walk the main yard." They said, "It's your decision." And so for the next eighteen years, I walked the main yard. There were some truly scary days. Again, I'm not going to lie about it. There wasn't a day that I didn't wake up and think, "This is going to be my last one."

STICKS: You never did do a name change or anything like that. You kept your actual name there. Correct?

SPENCER: They didn't change my name and at one point the officers knew who I was and one of the problems was they had access to go look at my file. And when I first went there and I ended up going to work, the officers in the unit said, "Look, we're going to put you to work outside, doing yard work outside the unit. We don't know what's going on, but this lieutenant calls every week wanting to know if you screwed up, so be careful. Whatever's happening, you know, they're out to get you."

One day, Spencer was outside working his prison job, doing yard work, when a man in a suit approached him. At first, Spencer thought he was some kind of religious volunteer.

SPENCER: He comes up and he goes, "How's it going?" I go, "Not bad." Then I see his ID and I said, "You're the lieutenant that keeps refusing my job applications." He said, "Yeah," he said. "Remember our captain in Washington?" As it turns out, this lieutenant used to work for DOC in Washington [State]. I said, "Yeah." He said, "He told me to bust your balls, and that's what I plan on doing." He said, "So don't expect to get work for two or three years. If I feel like it, I'll let you go to work."

Spencer was aghast but what could he do?

The answer was nothing at all.

Still, word got around, as it always seems to in prisons.

SPENCER: ... I think one of the officers in the unit called the deputy warden. And the warden called me in and I said, "Look, this is what's going on." So the deputy warden called this lieutenant and said, "You will hire him, and you'll stay out of this." Just a side note, years later that lieutenant was arrested and convicted of molesting his kids.

Now put yourself in Spencer's shoes. You've been transferred to a penitentiary in Idaho where you're living in the general population under your own name. Your background is an open book. In the world of the prison, you're known as both an ex-cop and a chomo.

Are you scared yet? You should be. So was Spencer. Turns out, he had to defend himself on a practically daily basis.

He had plenty of run-ins with prison gangs who felt it was their duty to purge the world of people they hated. Against such assailants, Spencer found that his training with the U.S. Navy SEALs came in handy.

"You have to get that rep that you're not going to be easy," he explained to me.

Meaning, not an easy target.

SPENCER: Probably the first six months, there wasn't a week that went by that I didn't fight, or got into it with somebody. There was this one old con who told me one time. "You know? I don't know what there is about you." My wife says I walk like a cop. I don't know what that means. But, apparently there was something about me that just didn't fit ... These are things that you deal with, and you just accept the fact that you're going to die in there, and you're just trying to put it off as long as you can.

One time, he landed in solitary confinement for defending himself. This is how it happened.

By that point, Spencer had been in prison about seventeen years. He had a job as one of the lead men working in the prison print shop. One of his workmates was a fellow convict whom the supervisor caught going through the area phone books, which the print shop had access to.

This convict would go through the phone books and write down the names of women he found. Then he would call these women collect. If they accepted the call, he would talk dirty to them.

Evidently, he'd been doing this so long, a number of complaints had been lodged. But no one, as yet, had traced the calls back to the Spencer's workmate. Until, one day, they did.

Spencer's supervisor caught his workmate red-handed.

SPENCER: So the supervisor fires him. About four days later, I'm at the gym. The guy comes up to me and says, "If I don't have my job back by Wednesday, your ass is mine." I said, "Partner, this doesn't wait til Wednesday. We do this right now." We used to fight down in the shower, where the guards couldn't see it unless they stepped in there. I get down there, and I take my jacket off, and the guy said, "Well, I don't want to fight." I said, "Look, dude. You started this. You brought this on yourself." He then says "I'm not going to fight." And he walks out.

The convict who started the fight went and told certain higher-ups in the correctional system that Spencer had threatened to kill him. Spencer was called in to answer some questions.

SPENCER: ... and they said, "We have this complaint. This guy said you threatened to kill him." I said, "No. I never said anything like that. But I will tell you if he puts his hands on me, I'll put him in a box. And that goes for anybody. I'm not going to be somebody's punching bag." An hour later, the tactical unit shows up. They beat me down, cuff me up, take me to the hole. I'm in the hole for about three days. The sergeant in charge of it comes back, and he looks over to see who's been locked up on his days off and he sees my name. He calls me out and he says, "Spencer, in seventeen years you've been on this yard, you've never been in the hole. What happened?" I told him. He said, "I'll tell you what." He said, "If this comes up again," he said, "Pour gasoline on the son of bitch and torch him off. He's a child molester. He's not worth the air we breathe."

Now during this time, while living in his six-by-eleven-foot prison cell, Clyde Ray Spencer had a sort of spiritual awakening.

As he told Katie Couric, "I was in maximum security and I wanted to bring closure to my life because I knew I would never see daylight again."

These thoughts sent his mind back into the past. Spencer found himself reflecting a lot on his first love, a woman named Norma Kohlscheen.

Spencer and Kohlscheen met when he'd been stationed on Guam in the late 1960s. They were both in their early 20s back then. Spencer was there as a military air traffic controller. Kohlscheen served as a nurse.

They'd had a whirlwind relationship and Ray had proposed marriage.

"I was very young, inexperienced, just learning about life and I needed more time. So I passed," Norma Kohlscheen told *20/20*.

They separated once they got back to the states.

Now Spencer tracked down Kohlscheen down. It had been decades since they'd seen each other.

SPENCER: I wrote her a letter. I said, "I just want you to know that you were the only woman I ever really loved. And this is where I'm at." I didn't tell her why. I said, "I'm never going to know freedom again, but I want you to know that I never forgot you."

He had reason to keep his expectations low. He had no idea how she felt about him. Also, imagine getting a letter from somebody you haven't seen in a generation or so. And this person reveals they are currently incarcerated in a maximum-security prison.

But it turned out Norma Kohlscheen had never stopped thinking of Clyde Ray Spencer.

"I still have the first picture that I got of him back there on my wall," she told *20/20*. "I've carried it all these years."

She went on: "He's always been the love of my life. And I made a promise to myself that if we ever got back together again, no matter what the circumstances, I would take it."

SPENCER: ... I spoke to her brother years later. He said, "You know, she cried that whole week." She wrote back, and then I told her, in the next letter, what the charges were. And she said, "I'm not buying any of this."

Norma Kohlscheen was still single. After a six-month courtship by mail, Spencer asked her to marry him. Again. This time she didn't hesitate. Norma Kohlscheen said yes.

"I had to be there for him," she told *20/20*. "Someone had to be there for him."

They got married in the prison in Idaho. Spencer recalls he was allowed to invite about half a dozen inmates. The ceremony took place in the prison's chapel.

"It wasn't bad," Norma Kohlscheen recalled on *20/20*, smiling.

There was no honeymoon. No conjugal visit. No opportunity for the newlyweds to spend time alone with each other. Directly following the ceremony, Spencer went back to his cell and Kohlscheen went back to her home in Los Angeles.

All this may have been off-putting to some brides. But Norma Kohlscheen was determined. She had no doubt whatsoever that her new husband, Clyde Ray Spencer, was innocent. And she made it her personal crusade to see that he was vindicated.

First, she shouldered the financial burden of his appeal. This meant that Kohlscheen had to work two jobs or about seventy hours a week. She traveled frequently to visit Spencer in Idaho, and later, once he was transferred, to his next home, a prison in Washington State.

During these visits, the husband and wife were not allowed to touch one another save for one kiss at the start of each visit and one at the end. Each kiss lasted approximately three seconds.

Then, starting in the early 1990s, Norma Kohlscheen hired Peter Camiel as Spencer's new defense attorney. She also hired private investigator,

Paul Henderson. These men got to work picking apart the original case against Spencer.

"She came up here month after month, year after year after year. She made the difference," Henderson told *20/20*.

Henderson and Camiel began by studying the testimony that Spencer's daughter, Katie, allegedly gave Detective Sharon Kraus way back in the early 80s when she was still only five years old. Both men couldn't help notice that Sharon Krause had interrogated Katie alone in a strange environment—Krause's hotel room. Also, that Krause had no evidence to back up the five-year-old's testimony. No video recordings. No audio. Not even handwritten notes. It was therefore Krause's word against Spencer's.

They then turned their attention to the testimony of young Matt Spencer. Here again, there was no evidence whatsoever to back up Detective Kraus's assertions. No recordings. No contemporaneous notes. But here, there was an additional red flag. Why had it taken Matt Spencer eight months for him to "realize" he'd been abused?

In November 2010, Matt Spencer, then age thirty-four, recalled that, as an eight-year-old boy, "I [was] just tired, exhausted of being questioned with the same question and ... I made up stuff."

As Camiel and Henderson kept digging, they discovered it was young Matt who'd been the one to propose that other police officers had been involved in his alleged molestation. Not Katie. Meaning that once the eight-year-old boy had finally broken, he had broken hard.

Here again, there wasn't a shred of physical existence proving that Matt and Katie Spencer had been molested by one police officer—their father—let alone many. Yet prosecutors had used the children's testimony as the fulcrum of their case against Spencer.

Then, in the summer of 1996, Henderson and Camiel uncovered a trove of records. These were the sexual assault exams performed on Katie and Little Matt just after Ray was accused of molesting them.

"Now those medical exams turned out to be completely and totally negative," Paul Henderson told *20/20*. "The examining physician didn't find any evidence that either one of them had been assaulted."

Yet Clyde Ray Spencer had been accused of both repeatedly and violently raping both kids. How was this possible? The two accounts didn't fit one another at all.

Around this time, Henderson and Camiel also dug into the curious behavior of Shirley Hansen. Why would a woman who said she feared her husband had molested his kids from a previous marriage then ask him to spend the night with her three-year-old son alone in a motel room?

"One of the explanations is that it was a setup," Peter Camiel told *20/20*. "Can I prove that? No. I can't. But it sure looks like it."

This assertion begs the question: Why would Shirley Hansen try to set up her husband?

We may never know for certain.

By this point, Spencer's kids were grown. Matt and Katie's growing curiosity about their father's whereabouts led them to uncover the truth. They began to realize that, not only was their father in prison, but they themselves had played a key role in sending him there.

It was a shocking discovery, the guilt of which weighed heavily on them. But guilt was just the beginning. They must also have felt confusion.

All along, they'd been told by a pack of adults —including people they trusted, like their mother, DeAnne—that the molestation was real. It had actually happened. They were victims.

DeAnne said their father had hurt them. But this didn't jive with their memories. And their memories didn't jive with what Detective Krause had told them to say.

As they grew older, Matt and Katie started to question everything.

The situation was so confusing. Katie later admitted to her own problems handling her guilt and shame over misrepresenting her father's actions.

Despite how futile he knew it to be, Clyde Ray Spencer continued to apply for parole.

About every three years or so, the prison system would take him back to the state of Washington for a hearing. But his choice of the Alford plea worked against him time after time.

In fairness, Spencer had known this would be the case. Judge Lodge had told him as much at his sentencing back in 1985. The system would not grant clemency unless and until Spencer admitted his guilt.

But he wouldn't. He simply would not.

As fate would have it, Spencer's fifth and final parole hearing was on September 11, 2001.

SPENCER: I had no idea what was going on [in New York] ... They told me, "You either admit guilt or you're going to die in prison." I said, "I already made that decision. I didn't do it." I would bring them things, something new that had been discovered since the last parole hearing, whatever it may be, new evidence, whatever. And they would say, "We're not going to rehash this case. We're not going to retry this case." And I said, "No, your responsibility is to determine how much of a threat I am to society. If there are mitigating circumstances, I think you should take those into consideration when you make your decision." Well, they weren't used to hearing something like that.

It was a cogent argument. But it didn't make one bit of difference. The board denied Spencer's parole. Again.

Now here's an interesting side story. The warden of Spencer's facility had been the head of Correctional Industries when Spencer first came to Idaho. He was also a retired Air Force colonel. Spencer had been in the Air Force, too. So the two men had some parity there.

This warden understood very well what a strange case Clyde Ray Spencer presented. He knew that the guards in his prison had read Spencer's case file cover to cover. Knew that they talked about him in the yard, which meant they discussed Spencer openly while patrolling the general population.

By then, it was already widely known that Spencer had gone through two FBI SWAT schools. That he'd trained with the Navy SEALs. But from there a sort of myth took root.

A few correctional officers mistakenly thought that Spencer was an undercover FBI agent. Eventually, very few people in prison had a clear idea of who Spencer was.

SPENCER: Some of the guards came up to me and said, "Look, we've heard some things about your case. If this place ever goes off, you get in touch with us, we'll get you out the front door." Other ones thought I was just a dirty cop, and every time I'd run into them, they would bust my balls.

Eventually, Spencer'd had enough.

SPENCER: ... I actually went to the warden. I said, "You know, Joe." I was the only inmate to ever call him Joe. I said, "You know, they're putting my life at risk here." I said, "You need to seal my records." He said, "I can't do that, Ray." He said, "In some ways, you're the worst inmate I've got here, as far as a threat goes." He said, "You know the ins and outs." He said, "Anybody that transports you back for a parole hearing or downtown for a medical, they need to know who they have, they're dealing with." He said, "I can't do that, but I will put a cover letter on it that none of this will be discussed amongst other inmates, or anything like that."

It's quite a thing to live like a legend when, really, you're just a man, like everyone else. Spencer told me how he made a point of never showing emotion while he was in prison. Emotion, he figured, equated to vulnerability. And vulnerability of any sort, real or perceived, could get a man killed.

SPENCER: I never showed emotion. One time I got called up in front of that lieutenant [who refused the jobs] and he said, "Spencer, I see you walking this yard." He said, "You think you're so cool. You never show emotion. But you're an angry man, and you better deal with that anger before you get out, or you're not going to make it in society." Well, discretion was never one of my big things so I wouldn't break eye contact with him. I said, "You know the problem with that, Lieutenant, is that the only one I see that's angry around here is you. And second of all, I'm never getting out, so I really don't have to worry about it."

After he got turned down for parole in 2001, Spencer was transferred to a facility back in Washington State. The board's rationale for this was simple. Seventeen years had passed since Clyde Ray Spencer went to prison. Who on earth would remember him?

They were right. It turned out nobody did.

This struck me as terribly sad when I heard it. After all that Clyde Ray Spencer had endured, the final indignity was that no one cared about him anymore. He was a non-person. In the eyes of justice, he simply didn't matter anymore.

He spent the next three years at the facility in Washington State without any hope whatsoever. He'd exhausted all legal avenues to affect his release. He therefore resigned himself to live out the rest of his life and die in prison.

Picture Clyde Ray Spencer here. He's now been in prison for nearly two decades, all because of some heinous crime people said he had done, when he didn't.

The handsome motorcycle cop was gone. He was heavier now. He moved slower, and with the wariness of an animal who knows that predators strike when you least expect. He'd lost his cock-eyed optimism, along with most of his hair. That youthful glint in his eyes was still there, but tempered now. It had faded.

For all intents and purposes, the man who'd once called himself Clyde Ray Spencer was gone, replaced by a darker, more somber version of himself. This new Spencer's eyes had seen aspects of life most people can never imagine. When you looked in them, you saw remarkable pain and a pragmatism stronger than steel.

But beneath all that? There was fire. Fire that burned. The fire of truth.

In the autumn of 2003, knowing that Spencer was out of appeals, his new attorney, Peter Camiel, figured they might as well go for broke.

He contacted the office of Washington's governor. At the time, a man named Gary Locke sat in that office. Camiel pled with Governor Locke and his team to commute Spencer's sentence.

SPENCER: The governor—this actually surprised me, because he was an ex-prosecutor. But he looked into the case.

More than a year passed. Then, to hear Camiel tell it: "December 23rd, 2004, I get a fax. 'Congratulations.' His sentence has been commuted to time served."

The governor of Washington State had ordered that Clyde Ray Spencer be released in a matter of days. As part of the deal, Spencer would have to endure three years of intense parole. This included wearing an ankle monitor and reporting to his residence every night by 10 p.m.

"Things like that?" Spencer told me. "I could care less."

According to the paperwork for Spencer's commutation, the governor's office had reviewed Spencer's conviction. It cited the complete lack of physical evidence proving the children had been molested.

Tellingly, it also cited the highly improper affair between the lead investigator for Clark County, Detective Sergeant Michael Davidson, and Spencer's second wife, Shirley Hansen.

The governor's office went on to cite other "troubling aspects" of the case.

SPENCER: In his commutation that he gave [Governor Locke] said, "This case disturbs me to no end. Not only has evidence been proven to have been tampered with, but the affair with the detective sergeant in charge of the case while Mr. Spencer's awaiting trial," he said, "just goes beyond words."

Ken Olsen was a reporter for *The Columbian* newspaper in Clark County. He told *20/20*: "Governor Locke is a very cautious man. For him to commute this sort of sentence meant there was something really rotten at the heart of this case."

In other words, it was finally clear that Spencer wasn't crazy. Someone higher up the ladder had reviewed the evidence against him—or really, the utter lack thereof—and they were questioning what had happened.

A few days after that fax arrived, Clyde Ray Spencer was released from prison. By that point, he'd served almost twenty years. It was the longest sentence for a sex crime in the history of Washington State. And of course, it was all predicated on a lie.

Paul Henderson met Spencer outside the wire. The PI asked Spencer how happy he was feeling. Spencer, rendered speechless, replied by thrusting both fists at the sky and grinning.

Finally, Clyde Ray Spencer and Norma Kohlscheen were able to spend time together. That in itself must have been worth all the effort.

Years later, Spencer told *20/20*, "She always gave me hope. She always hung in there. When it's all said and done, if you can end up with a woman who's the love of your life. Can't beat that."

But the drama wasn't over yet. Not by a long shot.

☆ ☆ ☆

Spencer's commutation had gotten him released from prison. However, he was still listed as a convicted sex offender. This meant that his freedom bore many restrictions. High on that list was the fact that he was restricted from traveling out of state. Among other things, this meant that his time with his wife, Norma Kohlscheen, was limited.

Legally speaking, Spenser was also a registered sex offender. He would not be fully exonerated until his kids broke their silence.

But the damage here was already done. Matt and Katie Spencer hadn't seen their father in more than twenty years. They had no idea who he was, no connection to him. They also had plenty of fears which had all been carefully stoked by various parties.

For instance, Spencer's ex-wife, DeAnne, evidently had told her children that, if Spencer was ever released, he'd track them all down and kill them. To put it bluntly, the challenges Spencer faced while struggling to reunite with his kids were huge.

But here, reporter Ken Olsen went to work on Spencer's behalf. Following Spencer's release, Olsen placed several calls to Matt Spencer, who was then living in Sacramento. Initially, Matt hung up when he heard that Olsen was calling on behalf of his father. Matt was still agonized over what had happened. He carried incredible loads of guilt for the part he perceived he'd played in the whole affair.

As he later told *20/20*, "We had been told that we had just suppressed [memories of being molested], that we're blocking everything out. And when I finally realized: I'm not blocking anything, I remember everything else."

Katie added, "I don't care if I was five or not. If something that violent was going on, I would have known."

"Deep down, I always knew that nothing happened, but didn't know what to do about it," Matt Spencer said.

"My life was kind of falling apart," he admitted on *20/20*. "Felt kind of like a walking dead-type person. I was just going through the motions."

Katie Spencer agreed. "It's just kind of being lost. And you feel like you've completely turned somebody's life upside down. It just kind of compiles on you, and it gets really difficult to deal with."

Several months passed. Finally, Matt decided he could no longer live with this burden. He reached out to his father through email. Slowly, they began to correspond.

"I told him whenever you want to talk, you can call me," Spencer said.

In the fall of 2006, Matt boarded a plane headed for Seattle, where his father now lived. He was hesitant, of course. The lies his mother and so many other adults had told him must have rung loud in his ears.

But he also knew he had a father. And he knew his father was innocent of all the crimes he'd been accused of. That he'd suffered outrageously for it. Suffered for Matt and Katie, from one point of view. He felt that he had to make things right.

Matt's plane landed in Seattle. Spencer met his son at the airport. One can only imagine how that must've felt. For both of them. Father and son reunited.

They began to rebuild their bond.

During this first trip, Matt confessed that he knew the molestation had never happened. That he'd lived with the guilt of that too many years. The confusion of being lied to and coerced to give false testimony.

"It didn't take but a day," Matt told *20/20*, "and I trusted that man with my life."

Ray recalled one of their initial conversations. "He said, 'I know you didn't do it. But they made me say it.' I said, my attorney is standing by. He said, 'That's why I came.' The next day, he gave a deposition and that started the ball rolling to get this thing overturned."

Matt was eager to recant the testimony he'd made twenty years earlier. Under oath, he recounted how, back when he was just eight years old, he'd felt threatened by the situation. Hounded by adults who clearly wanted him to say things and certainly put the time in to get him to do so. Eight full months.

SPENCER: [Matt] just told them anything just to get them to leave me alone. They had browbeat this little guy for eight months, until they finally broke him.

So he carried around this guilt all of those years thinking that he had lied and sent his father to prison.

When Matt got home from that trip, he spoke to his sister about their dad. By that point, Katie had started a family of her own. She and her husband lived in Sacramento. They had a one-year-old daughter.

Katie was understandably apprehensive about reconciling with her dad.

"You don't know how to admit to him that you don't think this ever happened," she told *20/20*. "How do you say that to someone you sent to prison for twenty years?"

It took another full year for Katie Spencer to contact her father. She emailed him on a Friday night and told him she wanted to know who he was. Not where he lived. Not to hash over all the details of what had happened. They both knew far too much about that.

No, she wanted to get to know the man who, in memory, far beyond all the confusion, she still knew and loved beyond all words. The man who was her father.

"I had to tell him that, look, I can't give you your life back," Katie told *20/20*. "But we can do what we can, you know, to make it good from here. We are your children and you now have grandchildren. You've missed enough."

Ultimately, Katie followed Matt's lead. She reunited with her father in 2007.

SPENCER: [Katie and her family] lived in a suburb of Sacramento. I go and I knock on the door and nobody answers. I think, "She changed her mind." What was going on was her husband and her were standing there, and she's holding my granddaughter. The last time I seen my daughter, my granddaughter was the spitting image of her. My daughter looks at her husband and she says, "Well, how are we going to work this?" [My son-in-law] just said, "I'll get this." He opens the door and he said, "Come on in, Pop." I walked in and I saw my daughter standing there with my granddaughter.

It was a strained visit in so many ways. As Katie and Spencer got to know each other, they also began to trade stories. For the first time ever, Katie got to hear her father's side of everything. She was forced to confront the fact that almost everything her mother had told her and Matt about Spencer was a lie.

Imagine being in that position. Imagine that one parent tells you your other parent is mean, vicious, evil. That they'd harmed you when you were little and that, if they ever met you again, they'd try to kill you. Just imagine that.

My heart goes out to Katie and Matt. The position they found themselves in as children was awful. Simply untenable.

Once Spencer told his side of the tale, he explained how hard it was for him to find work. Few employers wanted to hire a man who'd been in prison for twenty years. Fewer still wanted to get involved with a man who'd been to prison as a convicted child molester.

Again, despite Governor Locke's commutation of Spencer's sentence, he was still a registered sex offender. This designation would have to be legally changed, and the only way to do that was for both children to go to court and testify that they'd lied. More specifically, as children they had been pressured to lie by the two detectives who led their father's case on behalf of Clark County: Michael Davidson and Sharon Krause.

So that's what they did.

The judge assigned to Spencer's case welcomed the testimony of his children. He said that, if Matt and Katie's testimony was consistent with their sworn depositions, he was going to overturn Spencer's conviction.

Spencer later told Katie Couric that he wasn't angry with his kids about what the role they'd played in his tragedy.

"They were babies. These were little kids. [The detectives] took advantage of them. And then they had to live all those years without a father."

The more she got to know her father, the guiltier Katie felt about what she had done.

"The prime of his life was gone," she told *Esquire* magazine. "Everyone can say, 'You were a kid,' over and over, but they don't understand. You know you were used, and there is this kind of guilt in that. And there probably shouldn't be. But nobody can convince me not to feel guilty."

In July 2009, Katie and Matt were cross-examined in a hearing where they successfully recanted the testimony that, years before, had sent their innocent father to prison. Firmly and repeatedly, they stated their father had never abused them.

And this is where something remarkable happened.

Okay, fine. Let's call it a bombshell.

A videotape surfaced showing little Katie being questioned. By "little Katie," I mean this video was shot mere months after Katie told detectives she'd been abused.

The video is a chestnut. Everyone in it wears period clothes from the early 1980s. The image quality is grainy, typical of first-generation VHS recorders. Still, you can clearly see Katie, age two or possibly three years old. She's sitting in her mother, DeAnne's, lap while Jim Peters, who was then the Clark County prosecutor, questions her.

Peters was trying to gauge how the toddler would hold up if he called her to the witness stand. The video is disturbing in that it clearly shows questionable tactics being used to subvert the child's testimony.

But don't take my word for it. Listen to Dr. Stephen Ceci, an independent expert on child testimony, being interviewed by *20/20*:

"The prosecutor violates the child's space. He's about eighteen inches from her face. The worst of all, of course, is she's sitting on her mother's lap. She's [DeAnne is] prompting Katie. She's coaxing her. There were a lot of highly leading questions. If you do these things relentlessly to children at that age, you can be pretty confident that some of those kids will come to make false disclosures."

Dr. Ceci also found fault with the report filed by Detective Sharon Krause.

"She says the child said something. But did the child say that initially? Or was there denial, denial, denial—and then finally the child makes a disclosure because she wants to terminate what, for her, has become a harangue?"

Ceci noted that Krause's actions had sown the seeds for highly unreliable statements. He said that Detective Krause should never have taken the children to a private hotel room, nor bought them toys, cookies, candy, or anything else as part of her interactions with them. This simply defied common sense, not to mention proper investigatory procedures.

Without question, this videotape should have been made available for Spencer's defense during his original trial. Instead, it ended up collecting dust in Sharon Krause's garage.

You heard me right. The video tape that could have changed the course of Clyde Ray Spencer's life and exonerated a cop who was falsely accused ... had sat in Detective Krause's garage for something like twenty-five years.

I asked Spencer why Krause finally released the material.

SPENCER: I think she panicked. Because after the governor ordered my release ... and all charges were dropped. Then we started a civil case, and I think she was afraid that somebody would say, "Hey, whatever happened to these things?" She claimed that she didn't realize she had taken them home. She had cleaned out her desk. Which doesn't bode well for the fact that this was evidence. It should've been placed in evidence, not in her desk. So she turned them over ... I think she was afraid that if somebody started asking questions and they found out she had them and never turned them over that she could be facing some charges. So, she turned them over.

STICKS: Just twenty-five years later.

In 2010, the Washington State Supreme Court overruled the lower courts' rulings during appeals. A date was set for Clyde Ray Spencer to finally clear his name. In its decision, the court wrote harshly of the original investigators, stating: "the notion that the state would lose track of a videotape in which a prosecutor interviews a complaining witness is difficult to fathom."

All this notwithstanding, the court granted prosecutors the option to retry Spencer. A very real threat loomed that Spencer would have to go through everything all over again. He waited for months on pins and needles.

In September 2010, he went into court to withdraw his original plea. At that point, prosecutors revealed they'd decided not to retry him. After the hearing, the Clark County Prosecutor's Office issued a press release that included the following explanation of their decision to dismiss the case:

"First, to try the case at this time a jury would need to rely on the memory of witnesses to events from some 25 years ago. For example, the defendant's step-son, Matt Hansen [Little Matt], who is one of the victims, is now 30 years old. He was five at the time of the alleged crimes ... Second, even if a jury nonetheless were to convict the defendant in subsequent trial, the defendant, having already served a substantial prison sentence, would probably only have a duty to register as a sex offender with no additional post-release supervision or conditions. This is because his original sentence was conditionally commuted by Governor Gary Locke in 2004. Given this situation, the value to further prosecution would be far outweighed by the huge cost to our taxpayers of additional litigation."

Clark County Prosecutor John Fairgrieve later told *20/20*, "We just decided that in this particular case, at this point, that dismissal without prejudice was appropriate."

Clyde Ray Spencer summed it up like this: "I can't change what happened. I can't get those years back. So I have to take satisfaction in the fact that I walked out of that courtroom twenty-five years later a free man."

With the withdrawal of his original plea and the prosecutors' dismissal of the case, Ray's record was fully erased. But it wasn't the end. No, not by a long shot.

More legal cases would drag out for years as Spencer sought restitution for the damage done to his life.

In fact, years later, Clyde Ray Spencer found himself back in the very same courtroom. This time, he was participating in a civil judgment case against Clark County. Here again, fate would again take an unfortunate turn and rally its force against him.

The judge presiding over the trial was the same judge that once denied Spencer his release back in the '90s.

SPENCER: So it never seems to stop. They refused to pay the $9 million judgment after we filed it. Then the State Supreme Court reinstated it. Then they said they were going to appeal it to the U.S. Supreme Court. Then the county came back and said, "We don't condone these kind of actions, so we're not responsible for what these two detectives did." I'm saying, if somebody's driving a truck for your local market and they're drunk, and they hit somebody and kill them, they were driving in your capacity as an employee. What do you mean you're not responsible? So when it was all said and done, after I paid my attorney, I end up with $3 million.

During the time we spent talking, Spencer admitted to me what I already knew: There's no amount of money that can make up for the twenty-plus years he spent behind bars. No reparation will ever compensate him for being wrongfully accused of one of the most heinous crimes imaginable.

"The only thing that I was grateful for was I walked out of there. I went out of them prison gates with my head held high. They didn't break me. I kept my honesty and my integrity, and it meant so much to me," he said.

"When they take everything away from you but your integrity and your honesty, those are the things I had control of. And it meant more to me to stick with the truth than to lie to get out of prison."

Today, Clyde Ray Spencer is more than seventy years old. His life is better than ever. He has a loving wife and his relationship with his kids has never been stronger.

His son, Matt, told Katie Couric that their relationship is "incredible today. I have never had such a weight lifted off of me ... We're so very close now. And he's such an incredible man. I mean, who gets a PhD [in Psychology] in prison? I mean, most people go into prison and they come out a monster. He came out just an impeccable human being."

If you ask me, someone should make a movie of Clyde Ray Spencer's life.

There would be hurdles, of course. Maybe the biggest would be the most obvious.

How many people would really believe that what happened to Clyde Ray Spencer is based on a true story? Probably no one.

But there's this: If you'd like a deeper dive into the life, times, and false accusation of Officer Clyde Ray Spencer of the Vancouver, Washington Police Department, check out his book, *Memoirs of an Innocent Man.*

It's an incredible read that corresponds with the life of an incredible man.

CLOSING THOUGHTS

You've just read a variety of true stories about law enforcement officers, all of whom were falsely accused.

Obviously, these stories ranged in severity. In one, a routine traffic stop escalated to crazy proportions. In another, an innocent officer had his life ripped apart as he languished in prison for two decades.

But for all their dissimilarities, both cases tell the same tale. They recount how the system of justice these officers swore themselves to uphold failed them in their greatest hour of need.

I want you to think about that.

And while you're at it, think about this:

If you were to speak with every one of these officers, I bet they would all tell you how much they love or loved their chosen careers. That, even after all they've been through, they still believe in law enforcement.

They might have faced ridicule, public questioning over their actions and motives, and even time behind bars. But they still believe in the oath they took. They still believe in the job they did. They'd choose the same path all over again if given another chance.

To my way of thinking, each of their stories is a cautionary tale for society.

The way I see it, it doesn't matter which side of the law enforcement fence you're on. We should slow down and breath a bit more. We should all make sure we get the facts in every case right before making decisions.

There's an old saying that comes to us from the Far East. It goes like this: "He who knows does not speak. He who speaks does not know."

These days, I hear a lot of people speaking. But how many of them know what they're talking about? Not many, unfortunately.

We could all try thinking a little bit more before we open our mouths.

Critical thinking has become a lost art. I say it's time we brought it back. Because the truth is rarely black or white. It's hardly ever left or right. It doesn't care if you're red or blue. These are polarized notions that only make sense to people who don't want to do the real work of taking each moment, each case, for what it is, and only passing judgment after the facts have been thoroughly sorted.

The truth is the truth no matter who spins it. And as they used to say in the old days, VERITAS VOS LIBERABIT. "The truth will set you free."

Lady Justice might be peeking sometimes or holding her scales up crooked. But she always knows what the truth is. And she knows that the truth is worth fighting for.

She will never abandon that struggle. And neither will I.

That's what being a cop's all about.

So thanks for taking the time to consider my perspective. And if you're ever in Tulsa and happen to see me out on patrol with my guys, say hello, okay? We love it when folks introduce themselves and I love making new, good friends.

Until that day, I remain yours faithfully.

SEAN "STICKS" LARKIN
Tulsa Police Department
Tulsa, Oklahoma

ACKNOWLEDGMENTS

Thanks go first and foremost to my two children. They're the light of my life and, for various reasons, they've endured me working nearly seven days a week these past three years or so. I want to tell you both here and now what I hope you already know: You make me so proud to be your dad. You give me strength in ways I cannot describe. Thank you for that, and for so much more.

Thanks also must go to the Tulsa Police Department, to all my colleagues there, and in particular to Retired Tulsa Police Chief Chuck Jordan, Deputy Chiefs Eric Dalgleish and Dennis Larsen, Major Luther Breashears, and Retired Captain Nick Hondros; for your belief in me and for supporting me through the investigation of 2010.

To the Tulsa County District Attorney's Office, because at one point, they flat out told me they never once suspected I'd ever been untruthful in court. It's because of the Tulsa DA's office, I can still do my job. Also, in the eyes of the court system, I remain a recognized, expert witness on the subject of criminal street gangs based in Tulsa, Oklahoma. That's good for me but it's also good for our city. So thanks for that, guys.

To Dan Abrams, for having faith in me to take on this book project and for all the great experiences at Live PD and Live PD Presents: PD Cam on the A&E television network. To Mike Lewis, for putting up with my slow writing at times and helping craft some great stories for this book. To Damon DiMarco for batting cleanup on this book project for us. So much appreciated. To Korey Scott and Howard Doss, for listening when I needed help and then offering the best advice that, miraculously, always worked out. To José "Inkfather" Sanchez, for the incredible Lady Justice tattoo. To all the law enforcement officers who took the time to personally share stories of their false accusations with me. To the "Jump Out Boys," for hands down being the best group of police officers I could ever have hoped to work with.

To all the good people in the city of Tulsa who make life interesting and inspire me every day that I'm there. And, finally, to all my brothers and sisters in blue across the country. For showing up to work every day, especially during the last few tough years. For looking out for each other. For doing the job of keeping our town and communities safe. And always, always remembering we are there to protect and serve. I am proud to do so beside you.

SEAN "STICKS" LARKIN

ACKNOWLEDGMENTS

I want to thank my family for their abundance of patience and understanding as I devoted countless hours, yet again, to staring at my laptop screen and tickling the keys. But thanks must also go to Marilyn Allen, literary agent par excellence—thank you for your boundless advice and support. To David Wilk— I appreciate your trust in me and hope we can work on more projects together in the future. To Dan Abrams and all the great folks at Abrams Media. To Stephen Spignesi and Rachel Montgomery, for all your help. And, of course, to "Sticks" himself, Sean Larkin, and all the men and women in blue who keep us safe on a day-to-day basis. Yours is the song we sing in this book. May others learn the tune.

MICHAEL LEWIS

ABOUT THE AUTHORS

SEAN "STICKS" LARKIN is a police officer with the Tulsa Police Department in Tulsa, Oklahoma. His career, spanning nearly twenty-five years, has been spent trying to reduce violent crime in and around the city of Tulsa. Officer Larkin has worked in various divisions during his law enforcement tenure, including patrol, Street Crimes, Major Crimes, Homicide, Narcotics, SWAT, and the Gang Unit. He is currently supervisor for the Crime Gun Unit. Sean worked as an analyst for the hit television show *Live PD*. He was also the host of *Live PD Presents: PD Cam*. Both shows premiered on the A&E television network. He lives in Tulsa, Oklahoma.

MICHAEL LEWIS is a lifetime marketing and communications professional who has worked for more than twenty years as an editor at several major book publishers. He has acquired and edited more than 500 titles, works freelance to help authors to develop their proposals and manuscripts, and regularly lectures on how to get a book published. He has written fourteen books including *A Guy Walks Into a Bar*, *The 100 Best Beatles Songs*, *Outdated Advertising*, and *Random Commuter Observations*. He lives in Northern New Jersey.